T0356389

CHALLENGING
BOYS

CHALLENGING
B O Y S

A PROVEN PLAN FOR KEEPING
YOUR COOL AND HELPING YOUR SON THRIVE

J. TIMOTHY DAVIS

ROWMAN & LITTLEFIELD
Lanham • Boulder • New York • London

Rowman & Littlefield
Bloomsbury Publishing Inc, 1385 Broadway, New York, NY 10018, USA
Bloomsbury Publishing Plc, 50 Bedford Square, London, WC1B 3DP, UK
Bloomsbury Publishing Ireland, 29 Earlsfort Terrace, Dublin 2, D02 AY28, Ireland
www.rowman.com

Distributed by NATIONAL BOOK NETWORK

British Library Cataloguing in Publication Information Available

Library of Congress Cataloging-in-Publication Data

Names: Davis, J. Timothy (James Timothy), 1963– author.
Title: Challenging boys : a proven plan for keeping your cool and helping your son
thrive / J. Timothy Davis.
Description: Lanham : Rowman & Littlefield, [2025] | Includes bibliographical
references and index. | Summary: "Drawing on the author's years of experience
as a child psychologist and time as a volunteer firefighter, this book applies the
wisdom of the fire service to teach parents of challenging boys to plan and prepare
for challenging behaviors and triggers, enabling them to feel confident, relaxed, and
ready to support their child"—Provided by publisher.
Identifiers: LCCN 2024040170 (print) | LCCN 2024040171 (ebook) |
ISBN 9781538191125 (cloth ; alk. paper) | ISBN 9781538191132 (epub)
Subjects: LCSH: Parents of problem children. | Sons. | Parenting.
Classification: LCC HQ773 .D38 2025 (print) | LCC HQ773 (ebook) |
DDC 649/.153—dc23/eng/20241129
LC record available at https://lccn.loc.gov/2024040170
LC ebook record available at https://lccn.loc.gov/2024040171

For product safety related questions contact productsafety@bloomsbury.com.

♾ ™ The paper used in this publication meets the minimum requirements of American
National Standard for Information Sciences—Permanence of Paper for Printed Library
Materials, ANSI/NISO Z39.48-1992.

For my wife and children—
Your love means everything to me.

CONTENTS

AUTHOR'S NOTE

The concepts and strategies presented in this book are based on scientific research and years of clinical practice. They are intended to supplement, not replace, consultation or treatment with a qualified mental health professional. The names and identities of individuals mentioned have been significantly altered. Most of the cases described are composites of many families facing similar challenges. When I have presented examples that refer to specific families, I have obtained permission from those individuals to use their stories. These measures have been taken to protect privacy and confidentiality. Despite these changes, I have attempted to remain true to the essence of our work together. I hope these narratives resonate with you and help bring the ideas of this book to life.

Foreword

I first met Dr. Davis fifteen years ago when I discovered we shared a number of cases. As I was just beginning my career, I was looking for support and approached him for supervision, mentorship and consultation. I was always impressed by his deep thoughtfulness and reflection, as well as his ability to break down complicated situations, especially as it related to the *challenging boys* in my practice, with wise words and guidance. I'm so grateful that he's now written this book and made his perspectives available to more people than just one hour at a time.

I was honored when Tim reached out for some feedback and later for a foreword, and I looked forward to diving in. Let me tell you, as I began to read, that it seemed on every page I was not giving notes to him so much as wanting to take notes for myself—as a therapist to be sure, but as a father as well. I felt like I was getting gems of advice that I would be implementing in my own family later that afternoon, and I was learning great lines to share with clients and their parents. I think you too will not be disappointed. I hope that your copy of this book will become as marked up and beloved as mine.

What Dr. Davis succeeds in most is the weaving together of the science and research of child development with real-world examples of these concepts in action, translating for parents and professionals alike concepts that can seem distant, abstract, or impractical. I know too as a colleague with shared cases, that his clients and parents also find his empathic and practical approach empowering and helpful, never condescending, impractical, or distant like so many self-appointed parenting experts these days.

In a time in our culture when we are divided over not just how to raise children but even what it means to be a boy and a man, Dr. Davis is able to bring child development wisdom into the twenty-first century and directly to the crisis of masculinity. So many parents are fearful of what their challenging boys may become, and his work offers not just inspiration but confidence that we can help our most challenging boys grow up to confront the problems in our society and solve them in what we know will be a complex future.

Over the course of the book, Dr. Davis helps us to understand ourselves and what we may unconsciously be bringing to our own parenting. From there, we discover some of the more organic roots of our children's behavior and why even within families people can be so different. With the journal prompts, we go deeper into understanding why our own buttons are getting pushed and how we can more deftly respond to challenging episodes and learn to rebuild our relationships with our sons with new and better skills than those we were raised with. The communication and co-regulation chapters, where I took more notes than anywhere else in the book, not only offer critical insights for family harmony, but also guide us and our boys in the wider world as well. Lastly, Tim busts through myths, misunderstandings, and trends as they relate to rules, rewards, and consequences with a contemporary sensibility about how we can approach these skillfully and strategically.

Parenting a challenging boy is not easy, as you already know— I'm guessing you could write your own book on the topic—but Dr. Davis's empathic and empowering guide to this challenging phase in your family's journey will help you and your sons come out on the other side stronger and closer than ever.

—Christopher Willard, PsyD, Cambridge MA

Introduction

Parenting is often called "the toughest job you will ever love." If you have a challenging boy, you know how incredibly tough parenting can be, but you are probably frequently left wondering why you are not loving the "job" more. And while you love your child, you might not always like him.

Being a parent of a typical kid can be stressful enough—working your job, making ends meet, arranging daycare, getting kids to school and activities, feeding everyone, monitoring homework, managing bedtimes, and so on. If your child also challenges your authority at every turn, won't take "no" for an answer, argues every decision, and explodes at the slightest provocation, then parenting just feels like a grind. The rudeness, the disrespect, the entitlement make you feel crazy. It's confusing, overwhelming, and infuriating.

Having a challenging boy is also very lonely. Friends, relatives, even strangers judge you. They think that his misbehavior is the result of your poor parenting and offer unsolicited advice like "you need to be more consistent" or "you need to be firmer" (although when you try to follow this advice it somehow always makes things worse). The phone stops ringing for play dates as other parents distance themselves and discourage their children from hanging out with your son. It also can be lonely at home. You and your spouse increasingly find yourselves fighting about how to best manage your son. You become polarized, with one of you always too sympathetic to your child's plight and defending him, while the other is too hard-nosed, insisting that you need to crack down.

If all this sounds familiar, then this book is for you. In these pages, I will teach you the lessons that I've learned and insights I've gained from thirty years of working with challenging boys and their families. My approach is also grounded in the understanding of male development across the entire life course that I gained in my work as a fellow at Harvard Medical School's Study of Adult Development. I have also learned much from my experiences as a father of three.

There is another, somewhat unconventional place, where I gained valuable insights into working with challenging boys. It began when I was awoken on a frigid winter night in 1989 by my fire department radio. "Company 14. 609 Ogden Ave., fire investigation." I leapt out of bed and rushed down the street to the town firehouse where I was a volunteer firefighter. After getting into my fire gear, I climbed onto the back step of a fire engine as it left the station. It was only my third call since becoming an active-duty member. The first two ended a few blocks from the firehouse—false alarms. This night was different. Instead of heading back to the station, the truck sped up. The sirens screamed and I held on tight as I bounced up and down on the back of the racing fire engine. Soon we arrived at the address, and I looked up to see flames leaping out of a second-floor window of the house. I saw a couple with their child in the front yard in shock watching their home burn. "Oh s—! This is real!" flashed in my mind. Although adrenaline was coursing through my veins and my heart was pounding, my fellow firefighters and I acted calmly and efficiently to quickly bring the fire under control.

I often think back to my time as a firefighter when I work with parents who have a challenging boy like yours. Just like firefighters, parents of challenging boys need to remain calm and work effectively when things are hitting the fan. When a challenging boy is exploding, melting down, hitting, breaking things, etcetera, it feels like the house is on fire. We get triggered into fight-or-flight mode where we are overwhelmed by strong feelings and find it impossible to remain calm.

Maybe you can relate to the story of Ryan and his family. Ryan, a fourteen-year-old, was on his computer playing a video game when his dad alerted him that he had ten minutes until time to get ready for bed. Ryan ignored his father and continued playing the game. A little later Ryan's father returned and said, "Alright, time to shut it down." Ryan replied, "OK, OK, I just need five more minutes to finish my level." Ryan's dad agreed, "Fine, five minutes. That's it.

I mean it this time." He left hoping Ryan would turn his game off at the end of his level. Ryan's mom, overhearing the situation, was becoming increasingly annoyed that her husband hadn't stood by his initial limit. Fifteen minutes later she went into Ryan's room to find him still playing. "You agreed that you would turn the computer off at 9, it's 9:30 now!" Frustration saturated Ryan's mom's voice. She moved to turn the computer off. Ryan screamed "stop f—ing bothering me!" and knocked her hand away while trying to keep playing. Ryan's dad ran in from the other room, "What's going on in here?" Ryan ignored them both and kept playing his game. Fed up with this, and a hundred other similar instances of not listening, Ryan's mom yanked the computer power cord out of the wall. Ryan screamed, "you lost all my progress!" shoved his mom out of the way and stormed out of the room. She yelled after him, "No computer time for a week!"

Ryan's parents were left reeling. "Why does this keep happening?" they wondered. Ryan's dad was in shock, "I would never have dreamed of speaking to my parents that way." He turned to his wife: "We've talked about this. You can't lose it like that!" Feeling defensive, she responded, "I never would have, if you had gotten him off the computer when you said you would!" "I was in the process of doing that," Ryan's dad insisted. And so the fight began. Underneath their anger, Ryan's parents both felt ashamed for losing their cool, yet again, despite their resolve to stay calm. They felt angry, burned out, helpless, guilty, and like complete failures as parents.

Ryan's parents needed to think like firefighters. Firefighters remain calm and effective under extreme circumstances because they *plan* and *prepare* for emergencies. Anxiety and stress (at a fire scene, or with a melting down child) threatens to send us into fight-or-flight mode which disrupts our ability to think clearly and solve problems effectively. The best time to decide how to attack most of the problems that regularly and predictably occur at a fire scene is prior to the call (in the relatively calm and low-stress environment of the fire house). Doing so leads to much safer and more effective firefighting. You do not want to be trying to figure out how to fight a fire in the literal heat of the moment. It is best to have plans made in advance that are *executed* during the emergency.

Things are similar with challenging boys. You need to create a plan ahead of time for how you will deal with challenging moments. You might be surprised to know that tantrums, power struggles, explosions, and meltdowns occur in highly predictable circumstances and play out in very predictable ways. I'll show you how to identify those patterns so that you can plan and prepare for them like a firefighter and, like a firefighter, remain calm.

For Ryan, in the example above, a frequent cause of meltdowns was getting off the computer at night. By examining the computer blow ups, Ryan's parents and I were able to come up with a plan for getting him off the computer without an explosion. We also developed an emergency plan for managing those situations where he did explode—which were becoming increasingly less frequent. These plans helped Ryan's parents relax, feel more confident, and enjoy their relationship with him the rest of the time. In this book, I'll teach you how to make an emergency plan for dealing with your son's challenging moments. In executing this plan, you will respond effectively and calmly, de-escalate things quickly, and be less likely to say or do things you'll later regret.

Firefighters are prepared, always ready for emergencies. The equipment they need is carefully organized in storage compartments on the fire trucks. These trucks stand ready for a rapid response, fueled up and facing outwards in their garage bays. When you have a challenging boy you also need to be always ready. Just to be clear, "always ready" doesn't mean always on edge. A firehouse between calls can be a very relaxed and fun place. The reason they can relax and enjoy their time together is that they are prepared for when the alarm sounds, and they need to jump into action.

Similarly, being always ready as a parent means that you can finally relax. Most of you reading this book feel like you have to be on red alert 24/7—afraid of when the next meltdown or explosion will happen. This type of chronic hyperarousal wears us down, saps joy, and shortens our fuse. What goes into being always ready with a challenging boy? First, you need to know what circumstances trigger your son's challenging behavior. I will show you how to identify what your son's specific triggers are. Once identified, you'll be able to relax when these triggers aren't present. You'll also learn how to manage the triggers without an explosion when they are present. Second, you need to know how your son's challenging behavior typically plays out. Knowing the pattern that challenging episodes follow allows you to plan your strategy for de-escalating a meltdown when it does occur. I'll teach you how to identify the pattern of your son's challenging behavior. Knowing what triggers challenging behavior, knowing the pattern challenging behavior typically follows, and having a plan for dealing with these episodes is what it means to be always ready, rather than always on edge.

I helped Ryan's parents turn their situation around, as I have done with many other families in similar circumstances, and I can help you do it too. I know one thing right away. You are a loving parent, and your son is lucky to have you as a parent. I know this because you are taking time out of your extremely busy, stressful, and exhausting life to read this book. It means that you have not given up on your son and you have not given up the hope for a healthy, happy family life. It is my mission to help you turn that hope into reality. I am confident that if you follow the steps described in this book, you can dramatically improve your relationship with your son, as well as bring about big reductions in his challenging behavior.

You might be wondering why this book is for parents of challenging boys and not "challenging kids" more generally. It's perhaps never been more difficult to be the parent of a boy. We're in the middle of a mental health crisis created by the COVID pandemic. Even before that we have had years of skyrocketing rates of ADHD and autism, both much more common in boys. These current problems occur in the context of the fact that boys are still generally taught, as psychologist William Pollack pointed out in his groundbreaking book *Real Boys*, to suppress their feelings and to channel their distress into action—often harmful action. Lacking an understanding of their emotions and without constructive coping skills for dealing with painful feelings, boys' suffering can be expressed through destructive behaviors—at the extremes we see substance abuse, delinquency, and even suicide.

At the same time as traditional expectations continue to demand that boys hide their emotions—even from themselves—recent changes in our culture have called on boys to be more accountable for their actions. We no longer say "boys will be boys" to excuse their bad behavior. Boys should be accountable, and we all want to raise boys who will be good respectful men. Boys, more than ever, need greater emotional intelligence to navigate these new subtleties. However, they are frequently deprived of the opportunity to develop the emotional intelligence needed to meet these new expectations. This new reality may be most confusing for dads who are having to rethink their own masculine identities at the same time as they need to guide and be role models for their sons. In this book I will teach you how to help your son develop the emotional intelligence he needs for a healthy masculinity for the twenty-first century that embodies values of sensitivity and respect, in addition to strength and assertiveness.

I chose the word *challenging* to describe the boys who are the subject of this book for three main reasons. First, *challenging* refers to how these boys can make life challenging for parents, teachers, siblings, and peers. Labels like *oppositional, difficult, defiant, manipulative, willful, noncompliant, rigid, angry, temperamental,* and *rebellious* are often used but cast challenging boys in an unfairly negative light. This negative bias can lead parents to take challenging behavior personally and overreact to it which, in turn, can fuel more challenging behavior. You'll learn in this book that challenging boys aren't oppositional at all. They actually want to please their parents, but they often lack the skills to do so. I'll teach you how to identify what skills your child needs to learn and how to help him develop those skills.

Challenging also refers to the need to challenge our sons to pick their battles. They need to learn, as Aristotle said, to be angry with "the right person, to the right extent, at the right time, with the right motive, and in the right way." Being able to resolve differences is one of the most important skills for personal and professional success.

While we need to challenge our sons to learn how to get along, we don't want to turn them into "compliant boys." Success in today's world requires that an individual be an independent thinker. In this book, you'll learn how to teach your son to collaborate: to work with others while being true to what he thinks, feels, and believes.

Finally, *challenging* refers to the positive fact that challenging boys challenge us to grow. The role of parent is, perhaps, the greatest opportunity to learn about ourselves that any of us will ever have. We have a chance to reflect on our childhoods—particularly how we were raised—and to develop a deeper understanding of how these experiences have influenced the people and parents that we have become. Being a parent also stirs up relationship wounds from the past, giving us an opportunity to heal them in the present. As we grow in self-understanding, we are able to show up for our present relationships in a fuller and more satisfying way. With a challenging child we are also especially confronted with our limitations and our blind spots. We are challenged to be more patient, to communicate better, and to resolve conflicts more constructively.

Challenging boys aren't only challenging. Alongside the challenging qualities are the many strengths that are important to appreciate and cultivate. Being a firefighter taught me that challenging boys have interests and skills that, when pointed in the right direction, can be a powerful source for social good. Many of my fellow firefighters had been challenging boys. The environment of the fire department with its social service, high degree of structure, hands-on learning, and action were a wonderful fit for the skills and interests of challenging boys who were now grown-ups.

Additionally, challenging boys often have a well-developed sense of justice and fairness and a sensitivity to the needs of the weak and powerless. When I explained this to Allison, mom of challenging boy Michael, she said, "You're right" with an undertone of both surprise and relief. "I was so proud of Michael just last week when he stood up to his friends." Allison recounted a recent summer afternoon: Michael was playing in their backyard with a couple of neighbor kids, and they found a small frog. One of the boys caught the frog and wanted to keep it as a pet. Allison beamed as she described how Michael demanded that the other boy release it. He insisted that this was the frog's home and that it didn't want to be a pet. As she told her story, Allison could see Michael in a light that more accurately reflected the truth of who he is. "His greatest personal strengths are exactly those things that make it most difficult to be his parent." You can see in Allison's story about Michael that challenging boys do not merely instigate, they also advocate.

I have found that challenging boys are often creators and innovators. For example, their high energy, single-mindedness, and out-of-the-box thinking style makes them well suited to be entrepreneurs. Jason, a challenging boy who had clashes with his parents growing up and who performed poorly at school, was building a successful business when I met him in his late thirties. The high drive, intense focus on his "preferred activities," and a tolerance for risk that made Jason a challenging boy, enabled him to create a thriving company.

This book is based on the understanding that conventional parenting practices do not work with challenging boys. Conventional methods like "firm limit setting" work well with typical children because, frankly, almost every approach works well with them. You may have a typical child in addition to your challenging boy. If you do, you know how much easier it is to parent a typical child. Parenting a challenging child requires a specialized approach. In these pages you will gain the understanding you need to meet the unique challenges of parenting *your* challenging boy. If you follow the methods described in this book and work the exercises, you will feel more confident in your parenting, you'll become closer to your son, and he will become less challenging.

This book is not a one-size-fits-all approach because every challenging boy is unique and solving challenging behavior is a complex task. The approach presented is modeled on how I work with patients in my practice. I take you through the same steps of understanding the origins of your child's challenging behavior and then guide you through creating a plan for solving the problems that underlie it. This plan is based on your son's unique needs and draws on your individual strengths as a parent.

Many challenging boys would meet the criteria to be diagnosed with certain mental health conditions. Among the common diagnoses are ADHD, autism, anxiety, OCD, depression, and nonverbal learning disability (NVLD). Some children also get diagnosed with oppositional defiant disorder (ODD), although I think these children are almost always more accurately seen as challenging. I have used the *Challenging Boys* approach to help families and children with all of these diagnoses to improve their relationships and to reduce challenging behavior. Knowing whether your son meets criteria for one of these diagnoses is not necessary to begin doing the work presented in this book. It may be helpful, however, to have your son assessed by a qualified mental health professional. A diagnostic evaluation can assist you with getting services from your son's school, as well as in guiding you to find appropriate treatments and supports.

As you work your way through the exercises in this book, you will develop your customized plan for solving your son's problem with challenging behavior. You will also develop an emergency plan for handling challenging behavior when it occurs. This plan will empower you to remain calm and de-escalate things quickly and effectively. Finally, you will identify the skills your son needs to learn to overcome his challenging behavior, and you will learn the steps for teaching him those skills. I am certain that if you apply the concepts described in this book, you will dramatically shift the dynamic in your household from conflict and frustration toward closeness and connection. Instead of bringing the worst out of each other, you'll bring out the best.

You've always been a loving, dedicated parent; now you'll finally be a loving parent, who loves being a parent.

CHAPTER ONE

I Know I'm Supposed to Stay Calm. Why Can't I Ever Do It?

Once, during my firefighting days, I was preparing dinner in the kitchen of the garage apartment I rented in graduate school. I lit a burner under a pot to boil water for pasta and then briefly left the kitchen to get something from another room. I didn't see that there was a cookbook on the stove top touching the burner I had just lit. It quickly caught fire. The smoke detector started blaring. I ran back into the kitchen as smoke was filling the room. I hadn't prepared for this! I didn't have a fire extinguisher. I didn't have a plan. And I was embarrassed! All I could think about was how humiliated I'd feel if I had to call the fire department—*my fire department*—to put the fire out. "They'll never let me hear the end of this!"

Firefighters stay cool and effective amid the stress, confusion, adrenaline, and fear of a fire scene because they have *planned* and *prepared* for the emergency in advance. They aren't trying to figure things out on the spot. I also believe that this is the best way to handle challenging behavior: have a plan worked out in advance and be prepared by acquiring what you need for executing your plan.

Most of us, in contrast, deal with challenging behavior by winging it. It's like me with my kitchen fire. I had no plan, I was making up my response on the spot, and I wasn't prepared with what I needed to execute a good plan—I had no fire extinguisher.

When dealing with challenging behavior without a plan, we're vulnerable to getting swept up in the drama. We issue threats, offer bribes, or yell—whatever occurs to us in the moment to do. We are just desperately trying to make it through. This approach leaves us vulnerable to being overwhelmed by the intensity of the feelings that arise in challenging moments: anger, fear, or, like me in my kitchen, embarrassment. We get caught up in fight-or-flight[1] mode that makes us prone to overreact in ways that frequently make things worse.

There are obvious important differences between firefighters and parents. Unlike my kitchen mishap, firefighters don't usually set the fires that they are called to put out. They don't have to deal with the very bad feeling of having caused the problem that they are trying to solve. Not only are they not to blame, but it isn't their house that is on fire. They care deeply about doing a good job, but they aren't personally invested in the future of the house that is ablaze.

Parents of challenging boys, in contrast to firefighters, are extremely personally involved in the problems they are trying to solve. They worry deeply about their child. When responding to a challenging behavior incident, parents aren't just dealing with the stress of handling the explosion/outburst/tantrum happening in that moment. They are also dealing with a whole host of intense emotions that arise out of their personal investment like anger (How dare he speak to me like that!), fear of the future (How will we be able to manage him when he's older and bigger?), or shame (I'm a failure as a parent.). The emotional pressure is tremendous, and it makes staying calm much more difficult.

Consider the combustible situation at Mike and Jen's house. They were at their wits end with their eleven-year-old son Ethan who was

---

1. Walter Cannon coined the phrase *fight-or-flight* to describe an animal's response to threat. Over the subsequent one hundred–plus years, much research has been conducted to further elaborate this complex response. In a 2004 review, Dr. Stefan Bracha argued that "freeze, flight, fight, fright, faint provides a more complete description of the human acute stress response sequence." See H. Stefan Bracha, "Freeze, Flight, Fight, Fright, Faint: Adaptationist Perspectives on the Acute Stress Response Spectrum," *CNS Spectr* 9, no. 9 (September 2004): 679–85, doi: 10.1017/s1092852900001954. For the purposes of simplicity, I will use the original, and commonly used, phrase *fight-or-flight* to refer to the human stress response.

disrupting life for everyone in the family. Bedtimes and getting out the door for school in the morning were particular flashpoints. At night, Ethan would demand to stay up as late as his fourteen-year-old sister Clara. Mike and Jen would try reasoning with him: "You probably want to go to bed now because you're so tired in the morning it's hard for you to get up." Ethan wouldn't budge. He would insist they were wrong and, if he was in a particularly irritable mood, would tell them they were "annoying" or call them "idiots" or sometimes even tell them to "f— off!" Mike and Jen would look at each other in disbelief. "Where are we going wrong?" they wondered.

Sometimes they would yell at Ethan: "Turn off the TV and go to bed!" Or threaten, "You'll lose your Xbox for a week if you don't get to bed right now!" Unphased, Ethan would counter, "Go ahead. I don't care." Out of desperation to get Ethan and themselves the sleep they needed, they even tried bribes, "Go to bed and we'll get you that Red Sox hat you want." Often, they would feel defeated and go upstairs, leaving Ethan to get himself to bed. On these occasions of resignation, Clara would offer her critique of their parenting, "You let him get away with way too much. You need to put your foot down." Annoyed, Mike would tell Clara that they didn't need parenting advice from her. She'd reply pointedly, "I think you do."

Things were even worse in the morning. It was nearly impossible to rouse Ethan. When they did manage to drag him out of bed, he was in a terrible mood. It seemed like he intentionally moved as slowly as he possibly could. They'd nag him to get ready. "You're going to be late for school and make us late for work." He'd rudely reply, "That sounds like a *you* problem." Jen would think, "Oh my god, he has no empathy at all!" It was such a stressful situation. He was going to miss the bus and one of them was going to be stuck driving him to school. On some days, Ethan would be remorseful and promise that he'd "do better to be good." Inevitably, though, the evening would come around, and oppositional Ethan would return.

At school Ethan would get into arguments with his classmates over a playground game. At little league he would embarrass himself and his parents when he made an out—crying, blaming the umpire, throwing his bat and helmet. "The phone has stopped ringing for playdates," Jen expressed her worry about his social life. "I know the kids are getting together, but they aren't including Ethan. The other kids are getting less willing to put up with him." Their world was shrinking as the problems got bigger. She also was finding it increasingly difficult to put up with Ethan's challenging nature: "I am embarrassed to say this, but sometimes I don't like him. I feel like he's a bad kid." Mike and Jen were also too embarrassed to admit in our first meeting that Ethan's challenging behavior was leading to more tension and fighting between them as the stress and desperation of the situation wore on their nerves. They felt like their family was so dysfunctional and they were screwing everything up. With a nervous laugh, Jen said, "You probably think we're the worst parents."

Mike and Jen aren't alone in expecting their parenting to be criticized. While most parents feel that their parenting is negatively judged at least some of the time, the parents of challenging boys experience judgment and blame almost constantly. Parents of challenging boys feel stressed at friends' houses, worried about what their son might do. They endure parenting advice from relatives and get disapproving looks from strangers at the grocery store. Parents of challenging boys feel incredibly self-conscious because they know that others believe that their "bad" parenting is the cause of their son's disruptive behavior.

In Mike and Jen's case, even their own daughter, Clara, was critical of their parenting. Her words rang in their ears. "You're letting him walk all over you!" They almost didn't reach out for help because they feared that a therapist would also blame them for Ethan's problems. It's like not calling my fire department to help me with my kitchen fire because I felt embarrassed.

Parenting a challenging boy is very hard. You walk on eggshells and are on alert 24/7 because you never know what will set your son off next. It's unrelenting. It is a terrible thing to have a difficult problem to solve and on top of that to have to deal with the painful emotions that go with feeling blamed for it. The truth is nobody has any idea about how incredibly difficult it is to have a challenging boy (unless they have one themselves) but they will judge you and blame you anyway.

This ever-present criticism from others is painful, but it isn't even as bad as what is going on inside the head of the parent of a challenging boy. You agree with the critics! Like Mike and Jen, you also think that you and your co-parent must be doing something terribly wrong. You believe that you are bad parents and that the problems your child is having are all your fault. These negative feelings raise your internal emotional pressure and make it much harder to stay cool when your son is challenging. While it is easy to get into criticizing yourself and blaming yourself, you need to stop it. You shouldn't blame yourself, because it isn't your fault.

Psychologist James Garbarino points out that parents of typical kids just don't get it. It is easy for them to be on their high horses about what great parents they are because they don't realize that raising typical children is easy compared to having a challenging boy. Dr. Garbarino illustrates this point with a story from his own experience as a parent. He describes the contrast of how teacher conference day went for his two children—a challenging boy and a typical girl. Garbarino and his wife loved going to the meetings for their daughter because the teachers would talk about what a delight she was to have in class and would praise them for the wonderful job they were doing. It made them feel like great parents. However, they dreaded the conferences for their challenging son. In those meetings, the teachers would review his poor academic performance and his disruptive classroom behavior and would wonder what was going on at the Garbarino house. These meetings left them feeling like incompetent failures. The same parents, very different results. Parenting their son, because he was a challenging boy, was just much harder and often less satisfying than parenting their daughter.

My experience over almost thirty years of working with challenging boys and their families mirrors Garbarino's observations. I've yet to see a case where bad parenting caused the child's challenging behavior. At its heart, challenging behavior is largely the result of temperamental challenges (specifically high emotional reactivity and poor self-regulation) and executive functioning problems (poor inhibitory control, working memory, and cognitive flexibility). These are the things that make a child challenging—not inadequate parenting. Psychological research has shown that problems of temperament and executive functioning have a large genetic basis. I'll talk more about temperament and executive functioning in chapter 2 when we take a deep dive into the real reasons that your son is challenging.

That you didn't cause your child's challenging behavior doesn't mean that you are helpless to bring about change. In the words of Dr. Stanley Greenspan, "You aren't the cause, but you can be the solution." We aren't to blame for our son's challenging behavior, but we can help him learn how to be happier and get along better in the world. It's not just difficult to parent a challenging boy. It is difficult to *be* a challenging boy. As parents we can help our sons to appreciate the positive aspects of their challenging nature and to develop skills for better managing their challenging emotions, impulses, and behavior. "Being the solution" requires a clear understanding of your son, yourself, and your current family context. Before we can take an honest look at our situation, we need to clear away the misguided blame and accompanying bad feelings of guilt, anger, and shame.

LET GO OF BLAME SO YOU CAN FOCUS ON SOLVING THE PROBLEM

In the chapters that follow I'm going to teach you how to create and execute a plan designed to help you solve your son's problem with challenging behavior—a problem that you didn't cause. Not only are you not the cause, but getting caught up in the pain of guilt and shame just distracts you from focusing on the things you can do to "be the solution."

There's a great scene in the movie *Apollo 13* that takes place with the three astronauts many thousands of miles away from the earth in their damaged spacecraft. Tensions are running high. A very real possibility exists that they won't make it home alive and two of the astronauts (played by Kevin Bacon and Bill Paxton) start angrily pointing fingers of blame at each other. Finally, Commander Jim Lovell (played by Tom Hanks) interrupts the blame drama and says,

"We are not going to do this. We are not going to go bouncing off the walls for ten minutes. We're just going to end up right back here with the same problems, trying to stay alive." Lovell points out that they have problems that urgently need attention if they are going to make it safely back to earth. Blame, whether it's directed at yourself or others, leads to defensiveness, conflicts, and losing one's cool. It further takes up valuable time, energy, and mental space that could be devoted to working on finding solutions to the problems at hand.

Another problem with blame is that it alienates the people we need to team up with to have a chance to solve big problems. The astronauts in *Apollo 13* need to work together to survive. Their argument over who is to blame threatens that teamwork. Safety and success require collaboration. Firefighters never go into a burning building alone. It's too easy to get disoriented in the hot, smoky environment. You need a partner that has your back and helps you stay safe.[2] In families, challenging boys often create a wedge between parents. As parenting expert Jane Nelson says, parents need to be kind *and* firm. Challenging boys' behavior tends to polarize their parents such that one parent becomes almost exclusively kind (that is, so understanding of the boy's difficult feelings that they don't insist that he take responsibility for his actions) while the other parent becomes excessively firm (that is, so focused on rules, limits, and consequences that the boys' emotions are overlooked). In solving the problem of challenging behavior, you need teamwork between the parents, the child, and others including extended family members, teachers, special educators, pediatricians, and therapists.

One of our most important jobs as parents is to prepare our children for a safe and successful transition into the world of work and relationships. When we have a challenging child, we worry that there will be problems with the launch. We fear that if he struggles this much now, how will he ever manage college, have a relationship, or hold a job? We can feel like the Apollo 13 astronauts, claustrophobically

---

2. Typically, this partner will be your child's other parent. In the case of single parents, or when you can't co-parent with your child's other parent, others can be partners: grandparents, aunts/uncles, therapists, etcetera.

trapped together (we felt this acutely during COVID lockdown) with time running out on our efforts to prepare our son for life. This creates an emotional pressure cooker, like the Apollo 13 spacecraft, where fear and anger run hot, and blame follows.

When we're looking to place blame, it appears on the surface that we are trying to identify the causes of the problem. It must be somebody's fault. It's the bad teacher, or the school. We blame our spouse: if they weren't too harsh, or so lenient, then things wouldn't be this way. We blame our child: "he's lazy, oppositional, manipulative." We blame ourselves and feel like failures as parents. Blame isn't solution oriented. It is about criticizing, judging negatively, and determining who is the bad person deserving of punishment for the mess you are in. Blame encourages ruminating on backward-looking thoughts like, "How could this have happened?" "Why me?" or "This can't be my life!" We need to tell ourselves, as Commander Lovell reminded his crew, that blame only gets in the way of solving the very big and important problems we're facing.

Remember Ryan's parents fighting to get him off the computer in the evenings. Ryan was disrespectful to them and defied their rules. Conflicts over computer use weren't the only problems they fought about. Emails were coming in from teachers that Ryan wasn't doing his homework. He was verging on failing several classes. His parents, Tracy and Bob, tried punishing him by taking away his computer time. They tried bribing him with in-game purchases on his favorite video games. Nothing seemed effective. They had a hard time sticking with their consequences. Ryan had a hard time doing his part to earn the rewards. He didn't do some assignments because he said they were boring. Others he didn't do because they were difficult; he got frustrated and gave up. What dumbfounded his parents even more was that when he did do the work, he sometimes didn't turn it in. They wanted to try medication, but Ryan refused to take it. Tracy and Bob were desperate. They felt an urgent need for something to be done, but what?

Like the Apollo 13 astronauts, Ryan's parents started placing blame. On the school: "We did the testing. They should have given him an IEP." On his teachers: "They should know that he's not able to reach out for help. They have to go to him." On each other. Ryan's dad blamed his wife's volatility for causing the fights with Ryan. Ryan's mom blamed her husband's conflict avoidance. Both blamed Ryan for being lazy. When they met with me, they blamed themselves. Then and now they were very embarrassed by Ryan's behavior at school. Tracy and Bob felt like failures. They were alienating each other, and they were at risk of alienating the school. Although there was some truth in these "blame statements," the blame interfered with finding solutions. What they needed was a plan for how to change things going forward.

Blame triggers the fight-or-flight response which shuts off rational thinking. Sometimes blame sends us into fight mode—yelling at our child (for making us feel like such a failure as a parent) or at our spouse (for causing our child's problems). More frequently, blame evokes intensely painful feelings of shame and guilt, which lead to a flight response.[3] We retreat into defensiveness. We avoid thinking about our family problems because, when we do, we just end up feeling bad about ourselves and our sons. Blame further interferes with our ability to learn what's really causing our problems and figuring out what can be done to correct them. It leads to a focus on faults and defects—ours, our co-parent's, our son's. Blame doesn't just divert our attention from constructive problem-solving, it also disrupts the type of thinking necessary for developing solutions.

Obviously, avoiding thinking about problems never solves anything—usually the problems just get worse from neglecting them. Even if we try to think about the problems we're having with our child, the guilt and shame of blame disrupt our thinking. They create a negative bias in how we evaluate problems. Guilt and shame make problems seem much harder to solve than they actually are. These

---

3. Many psychologists distinguish "guilt," the bad feeling associated with having done something wrong, from "shame," the bad feeling associated with believing oneself to be bad, defective, inferior. In my experience, when it comes to the parents of challenging boys, they experience a painful mixture of guilt and shame that is very harsh. I use the words *guilt* and *shame* more or less interchangeably to refer to this painful experience of feeling bad and at fault.

emotions also interfere with the creative brainstorming necessary for generating possible solutions to problems; instead, we remain stuck in inside-the-box thinking. Finally, guilt and shame evoke a depressive response: decreased energy, diminished motivation, and feelings of hopelessness and helplessness. This depressed state is the opposite of the grit, resilience, and persistence that we need for improving a challenging situation.

Perhaps the most destructive aspect of blaming yourself is that it creates a cycle of guilt and anger that makes everyone involved unhappy. When you feel you have caused your son's problems, your self-esteem and mood suffer accordingly. Tracy and Bob felt very guilty and ashamed about not supporting Ryan better with his difficulties at school. This guilt led them to let a lot of his disrespect and defiance slide by.

Guilt, however, is not a stable emotion. It's one side of a coin that has anger on the other. Eventually, when the guilt feelings grow to the point where they become overwhelming, the coin flips and the feelings change to anger. You can only take so much. It's as if you can't help saying, "Wait a minute, it's not my fault. It's theirs!" (referring to your son or your spouse). As the anger intensifies, you are increasingly at risk of losing your cool and blowing up at your son or saying something to him that will be hurtful and that you will later regret. Ryan's behavior was incredibly provocative. Tracy and Bob, like all people, had their limits. One day at her wits end, Tracy flipped from her self-blame into Ryan-blame and screamed, "You don't need to live here! You can go to boarding school!"

We're all human and we all, like Tracy, lose it. We yell, threaten, or shame our child when he's being challenging. You might want to stop me and point out: "That *is* bad parenting." Definitely, these reactions do not help solve the problems of your son's challenging behavior and they can even make the problems more ingrained. Challenging behavior is stressful to deal with and frequently provokes reactions from us that escalate the situation. However, I believe it's more accurate to think of yelling, threats, and other regrettable parenting behaviors as *reactions to* challenging behavior rather than a cause. When faced with meltdowns in the supermarket, refusal to do homework, or disrespectful backtalk, parents feel helpless and are desperate to get through the challenging event using any means they can. We threaten, bribe, yell, beg, cave, all in an effort to survive the stressful situation our child has created. You feel like you must be a terrible parent given the way your child acts and given the way you are constantly losing your cool and doing all the things that parenting books tell you not to do.

Instead of taking the blame (which you shouldn't because you aren't the cause), I want to help you take *responsibility* (which you are already doing by reading this book). Responsibility is empowering. It aims at understanding the problem: What happened? What is my contribution? What can I do to change things? While blame is stuck in the past, responsibility accepts present circumstances as they are and focuses on creating a path to a better future. Blame asks, "Who should feel bad about getting us here?" Responsibility asks, "What are we going to do now to make things better?" Blame focuses on pain and regret around past choices. Responsibility focuses on the choices you are currently making and the ones you will make in the future. Blame is about condemnation; responsibility is about accountability.

We are responsible for our own behavior. When we *react* to our child's behavior unthinkingly from impulse, or from fight-or-flight, we are not being responsible. We are reactive. When our *response* to our child, like a firefighter's, occurs with a clear head and according to a predetermined plan—we are taking *response*-ability. I'm going to teach you how to be responsive, not reactive. Letting go of blame helps us take responsibility.

I hope by now I've convinced you that blame generates bad feelings that make us more reactive and make it harder to keep our cool. Responsiveness implies calm, thoughtful, planful action. Reactive behavior is immediate, reflexive, and unthinking. One of the most important capacities that your child can possess is the ability to take responsibility for himself, his feelings, his actions, and his life. Cultivating responsibility in our sons is one of the key objectives of this book. The most powerful way we can teach responsibility is by modeling it. You begin to model responsibility by bypassing blame and focusing on effective problem-solving.

Firefighters don't have to fight the additional burden of dealing with blame and judgment when fighting a fire. They didn't start the fire. Parents didn't start the fire of challenging behavior, but as a culture we blame them, and they blame themselves. We can't do much to prevent the judgment of others, but if we can avoid judging and blaming ourselves, the judgments of others won't sting so much. It's when the judgment of others echoes our own self-blame that we are especially vulnerable to being reactive. It just hurts so much more. It's as if our self-criticism and the other's criticism team up to make us feel really bad. Freeing oneself from blame so that we can remain calm and responsive and be part of the solution is one of the most important tasks for parents of challenging boys.

DEALING WITH OUR BAGGAGE FROM THE PAST

I've made my argument as to why you shouldn't blame yourself for the problems your son is having. First, you aren't the cause of the problem, even if you have unintentionally contributed to it. Second, blame makes it harder to keep our cool. Finally, blame diverts attention from finding solutions and interferes with engaging in the type of thinking needed for good problem-solving. I hope I've been convincing. However, even if you are persuaded that it's not your fault, you still might find it difficult to let go of blame. Even if you feel appropriate relief reading the preceding section, it is my experience that most parents of challenging boys eventually drift back into blaming themselves for their child's problems.

This almost inevitable return of blame relates to the fact that being a parent places us once again in a parent-child relationship. Conflicts with our challenging kids stir up unprocessed issues from our own past. So, when we are dealing with our children in the present, we are also emotionally transported back in time to our own childhoods. The shocking truth is that most adults experienced some form of serious hardship growing up: abuse, neglect, domestic violence, parental substance abuse, and so on.

Even if we are among the minority who had the good fortune to grow up in a safe and stable home, unresolved issues from childhood can still resurface in interactions with our challenging sons. There is good news in this. Because being a parent revives unprocessed issues from our childhood, we are given a wonderful opportunity to heal old wounds. However, it explains why it can be so difficult to avoid blame and so very difficult to remain calm in challenging moments—our childhood experiences weren't always positive. Children tend to blame themselves for the bad things that happen in their lives—a common example is parental divorce. It's very painful to feel blame, but it creates the illusion for the child that they at least had some control. They might falsely believe that, if they were good enough or fixed their faults, they could prevent more bad things from happening. This is a big part of the reason that blame is so difficult to let go of now.

In reality, as small children, we were essentially helpless in the face of family circumstances where we were neglected, hurt, or frightened. When bad experiences like these are buried and moved past—left unprocessed and unresolved—they leave an emotional residue. These buried feelings make us vulnerable to being emotionally "triggered" by situations in our current life that are reminiscent of the bad past events. Old feelings of danger from your childhood can make being in your family today feel unsafe, especially in times of conflict, even though you are no longer a helpless child. You are now an adult, and you are the parent. The beginning of healing is realizing that these very painful feelings aren't the result of things happening now with our challenging sons, but instead they are emotional memories of events that happened in the long ago and far away time of our own childhoods.

An illustrative example comes from the Ross family. Eight-year-old Josh would have intense meltdowns. He'd scream and cry when his parents would turn off his video games. He loved playing sports, but he'd often refuse to go to practice or even a game. His parents, Chris and Andrea, would encourage him to go. They'd talk to him about the commitment he made to his teammates. The more his parents pushed him to go, the more out of control he would get, sometimes hitting or kicking them. Once Josh even threatened to jump out of his bedroom window. Because of these extreme explosions, Chris and Andrea didn't feel safe leaving him with a babysitter, they felt trapped in their own home.

During Josh's outbursts, Chris used threats and punishments to try to assert control. He was incensed by Josh's disrespectful and defiant behavior. When things would inevitably escalate, Chris would walk away leaving Andrea alone to wrestle and restrain Josh to keep him from hitting her.

Andrea was extremely stressed by Chris's behavior. She hated how he started out harsh, then disappeared. When Andrea would complain to Chris about his walking away, he'd get defensive and say he was trying to not make things worse. This was all having a terrible impact on their relationship.

Josh very much reminded Chris of his brother. Chris's brother and father would have huge escalating fights that sometimes got physically violent. Chris's father believed in absolute parental authority and thought the worst thing would be to back down in the face of Chris's brother's defiance. In these awful episodes, Chris would hide in his room and tune out, sorting through his baseball cards waiting for the fight to be over.

Josh's behavior now was evoking these feelings from Chris's childhood: rage, fear, and helplessness. These past feelings confused Chris. He would try to assert his authority at first, then become paralyzed. Because he was triggered, he couldn't be there for his wife and son in the present.

Chris felt very confused about how to be a father to Josh. He was terrified that Josh would turn out to be like his brother whose adult life has been a disaster. Chris's brother has never been able to hold down a job or keep a relationship. Chris was stuck in a fight-or-flight reaction from the past. He didn't want to fight with Josh like his father and brother did, so he thought the only option left to him was to flee. Being triggered into fight-or-flight mode limited Chris's ability to imagine ways of responding that were neither fighting nor fleeing, but instead would allow him to remain present to help his wife and son.

When we are triggered, we often don't remember the corresponding childhood situation consciously. Chris didn't initially make the connection between his feelings about Josh's explosions and his childhood experiences of the awful fights between his father and brother. The metaphor often used is that we have a "button." Interactions with our child can push these buttons of ours. It's like the button on a time machine that takes us from the present moment back in time to the feelings and reactions of some unremembered past. Instead of recalling past events, however, we reexperience the emotions and physiological reactions as if they belong to the present situation. We confuse past and present. It's difficult to recognize that we're triggered by our son's challenging behavior because our reactions feel very vividly to be about the present situation, even though they actually come from our unhealed past. We can only see evidence that we are triggered indirectly.

When you have a challenging boy, triggering situations occur over and over again. Your son keeps exploding, defying, melting down, harassing you or his siblings. These episodes often happen at the most inconvenient times and in the most embarrassing circumstances. It is extremely upsetting, and if we haven't planned ahead, we can feel like Chris did, that we have no good options about how to respond. Although they all feel terrible, any given episode of challenging behavior isn't actually that big a deal. It is the overall accumulation of these episodes over time and whether the trajectory is worsening or moving toward improvement that really matters. However, when we're triggered, each episode can *feel* like it is practically life or death, and we *feel* we are to blame for what is happening. It's almost impossible to remain calm when the stakes feel so high.

Our unprocessed traumas leave hazards behind, like faulty wiring in an old house. A hidden problem that can spark and cause a fire when circuits get overloaded. Just as flickering lights, strange odors, or hot outlet covers can indicate the presence of potentially dangerous electrical problems, getting triggered in interactions with our challenging sons gives us clues to the presence of emotional "wiring issues" that need to be identified and healed.

Signs we are triggered include experiencing sudden strong feelings of anger, fear, or helplessness. We act impulsively—often too aggressively. Overall, our feelings and reactions are too intense; they don't match the situation we are in. Or we get shut down, paralyzed, numb. After an episode is over, we can often see signs that we were triggered in the "hangover" of shame, hopelessness, and despair that is left behind. You also might find that you have a hard time remembering exactly what happened, because you were in an altered state and not processing what was going on. Anything can be a trigger, although some common examples include backtalk, lying, disrespect, ignoring you, getting in trouble at school, and bullying siblings.

Frequently our son's challenging behavior can trigger us by reminding us of some difficult person from our early life. Like Chris, your son can evoke old feelings about the brother who bullied you, an impaired sibling who took up all your parents' attention, or a rigid father who was prone to outbursts. It's very likely in instances of challenging behavior that your reactions are shaped by your experiences with that person. You can flashback to terrifying fights in your house growing up. You can also feel worried that your son will turn out like your relative, especially if things have gone badly in that person's life.

Getting triggered by challenging behavior can also lead to fights between spouses because frequently we are both triggered by the episode. In the case of Chris and Andrea, Chris was triggered and left Andrea alone to handle Josh's meltdowns. Andrea was also triggered by the situation. Growing up she felt abandoned by her father when she got into conflicts with her volatile mother. Andrea wanted her father to defend her, but he was often at work or otherwise unavailable. Chris's retreat during fights with Josh brought up these old painful feelings of being alone and unprotected. In their triggered states, Andrea and Chris blamed and criticized each other, leading to increasing tension, conflict, and escalating fights between them. They both felt terribly upset and alone.

Signs That You Might Be Triggered

- You experience a rush of feelings of anger, fear, or helplessness.
- You have feelings that are too intense and don't match the circumstances.
- You feel you are in a near life-or-death crisis and that something must be done now.
- You feel your heart racing, your skin flushing, you feel out of breath, or even that you are having a panic attack.
- You act impulsively, sometimes shocking yourself or those you are with.
- You raise your voice.
- You interrupt.
- You say hurtful things you don't really mean or make extreme threats.
- You overreact, or "snap."
- You become overly aggressive.
- You shut down or become paralyzed.
- You feel mistrustful of your spouse—that they are leaving you alone in the crisis or actively working against you.
- After the event you feel a hangover of bad feelings: shame, hopelessness, despair.
- After the episode you feel like you don't know what came over you. You didn't act like yourself.
- After the episode you find that you can't remember what happened very clearly.
- After the episode you feel numb or are consumed by fearful rumination.
- After the episode you can't believe that you acted in the same repetitive, unproductive way that you swore you wouldn't.

Once, when my middle daughter was fourteen, she announced to us she was going to be sleeping over at a friend's house that weekend. My wife responded pointedly, "You mean you're asking us if you can go?" Our daughter grunted "yes." My wife and I told her that we wanted to speak with the girl's parents. My daughter yelled, "You're so embarrassing. Nobody does that!" Thrown off momentarily, I wondered if we were somehow the crazy strict parents our daughter was painting us to be. She pushed further, "Don't you trust me?" I was starting to feel irritated.

We went back and forth like that for a while with her insisting that we were asking for something ridiculous and us responding that we would feel more comfortable speaking with the parents. It started getting increasingly difficult for me to remain calm in the face of her opposition. Finally, something in me snapped and I found myself yelling "*my* feelings matter!" My wife shot me a look that said, "What the hell is up with you?"

This type of interaction had been repeated many times with my daughter in those years. She'd do typical adolescent things: not completing her chores, fighting against her curfew, and saying things to me like "I'm too busy for that" when I would ask her to do something for me. I'd be determined to stay calm, but I often ended up getting very angry. To my frustration and dismay, each time I reacted angrily, she'd feel more convinced that she was justified in not listening to me. I would feel upset at myself for overreacting. I felt like a bad parent.

These episodes always left me feeling disappointed in myself for losing my cool. I wasn't teaching her anything. My anger was only convincing her that I judged her unfairly and that I didn't understand her. The repetitive nature of these interactions and my angry overreaction were both signs that I was triggered. So, I did what I'm going to recommend you do throughout this book. I wrote about the sleepover fight in a journal. I wrote about what happened, including as much of the minute-to-minute detail as I could remember from how it began, to what I did, what I said, what she did and said, what emotions I experienced, and what sensations I felt in my body.

Most of us don't like thinking about (much less writing about) upsetting events we have with our children. Once the episodes are over, we want to move on. Thinking about it can feel like picking at a wound. When things are calm, we don't want to return to the event and its bad feelings. However, getting it out on the page is cathartic.

Writing about upsetting events helps process and dissipate the bad feelings. Writing also helps us get clearer about what is going on during these repetitive challenging moments.

As I wrote about my episode with my daughter, I wondered why I started yelling. It made no sense. My wife and I had all the power in the situation. She couldn't go to the sleepover if we didn't give her permission. In talking about the situation with my wife, she said, half-jokingly, "She was just being a teenager. Teenagers are annoying." Something suddenly clicked for me: "She's right!" Teenagers are self-centered and it's normal for them to push for more independence. My daughter wasn't supposed to be focused on my feelings. I was starting to see how I was triggered. My anger was misdirected. It *felt* intensely real that the reason I was angry was my daughter not taking my feelings into account. However, it was becoming clearer and clearer that the feelings mainly belonged to another time and place. This is the thing about childhood issues, we remember the past in our feelings and our bodies. We do not consciously recall the times and places that those emotional memories were formed. My feelings with my daughter felt like they were in response to what was happening with her in the present moment, but they were more about events from decades ago in my childhood relationship with my parents.

Growing up with two mathematicians as parents, rationality and order were valued much more in my house than the messiness of emotions. The pain of my feelings not being paid attention to as a kid was being placed on my daughter now. This button getting pushed, along with the resulting anger, was harming our relationship. It was also interfering with working out the issues that were occurring now. My anger only led to her tuning me out more. With the recognition that her behavior was pushing my buttons, and with the understanding of what button was being pushed, I could prepare for the feelings that would be evoked in me the next time she acted this way. I would still feel the feelings, but I would also know that they weren't giving me useful information about how to parent her now.

How did I discover that I was being triggered? There were clues. One was the intensity of my feelings. They didn't match the situation we were in. Also, I felt extremely bad afterward. I was upset at hurting her and confused with how I'd gotten sucked into the same old pattern once again. Another clue was that I wasn't acting like myself. I'm typically a fairly calm person and I don't usually get angry quickly, but in this moment with my daughter I got very angry, and it came on suddenly.

Writing about the upsetting interaction with my daughter helped me get some objectivity about what was going on. It also recalled a particularly painful episode of my parents not listening to me when I was twelve. This is another important benefit of writing about our challenging experiences with our children. Sometimes it helps us identify specific wounds from our own childhoods that need to be healed.

With my daughter and the sleepover, I was able to see the situation in a new light. Once I calmed down, I understood that my daughter's opposition was the result of her feeling anxious. I knew that she was very sensitive to anything that might embarrass her in front of her friends. In this non-triggered state of mind, I was able to approach the problem of the sleepover in a much more compassionate *and* effective manner. We were lucky that the conflict eventually subsided without too much more fighting.

PARENTING JOURNAL

Throughout this book you will be using a parenting journal. The parenting journal is where you will work through exercises that will enable you to make a plan for solving your son's problem with challenging behavior. The parenting journal is also the place where you will process the difficult feelings that arise in the course of raising your challenging boy. When bad feelings and bad events are buried and not processed, they have a negative effect on our emotional and physical health. Also, unprocessed negative feelings have a negative impact on our relationship with our son. They leak out in irritated tones of voice, in overreactions to minor offenses, in sarcastic reactions, and so on.

Writing in the parenting journal is the cornerstone of the approach presented in this book. It creates a record of challenging episodes. Once written down, we can look at situations more objectively. We can identify where we are being triggered. We can also see what triggers our child. As we learn more about our child's "buttons" and our own, we will begin to see ways to avoid or de-escalate moments of challenging behavior. Additionally, in the process of writing about our experiences of conflict with our child, we might find that painful memories of childhood come up needing to be healed. The exercises in subsequent chapters will lead you through analyzing your journal entries of challenging moments to extract triggers and patterns and use this data to devise a plan for dealing with challenging behavior going forward.

Most of us don't take the time to process upsetting events. We don't want to think about the awful past pains; we want to forget and move on. Bottling up feelings can cause physical and psychological stress, make us more reactive or numb and paralyzed, and prevent us from learning the important lessons that can be learned from the episodes. Psychological research shows that people who write journal entries about upsetting events get over the bad feelings faster than those who try to forget and move on. Writing about painful events is physically healthier too. It is associated with a reduction of health-damaging stress hormones in the body. Perhaps most significantly for you and your challenging boy, writing about regrettable events helps improve people's relationships. Additionally, writing about and reflecting on these upsetting episodes helps us see and own our share of responsibility in the conflict and to take the steps necessary to repair things with our son. We'll discuss more about repair in later chapters.

First select your journal. There is some evidence to suggest that a handwritten journal may lead to better emotional processing. An advantage of using one of the many journaling phone apps is that your phone is always at hand and many of them include password protection so that even if someone has access to your phone, the contents of the journal can be kept secret. What matters most, whether you choose paper or electronic, is that your journal can be kept in a place where you can access it relatively easily, but you also can be sure that others, especially your children, will not be able to read it. You need to feel safe being open about your feelings.

KEY IDEAS
Blame
- Parents of challenging children need to plan and prepare for challenging moments (just like firefighters do) so that they also can remain calm and effective.
- Blaming ourselves or others for our son's challenging behavior interferes with solving the problem.
- Challenging behavior originates in temperamental problems and executive functioning problems, not bad parenting.

Trauma, Triggers, and Buttons
- Our son's challenging behavior can trigger strong feelings in us that *feel vividly* like they relate to what is happening in the here and now of our relationship with our son, but they actually are related to painful experiences from our own childhoods.
- We need to learn what our triggers or "buttons" are, so that we can recognize when we are triggered to avoid overreacting to our son's challenging behavior.
- Writing about our challenging interactions with our son, and our painful childhood experiences, helps us heal our childhood wounds and respond to our son more effectively in the present.

PARENTING JOURNAL EXERCISE
To jump start your journal, I'm going to ask you to write for fifteen minutes a day for the next four days. Set a timer to let you know when time is up. I want you to write about the most painful and upsetting moments you have experienced in parenting your challenging son. It might be a moment that you can't quite forgive yourself or your son for. It might be a moment that you feel strong embarrassment or shame about. Once you have decided upon what you will be writing about, let your thoughts and feelings flow freely onto the page. You might find that your writing takes you to your own childhood, to your

relationship with your parents or siblings, to your relationship with your spouse, to your feelings about yourself as a parent, or to some unexpected place. You may end up writing about more than one incident over the course of the four days. Follow where your writing takes you. Most people ultimately find this exercise liberating and it can lead to renewed joy in parenting and a revived determination to finally address your son's challenging behavior effectively. However, you might find that you initially feel strong feelings like sadness, anger, fear, or depression. These feelings should subside over the course of a few hours. If, in your writing, you find that the feelings evoked are too painful or overwhelming, stop writing or write about a different topic.

Things to reflect on as you write:

- Describe what happened in as much detail as you can remember. Starting from before the event began. How were you feeling? Happy, sad, neutral, tired, agitated? What do you think influenced your behavior? How was your son doing? What factors might have been influencing him? We're looking for clues about what was going on in you and your son that might have triggered the episode.
- What feelings did you experience?
- What do you think your child was feeling?
- How did it make you feel about yourself?
- How has it influenced you as a parent?
- How has it impacted your relationship with your child's other parent?
- What childhood experiences are you reminded of?
- If you find yourself getting stuck in ruminating about blame (whose fault it is/was), try to redirect your attention to the sadness you feel about the pain that you suffered, your family has suffered, or your son suffers.

To read an example of this type of journal writing, refer to the accompanying pdf found at www.challengingboys.com/book.

CHAPTER TWO

The Real Roots of Challenging Behavior
Temperament and Executive Functioning

After a blaze has been extinguished and the scene has been secured, fire investigators arrive and sift through the charred remains to identify the cause. Of particular concern to the investigators is determining whether or not the fire was deliberately set. Challenging behavior feels like deliberate defiance, but like fire investigators, we need to conduct a more thorough examination of its causes.

I hope I convinced you in chapter 1 that you aren't to blame for your son's problems with challenging behavior. So, if you aren't a bad parent, does that mean that your son is a bad child? Is he just willful and oppositional? It can feel like it. In describing their sons, parents of challenging boys will say to me things like: "he won't accept 'no' for an answer," "he only wants to do what *he* wants to do," and "he thinks the rules don't apply to him." When they try to set limits and apply consequences he says, "Go ahead and punish me. I don't care!" He can be rude and disrespectful, swearing at you and calling you stupid. You have to walk on eggshells and yet somehow your son always feels that *he* is the victim, often blaming others for his misbehavior. It's easy to conclude that challenging boys just don't care about the rules or the feelings of others, that challenging behavior is deliberate and intentional. It feels like your son doesn't cooperate because he doesn't want to, that he misbehaves to get what he wants.

Despite how it feels, challenging behavior rarely is intentional misbehavior. In fact, over the course of thirty years of working with challenging boys and their families, I've yet to meet a challenging boy who wouldn't do anything to have friends and be successful at school, to get along with siblings and peers, and, most importantly, to feel that his parents love him and are proud of him. But if challenging behavior doesn't start with incompetent parents or bad kids, where does it come from?

Consider this: to comply with a request, expectation, or demand from others (e.g., a parent, teacher, or peers), a child must rely on several skills or capacities. Responding appropriately requires that the child be able to stop what he is doing, pay attention to the request, comprehend the request, regulate his emotions/body/impulses, and suppress any inappropriate responses he might be inclined to give. That's a lot of steps!

Challenging behavior occurs when a boy is faced with circumstances that he doesn't have the emotional or cognitive skills to handle. Most frequently it's triggered by a teacher or parent asking him to follow a rule or comply with an instruction, but it can also happen when the boy has to accept a disappointment (like losing a game), deal with a frustration (like difficult schoolwork), or navigate a conflict with a sibling or peer. In these moments, a challenging boy is vulnerable to the experience of "flooding" or "fight-or-flight," where he is psychologically and emotionally overwhelmed. Fight-or-flight evolved to help our animal ancestors in situations where survival required immediate action. Adrenaline surges through the body to prepare to fight the threat or to run away. The rational mind is shut down because there's no time for thinking. Challenging behavior results from this emotional flooding. A challenging boy will try to avoid or evade the demand—that is, flee—or he will fight against the person making the demand (yell, hit, etc.) to get it withdrawn. It is not premeditated, manipulative, or seeking to get one's own way. It's not willful or oppositional. Challenging behavior is a sign that the child simply doesn't have the skills he needs to meet the challenges facing him.

When a challenging boy is flooded, he can't think straight. He can't take in information. He can't listen to reason. He can't have a constructive problem-solving conversation. He can't learn any lessons. He can't communicate his big feelings effectively. His brain has been hijacked by his emotions. All of us get flooded from time to time when we feel under attack or overwhelmed. The most frequent occurrences are in conflicts with our spouse or when facing challenging behavior from our sons. In these moments fight-or-flight mode shuts down *our* thinking and we respond in ways that we often regret later, just like our sons.

Why are challenging boys so prone to being emotionally flooded by expectations that typical kids can handle with relative ease? For an answer to this question let's turn to a discussion of temperament and executive functioning problems.

TEMPERAMENT

Typically, challenging behavior problems do not appear suddenly in grade school. Parents tell me that their son was a fussy baby who was sensitive to noises, lights, and other environmental stimulation. I hear that he cried a lot and was difficult to soothe. There will be stories of parents who were exhausted to the bone because they couldn't get their son on any kind of a sleep schedule; he was difficult to settle and to get to sleep and woke frequently in the night. Often challenging boys were infants who had problems with breastfeeding, digestion, and later with toilet training. There will be tales of epic toddler tantrums that wouldn't quiet down for hours. You can see that challenging boys begin life as challenging infants and challenging toddlers.

Understanding challenging behavior problems begins with temperament. The study of temperament seeks to identify the biologically based differences in emotional reactions and behavior that are visible from the first months of life. Temperament forms the building blocks of later personality development.

While the study of temperament goes as far back as ancient Greece, contemporary research on infant temperament began with husband-and-wife team Alexander Thomas and Stella Chess in the 1960s who sought to understand the behavioral differences they observed in their adopted children. Thomas and Chess grouped infant temperamental differences into three broad categories: Easy, Difficult, and Slow to Warm Up. Easy babies are generally happy and smile frequently. These babies tend to have regular and predictable patterns of feeding, sleeping, and elimination, which makes it much easier for their caregivers to establish routines. Easy babies adapt well to new situations and are easy to soothe. Babies that are slow to warm up are anxious, cautious, and take time to adapt to new circumstances. Finally, difficult babies tend to experience frequent and intense negative emotional reactions; they are quite prone to getting emotionally flooded. They cry more often and more intensely. These babies are difficult to soothe, have a hard time with transitions, and adapt poorly to change. Difficult infants generally have problems with self-regulation and have irregular patterns of feeding, sleeping, and elimination.

The Thomas and Chess categories capture something essential about the experience of raising these different types of kids. It's easy to parent easy babies. They require less effort to meet their needs. It's more enjoyable to care for them and they make their parents feel like great parents. By contrast, parenting difficult babies is difficult. They leave parents feeling frustrated and like failures.

Research on temperament has progressed considerably since Thomas and Chess's groundbreaking work. Most researchers today find that the key elements of temperament include Negative Emotion (the tendency to experience anger, sadness, fear, and getting emotionally flooded) and Self-Regulation (the ability to regulate emotion, attention, and behavior and, in particular, to inhibit inappropriate responses). Consistent with this temperament research, most parents of challenging boys say that their sons were temperamentally "challenging" as infants and toddlers. Challenging boys tend to be high on negative emotion. They experience anger, frustration, sadness, and disappointment more frequently and more intensely and the feelings take longer to calm down. Challenging boys are also low on self-regulation. They struggle to handle emotions, impulses, and distractions. Having big negative feelings combined with a poor capacity to regulate oneself makes life difficult for challenging boys and their parents.

Emotional flooding makes it hard for challenging boys to meet the demands placed on them at school and home. Their intense internal distress further means that external consequences (like punishments from parents or teachers) feel less important. Big negative emotions also interfere with challenging boys engaging the self-control capacities that they do have. This emotional flooding shuts down parts of the brain associated with self-control. It's a vicious cycle. To make things even worse, not only do challenging boys frequently feel bad, but they also frustrate and exhaust the caregivers that they desperately need to help them regulate their bad feelings.

By now you're starting to get a picture of where challenging behavior comes from. Challenging boys' big negative feelings overwhelm and disrupt their fragile ability to control themselves. When any of us is overwhelmed by negative emotion, it's extremely difficult to turn our attention away from our inner distress onto the things we need to take care of in the outside environment. In a challenging boy's case, the task of shifting his attention from his big feelings onto following rules and complying with instructions is nearly impossible.

From the outside, a challenging boy looks like a spoiled child when he throws a temper tantrum because he doesn't get what he wants. On the inside, we now understand that he's losing it because he's overwhelmed by intense feelings of disappointment and frustration that he can't bring down to size. From the outside, a challenging kindergartener who bothers his neighbors, talks out of turn, and eventually leaves the circle during story time looks disobedient and disrespectful. On the inside, we see that he is unable to regulate himself—particularly his attention, his body, and his impulses.

In fact, when kindergarten teachers were interviewed about what factors are most important for school readiness, they focused on the child's ability to regulate their emotions, attention, and impulses. Academic factors like being able to count or identify letters were considered much less important. Children high on emotional negativity and low on self-regulation are absent from school more, struggle to participate while at school, and like school less.

We are beginning to see a new explanation for challenging behavior other than opposition or defiance. In our new understanding, a susceptibility to experience emotional flooding combined with a poor ability to control those emotions sets the stage for challenging behavior. These temperamental disadvantages—frequent experience of intense negative emotions combined with poor self-regulation—become bigger and bigger problems as a child grows up and the demands at school and home increase. For typical children, their capacity for self-regulation grows in parallel to these increased demands. Challenging boys, however, frequently fall further and further behind their peers in the development of self-regulation and are increasingly unable to meet age-related expectations. Temperament also plays an important role in a child's social development as poor self-regulation leads to inappropriate social responses, which in turn can lead to rejection by peers.

EXECUTIVE FUNCTIONING

As a child grows from infancy, to toddlerhood, to school age and beyond, his temperamental predispositions to feel intense negative emotions and to struggle with self-regulation continue to unfold and are also shaped by life experiences. The study of executive functioning focuses on the development of the capacity for self-regulation. Just as executives are in charge of managing organizations, executive functions are the effortful, self-directed thought processes that we all use to manage ourselves: our emotions, our attention, our impulses.

Without executive functions we are trapped in automatic, habitual, impulsive responding. Without them we can't stop and think about what we are doing or might want to do. We can't learn from the past or look to the future. We can't adapt to changing circumstances, motivate ourselves, or pay attention. Employing good executive functioning takes effort. It's much easier to just do what we always do, to get distracted by shiny objects, and to give in to temptations.

Executive functioning is what allows us to shape our lives through intentional choice, rather than being constantly shaped by forces outside ourselves. As an example, we've all heard how important it is to delay gratification. Eat your vegetables before dessert, do your homework before playing video games, and so on. Delayed gratification is associated with all kinds of positive outcomes across life. It is executive functioning that enables us to delay gratification: to stop the initial impulse to get our gratification immediately, to imagine a better future gratification, to keep our attention focused on that future gratification, and to stay motivated until we reach it.

I was fortunate in graduate school to work with Adele Diamond, a leading researcher in the field of executive functioning. According to Dr. Diamond there are three core executive functions: inhibitory control, working memory, and cognitive flexibility. I'll describe each below.

Inhibitory Control (or Inhibition)

Inhibitory control is what allows you to stop yourself. It's the foundational skill that all forms of self-control are built on. With inhibitory control we can stop ourselves from acting thoughtlessly on our impulses, our habits, and our temptations. Inhibitory control also enables us to stop distractions—both internal (unwanted thoughts and memories) and external (shiny objects and other temptations in the environment)—from interfering with us focusing our attention. This stopping of automatic reactions creates a space to insert thought. It allows us to think before we act. It empowers us to make intentional choices over what actions to take, what to pay attention to, and what goals to pursue.

You need inhibitory control to wait your turn, to not get distracted, to stick with difficult tasks, to not rush, to not retaliate, to follow the rules, and to stay physically safe (by not doing stupid things on impulse). In Dr. Diamond's words, "Without inhibitory control we would be at the mercy of impulses, old habits of thought or action (conditioned responses), and/or stimuli in the environment that pull us this way or that." When challenging boys aren't paying attention, are interrupting, aren't listening, are saying hurtful things, are responding aggressively to conflict, are procrastinating, etcetera, we are seeing problems with executive functioning—in these cases, largely problems with inhibitory control.

Working Memory

Working memory is what allows us to hold information in mind so that we can work with it. Without working memory, we are limited only to thinking about and working with things that are immediately in front of us. We need working memory to bring to mind information about factors that are not present—past experiences, future hopes—information that is crucial for our adaptive functioning. As Diamond eloquently points out, working memory allows us to shift from only dealing with information we can immediately *perceive* to also working with information that is not present but that we can *conceive* of—that is, bring to mind as an image or an idea. With working memory, we can recall past experiences and apply lessons learned. With working memory, we can imagine a future, set goals for it, and make plans to achieve it.

An example of working memory occurs in playing strategy games, even simple ones. We have to hold the rules of the game in working memory along with what's occurring in the game, as well as our strategy for winning. Another example of working memory is reading comprehension. Students use working memory to keep track of information from one paragraph and connect it to the next, and to hold in mind information from the whole essay to answer comprehension questions at the end. Working memory is also involved in executing multi-step instructions. For example, instructions for getting ready in the morning: "get dressed, brush your teeth, and pack your backpack for school."

Working memory is what allows you to experience time. Without working memory, we are forever stuck in the present, only able to think about what we are taking in immediately through our senses. Being in the present moment, as in meditation, is wonderful if it means not being lost in past regrets or future worries. Fulfillment in our relationships and our lives, however, requires that we can leave the present moment and bring to mind the lessons learned from past experiences and imagine future goals.

Psychologist Russell Barkley has described people with working memory deficits as "time blind." Timing is very important. When we do things, and the order in which we do them, matters. Working memory lets us hold in mind the *what* (relevant information) as well as the *when* so that we can start things on time, proceed in the right order, and finish them by the time they are due. When kids don't get to work on school projects until the last minute, it looks like laziness and procrastination, but a big part of it is often being unable to accurately estimate how much time a project will take.

Working memory is crucial for maintaining our motivation to pursue future goals. If we can't hold in our minds a vivid enough image of what we're working toward, we won't be able to resist the present temptations to do something else. To anticipate consequences, we need working memory. We also need it to follow the rules. Working memory allows us to hold the rules in mind while our impulses are directing us to do other things. Working memory is also important for reciprocity, the foundation for social relationships. We need it to hold in mind that it was my turn before, so it's your turn now.

When challenging boys lose their jackets, their headphones, their homework; when they can't do their chores without nagging and reminders; when they don't remember what homework they have to do, or don't remember to turn completed homework in, or turn it in late; when they aren't ready to go on time (even for things they want to do); when they don't anticipate the consequences of their actions (like lying about something where they're sure to be caught); when they don't follow directions; when we tell our sons to get dressed for school and brush their teeth, only to find them later in their room half-dressed playing with Legos—these aren't oppositional or defiant behaviors. These are more examples of executive functioning problems. In this case, largely problems with working memory.

Cognitive Flexibility

Cognitive flexibility emerges later in development and relies on both inhibition and working memory. To be flexible in our thinking, we need to be able to inhibit our current thoughts, feelings, impulses, and point of view and then imagine a new one (i.e., hold it in working memory). We need cognitive flexibility to shift our approach if our initial plan isn't working, or if circumstances change. We need cognitive flexibility to be creative, to think outside the box and outside of what is conventional. From a social standpoint, we need cognitive flexibility to have empathy, to shift our perspective to hold in mind the mind of another while our thoughts, emotions, and impulses pull us to only think about our own point of view. To change perspectives, we need to stop focusing on our previous perspective and bring into working memory a new one.

When a challenging boy won't share toys or wait his turn; when he can't compromise and accept half a popsicle when there was only one left and he and his brother both wanted one, but instead grabs the other half out of his little brother's hand; when it's time to leave the park and he can't handle the transition and refuses to go; when he can't cope with changes in plans; when he explodes because something promised to him can't be delivered (for example, you get to the theater and find that the movie you were going to see is sold out and he won't accept seeing any others); when he seems unable to recognize or is unconcerned with other people's feelings; when he says hurtful things to others (for example, telling a teammate they lost the game because the other kid played badly); when he cries or throws things because he can't handle losing, whether it's a board game or a sports game; when he gets stuck on a math problem and gives up rather than trying another strategy, or asking for help, or moving on to another problem—this isn't stubbornness, selfishness, or inconsiderateness. These are examples of executive functioning problems, specifically with cognitive flexibility.

These core executive functions—inhibitory control, working memory, cognitive flexibility—are the basis for monitoring and controlling thought, emotion, and action. They also form the foundation for higher-order executive skills that become increasingly essential as the boy grows: planning, organization, time management, self-reflection and self-monitoring, sustained attention, and goal-directed persistence. Also, these core executive functions are crucial for the development of the capacity to understand the minds of other people, their experience, intentions, and motivations. This is the basis of empathy and other forms of social intelligence.

A Child with a Problem Becomes a Problem Child

We've learned that a challenging boy faces life with strong negative emotions and self-regulation challenges that lead him to be a challenging child. These are big problems to have. In fact, according to psychologist Russell Barkley, challenging boys are as much as 30 percent behind their peers in the development of executive functioning—so a ten-year-old will have the self-regulatory skills of a typical seven-year-old. Despite this, he's still a child who wants to be successful. He wants to have friends, do well in school, and have his parents love and be proud of him. A tragic shift often occurs in a challenging boy's life where he comes to believe that he can't succeed and that he's actually a bad kid.

Imagine a life where you do your best only to be criticized and reprimanded over and over for doing things in the wrong way. Imagine receiving countless lectures about how you're supposed to be different from how you are. Imagine wanting to have friends only to find yourself rejected and picked on. And then, on top of that, imagine that *you* get into trouble for trying to defend yourself. The adults tell you that you won't have any friends if you keep acting like this. Or they ask, "How would you feel if someone did that to you?" instead of punishing the other kids for bullying you.

This is what a challenging boy frequently feels: disappointment, hurt, criticism, and rejection. Eventually the boy can come to believe that he *is* stupid, that he *is* a failure, that he *is* a loser. He becomes convinced that he is bad, and he starts to give up or get angry or both. I refer to this very unfortunate change as the transition of the boy from being a "child with a problem" into the boy feeling like he's a "problem child."

A child with problems (or challenges) is like any of us. We all have struggles, limitations, and areas where we need to grow. Having problems doesn't define us. It just makes us human. When a child starts to feel that he is a "problem child" (maybe he's even been called it) he feels that his problems define who he is, that he's fundamentally defective, and that he's always going to be this way. It becomes an entrenched identity. He feels ashamed of who he is. As a result, the boy feels that he can't get what he wants and doesn't even deserve it. Eventually he comes to feel that it is pointless to try to cooperate, to try in school, to try following the rules, to try making friends.

Psychologist Ross Greene, in his excellent book *The Explosive Child*, says "kids do well if they can." Sadly, in the case of a child who has come to see himself as a problem child, it's no longer true. He's stopped caring about doing well. He's stopped caring about getting along. He no longer tries.

Some boys in this state give up and fall into hopelessness, help-lessness, and depression. Others get angry. They decide that the world is against them, and they need to fight or cheat if they are going to have a chance. It's as if they are saying, "OK world, you say I'm a bad kid. I'll show you just how bad a kid I can be!" They come to believe that being bad is the only way they can get attention. They might even think that being bad is the only thing they are good at.

You might hear these boys say, "I'm a bad kid," or "it would have been better if I'd never been born," or scarier still, "I wish I was dead." Although it might feel like a guilt trip, or manipulation, it's not. These are sincere expressions of how absolutely terrible it feels to experience yourself as constantly falling short, constantly at odds with the world, and constantly a source of disappointment to your parents. Sometimes the boys don't feel anything at all. They'll say "I don't care" when they have hurt another person or are threatened with a punishment. It's not because they are monsters or sociopaths. It's because they have entered this place of feeling like a problem child.

Further complicating things, feeling like a problem child makes it even more difficult for a challenging boy to learn from the past. Reflecting on his challenging episodes with his parents does not feel to the boy like a learning opportunity. Instead, because of the challenging boy's temperamental tendency to experience big negative feelings, revisiting the regrettable event just becomes an opportunity to be emotionally flooded by bad feelings once again. It's also possible, because his bad feelings decay slowly, that he still feels badly about what happened even though his parents think he is well beyond it. In an activated state it's very difficult to learn anything. It just feels to the boy like his parents are rubbing it in his face how badly he acted or how bad he *is*. The shame the boy feels is exceptionally painful, so he avoids the processing of challenging episodes with great intensity by fighting or fleeing. It looks like the boy is avoiding taking responsibility, but it's really the boy desperately trying to preserve what little good feeling he has left about himself.

When I meet with the parents of young challenging boys, I stress the importance of helping the boy get a handle on his issues before he becomes identified with them and begins to see himself as a "problem child." If you are reading this before that has occurred, that's wonderful. It's one more thing you won't have to deal with. For most of you, your child probably has already come to see himself as a problem child. Don't worry, we can solve this and help him see that he has problems and challenges (like everyone) rather than that he's defective.

ETHAN

Let's return to Ethan from the last chapter. He and his parents would fight over bedtime. Every night he'd stay up too late and every morning they'd have to drag him out of bed. It was very stressful for his parents who were trying to get ready for the day themselves. They'd have to stay on top of Ethan to get dressed, eat his breakfast and get out the door. Often one of his parents would end up late for work because Ethan would miss the bus and they would have to drive him to school. Trying to reason with Ethan had no impact. He'd deny that he had a problem getting ready in the morning.

Mike and Jen were worried that they were being too lenient with him. Maybe they should try giving him tougher consequences, but what consequences to use? They couldn't punish him by making him walk to school after he missed the bus. Ethan just wouldn't go. When they threatened to take away his Xbox, he'd say "I don't care." If they followed through with taking the Xbox away, he'd harass them with complaints about how unfair they were being or plead with them for another chance. It would make everyone in the family miserable. It just seemed easier to give in and give the Xbox back. Even when they did stick with the punishment, it made no impact on the problem of his getting ready for school on time.

Sometimes Ethan's nightly opposition or his morning delays would lead to big blow-up fights. Afterward he would typically refuse to talk about it. Ethan would say he didn't remember what happened. If his parents tried to remind him of the events, he'd run away. Occasionally Ethan would feel very guilty and tell his parents he was very sorry for being "bad." He'd say he wished he'd never been born and that his family would be happier without him. Ethan would promise to do better. He'd swear that he'd go to bed early that night, but he never did.

Looked at through a traditional parenting lens, Ethan was oppositional, aggressive, disrespectful, and rude. But now that we understand how temperament and executive functioning contribute to challenging behavior, we know there's something very different going on inside. Ethan has big temperamental challenges. When stressed, he experiences negative emotions (in his case anger, frustration) quickly, intensely, and they are slow to dissipate. These strong emotional reactions overwhelm his executive functioning, which already has weaknesses.

Bedtime is a big challenge for Ethan because it requires that he stop what he is doing and start getting ready for bed. This requires inhibitory control and cognitive flexibility. Bedtime also requires that Ethan shift his arousal level and begin to unwind, calm down and move toward sleep. This is a big challenge for him temperamentally. His motor runs high and it's hard for him to slow down.

Bedtime is a big working memory challenge for a lot of kids. There are many steps: take a bath or shower, put on pajamas, have a bedtime snack, brush teeth, and use the toilet. For Ethan there are additional working memory challenges at bedtime. When it's time for bed he is only experiencing his here-and-now wish to stay up. He isn't holding in mind the future of the next morning when he's going to feel very tired, irritable, and have a hard time getting to school. He also doesn't think about how his parents will be upset with him and will take away his Xbox. When they remind him, he says he doesn't "care" partly because he can't bring a vivid image of the consequence to mind in working memory. All he cares about is his strong in-the-moment feeling of not wanting to go to bed. He also can't bring to mind the promise he made that very morning to go to bed early, or his very guilty feelings about upsetting his parents so much.

Ethan needs cognitive flexibility to be able to put himself in his parents' shoes. Without it he can't see that they are trying to help him. It feels to him like they are "bugging him" and just wanting to get him out of their hair in the evening. He can't use cognitive flexibility to set aside his feelings and think about where his parents are coming from—that they are concerned about his being tired at school the next day.

Ethan feels terribly frustrated. He needs inhibitory control to stop his impulse to say rude and hurtful things to his mom and dad. He needs working memory for additional motivation to stop himself by holding in mind how much he doesn't want to upset his parents, whom he loves.

Finally, Ethan has come to view himself as a problem child. We see it in the tremendous guilt he feels at hurting his parents. It's evidenced in his statements that he wishes he was never born. It's also reflected in his feeling that his parents favor his sister.

Ethan's challenging behavior created a painful dynamic that he and his family were finding difficult to escape. It wasn't the result of his parents' incompetence. It also wasn't caused by Ethan's willfulness. Rather, it had its origins in his lack of *skillfulness*—specifically a lack of executive functioning skills worsened by a challenging temperament.

To sum up, challenging boys face life moving against some stiff headwinds. Their big, negative emotions and their self-regulation/ executive functioning weaknesses create conditions where they are vulnerable to being triggered into fight-or-flight mode. The challenging behavior that results from this emotional flooding places the boy frequently at odds with his parents, teachers, coaches, siblings, and peers. To make matters worse, most people don't understand how temperament and executive functioning impact behavior. Instead, challenging behavior is typically viewed to be opposition, disobedience, defiance, laziness, or some other moral failing. All the negative feedback a challenging boy receives from the world can lead him to experience himself as shamefully bad and defective. He no longer is a child with a problem but comes to experience himself as a problem child. He can give up trying or fight back. It's a lot for challenging boys and their parents to face.

Now we understand where challenging behavior comes from, we can turn to solving these problems.

KEY IDEAS

- Challenging behavior rarely is intentional misbehavior. Challenging boys are desperate to be successful, get along well with others, and have their parents love and be proud of them.

- Challenging behavior occurs when the expectations placed on a boy exceed his ability to manage them and he becomes emotionally flooded and shifts into fight-or-flight mode.

- Challenging boys are especially prone to emotional flooding because of temperamentally based tendencies to experience big negative emotions and difficulties with self-regulation.

- Challenging boys struggle with the core executive functions of inhibitory control, working memory, and cognitive flexibility. These executive functioning deficits make it difficult for challenging boys to respond appropriately to many of the ordinary demands they face at home, at school, and on the playground.

- Because they are so frequently at odds with the world, challenging boys can lose their motivation to do well. The challenging boy goes from being a child with a problem to experiencing himself as a "problem child"—that is, defective, bad, and unwanted.
- Understanding the true origins of challenging behavior empowers families to identify the steps necessary to solve the problem.

Parenting Journal Exercise

Let's start identifying areas where our son has skill deficits that contribute to his challenging behavior. Look at the items below and note in your journal which ones apply to your son and record examples of your son exhibiting the item. Notice which executive functioning/emotion regulation skills seem to be most frequently involved in your son's challenging episodes.

Negative Emotion
He is moody.
He has angry outbursts and meltdowns.
He overreacts emotionally.
He gets more emotionally upset, more quickly than his peers.
He doesn't notice when he upsets others or makes them mad.

Inhibitory Control
He interrupts and talks over others.
He says mean or hurtful things to others when frustrated.
He doesn't think about the consequences that might result from his actions.
He rushes through schoolwork and frequently makes careless errors.
He gets behaviorally out of control (silly or angry) more often than his peers.

Working Memory
He frequently loses things.
He frequently needs reminders from adults to stay on task.
He has trouble remembering assignments, even for the few moments it takes to get them into his assignment notebook.
He frequently forgets to do things he said he would do.

He has trouble with tasks or assignments that have multiple steps.

Cognitive Flexibility
He gets very upset when plans change.
He has trouble shifting from one activity to another.
He has trouble compromising when working with others.
He has trouble thinking of a different strategy for tackling a problem
   when he gets stuck.
He has difficulty seeing things from another's point of view.

CHAPTER THREE

Using Your Parenting Journal to Understand Challenging Episodes

Now that we know that challenging behavior doesn't come from *willfulness* but a lack of *skillfulness*, it's time to start the process of figuring out what specific skill deficits underlie our son's problem with challenging behavior. To do this, we're going to get out our parenting journals and begin keeping a record of challenging episodes. The goal is to use the journal entries to help us identify patterns. We want to find clues about what triggers the episodes, what signs indicate that challenging behavior is about to occur, and what sequence challenging episodes typically follow as they play out. You will ultimately use your journal entries as the foundation upon which to build a plan for solving your son's problem with challenging behavior.

In my experience, parents of challenging boys are frequently on edge, worrying about when the next challenging episode will occur. It feels to them like challenging behavior can occur anytime, anywhere. You'll soon learn from your journal entries that your son's challenging behavior episodes actually occur after fairly specific triggers, in predictable circumstances, and follow a consistent sequence.

The predictability of challenging behavior is very good news. First, once we learn from our journals what circumstances put our son at risk of a challenging behavior episode, we can relax when those signs aren't present. It's a big relief to not have to be on alert 24/7. Second, because challenging behavior has specific triggers and plays out in specific ways, we can make an emergency plan in advance for managing challenging episodes. We can be like firefighters who stay calm and effective because they have a plan to follow. Finally, once we know what specific circumstances lead our son to act in challenging ways, we can make a plan for teaching him the skills he needs to deal with these situations without becoming challenging.

Going back over these upsetting episodes might be painful—and you might not want to do it. Maybe it makes you feel like a "problem parent" rather than a parent with a problem. If so, please review chapter 1 and remind yourself that *you aren't the problem, but you can be the solution.* In fact, writing about your son's challenging episodes will likely help you process them emotionally. Research by psychologist James Pennebaker found that people who journaled about upsetting events experienced many emotional and physical benefits. Unprocessed upsetting episodes tend to fester in us, but they can heal when brought into the light of day. Writing about challenging episodes will help relieve lingering distress and it will lead the way to making challenging episodes occur with increasingly less frequency. You'll feel less and less like a problem parent, and you'll experience your child less and less as a problem child. Instead, you'll find that your whole family is better able to focus on solving problems.

In addition to alleviating the painful feelings of shame and hurt that go along with challenging episodes, the purpose of your journal entries is to help you get a more objective perspective on what is going on—to simulate what you'd get if you were telling the story to me or another child psychologist. If you find yourself getting too upset or overwhelmed by this exercise, take a break and, if it persists, consider doing it with someone: your co-parent, a friend, or a therapist. If you discover through your journaling that most of your son's challenging episodes escalate into physical altercations, or the bullying of a sibling or other family member, seek professional help right away.

Grab your journal and let's go. You can write a complete narrative, or a bullet point list. Think about a recent challenging episode that especially captures the type of challenging behavior that is disrupting your lives the most. The type of episode that if you could stop it from happening, it would have a huge positive impact on family life.

First, set the scene. When was it? Where were you? Who was there? Next, tell the story of what happened with as much detail as possible. Begin the story with the last moment when things seemed fine. Describe the events that led up to the challenging behavior as specifically as you can. Document how the challenging behavior unfolded through to whatever brought the episode to an end. Try to get down as much of what everyone said and did. Also try to write about what you thought and felt. Record your emotions and behavior as honestly as you can, this journal is just for you.

Try to get the order of events recorded as accurately as possible. Don't worry if your memory is fuzzy. The strong emotions that can be evoked by these episodes make it difficult to remember exactly what happened. Do your best.

Let's return to Ryan, age fourteen; his mom, Tracy; and his dad, Bob. We've discussed Ryan's challenges getting off his computer to get to his homework, or to get to bed. Here's Tracy's first journal entry.

Things were pretty calm in the house until Ryan came home from school. He slammed the front door and went straight to his room. I knew he had his first big assignment of high school due later in the week for history class and I was worried he was on his computer playing games rather than getting to work on the project. I went up to his room and knocked on the door. I kept it light. I didn't want to start a fight. I said something really low-key like: "Honey, you've got that history thing due Friday. This might be a good time to get some work done on it before we have dinner." He didn't respond. I knocked again, and again no response. I asked him to please open the door, but he kept ignoring me. I thought to myself "what the f." As I went to open the door, he pushed it back closed on me. We were both shoving against the door. I yelled that he better let me in or there would be big trouble. He stopped pushing and I opened the door and saw he had been on his phone. He told me I was a crazy person and I had better get a grip on myself. That made me furious. I grabbed his phone and he tried to grab

*it back, but I got out the door and headed to the kitchen. He came
downstairs and grabbed my phone that was sitting on the counter.
Somehow, I managed not to yell. I told him calmly to give me my
phone back. He said he'd give it back when he got his back. I told
him that I wouldn't respond to blackmail. I said I was going to
call Lucas's mom and tell her that he won't be going to the game
with them this weekend. He yelled that I always ruin everything.
Bob came home about this time. He seemed very stressed and acted
like he was negotiating a prisoner exchange: getting my phone
back for me and Ryan his. I told him that Ryan needed to give
me my phone before we talk about anything. Ryan starts pleading
with Bob and saying that he took a short break after school and
was about to get to work when I broke into his room and stole his
phone. Bob asked him to please give me my phone back. Eventually
Ryan put the phone down and went upstairs shouting something
as he went.*

Once your narrative is written, ask yourself the following questions about the situation. You don't have to answer every question.
The point of the questions is to help you get a new perspective on
the challenging episode and learn about the factors contributing to
it.

- How was your son doing before the episode? Had he woken up
  on the wrong side of the bed? Was he tired? Hungry? Sick? Had
  he been through something stressful earlier that day?
- What has the climate in the house been? Have you and your
  partner been stressed? Has there been tension between the two
  of you about your son or something else?
- Was there anything about the situation that made it especially
  difficult for your son to comply?
- How were you doing before the episode began? Were you
  stressed about anything not related to your son? Were you tired?
- What feelings did you have during the episode? (Refer to the list
  in the following box)

CHALLENGING EMOTIONS

Angry, annoyed, frustrated, furious, disgusted, critical
Defiant, resentful, defensive
Jealous, envious
Criticized, blamed, under attack, misunderstood
Incompetent, inferior, inadequate, self-conscious, like a failure
Worthless, unlovable, unwanted
Guilty, regretful, remorseful
Ashamed, embarrassed, humiliated, defective, like a bad person
Confused, hurt
Anxious, worried, nervous, frightened
Rejected, lonely, abandoned, isolated
Sad, depressed, disappointed, despairing
Hopeless, helpless, stuck, defeated, discouraged, pessimistic

---

- Try to identify a thought or thoughts that accompany the two or three most prominent emotions that you felt during the episode. For example, a thought that might go with a feeling of fear is: "What kind of life is he going to have if he can't do something as simple as _____?"

- Did your son remind you of anyone—you, your spouse, siblings, parents? If it is a sibling or parent, did that person cause problems in the family? Did you fight with that person? Did they bully or abuse you?

- Did the episode lead to conflict between you and his other parent?

- What did you do to try to manage the situation?

- How did your son react to your actions?

- What things did he say? What clues did your son give you about what was going on for him?

- What emotions do you think your son was feeling (refer again to the list above)?

Once you have examined your narrative with the help of the questions, try to write an account of the challenging episode from your son's point of view. Here are Ryan's mom's answers to the questions about her narrative:

- How was your son doing before the episode? Had he woken up on the wrong side of the bed? Was he tired? Hungry? Sick? Had he been through something stressful earlier that day?

  School is stressful for him. Socially, things are stressful for him. He's always worried that people aren't going to like him. School work is stressful too. Maybe he feels this assignment is too much for him. He's so much easier to deal with in the summer.

- What's the climate in the house been? Have you and your partner been stressed? Has there been tension between the two of you about your son or something else?

  Bob is stressed about his job, and I've been stressed having to pick up the slack while he's been so busy at work. I guess we've been a little snippy with each other.

- Was there anything about the situation that made it especially difficult for your son to comply?

  I don't know.

- How were you doing before the episode began? Were you stressed about anything not related to your son? Were you tired?

  I haven't been sleeping well worrying about him. But on that day, I was feeling pretty good before he came home. I was starting to feel like we were through the worst of the school transition. That I was feeling good made it even more of a bummer that he was in a bad mood.

- What feelings did you have during the episode?

  Angry, critical, blamed, regretful, under attack, like a failure, worried, afraid, discouraged.

- Try to identify a thought or thoughts that accompany the two or three most prominent emotions that you felt during the episode.

Worried: Is this how it's always going to be? Am I going to have to nag and fight him to do his homework all through high school? How is he going to go to college?

Afraid: He's getting big. It's not going to be long before he's a lot stronger than me. What am I going to do then?

Regretful: We should have put tougher rules on screen use when he was younger. Now it's too late.

- Did your son remind you of anyone—you, your spouse, siblings, parents? If it is a sibling or parent, did that person cause problems in the family? Did you fight with that person? Did they bully or abuse you?

  Ryan reminds me of Bob in being so high strung. He reminds me of myself in being so stubborn. He is also a lot like my brother. He just does whatever he wants, whenever he wants. My brother was always stressing my parents out. He and my dad would get into these big fights. It was pretty scary. I tried to stay out of my brother's way.

- Did the episode lead to conflict between you and his other parent?

  Not really. Bob tried to make peace at first but backed me up when I drew the line. I'm glad he came home when he did. He helped cool things down and got my phone back without a big fight.

- What did you do to try to manage the situation?

  I tried to be calm at first, but I needed to hold my limit once he started fighting me.

- How did your son react to your actions?

  He kept fighting me, he didn't listen. I had to really raise the stakes for him to back down.

- What things did he say? What clues did your son give you about what was going on for him?

  He said I was crazy. He said that I always ruin everything. He told Bob that he was just taking a break and that he was about to work when I took his phone. That was a lie. I guess he was trying to de-stress by playing a game on his phone. Or maybe he wanted to connect with friends. Maybe he really believed that he was going to stop at some point and get to work.

- What emotions do you think your son was feeling (refer again to the list above)?
  Angry, criticized, defiant, resentful, under attack, maybe incompetent, anxious about the assignment, maybe anxious socially.

Here's Tracy's attempt to write the story from Ryan's point of view.

I hate school. I had been waiting all day to get online with my friends. My mom kept interrupting and bugging me. She's so annoying! Why didn't she just leave me alone? What is her problem? She threatened me so I had to let her in. She grabbed my phone. She always invades my privacy. I tried to stop her, but she took off with it. I followed her. I grabbed her phone. I figured I'd show her how crazy she was being. She threatened me again. I can't go to the football game with Lucas. I felt so upset and angry. My dad came home. He tried to help, but she overpowered him too. I had to give in so I could go to the game. She won.

From writing this journal entry and several others, Tracy could see patterns starting to emerge. She already knew that finishing homework and screen use were problems for Ryan. Now she was coming to understand more fully how they triggered challenging episodes and why her previous efforts to solve the problems hadn't worked.

Tracy was always looking for solutions and had read several books before this one. She had tried many good ideas like having Ryan work at the kitchen counter where she could help him if he got stuck on something and keep him from getting distracted. She hired a tutor. She and Bob even tried parental controls on his phone and turning off the Wi-Fi to his computer. He resisted the kitchen counter in favor of shutting himself in his room. He wouldn't meet with the tutor or would barely do work while she was there. He also always found a way around the internet restrictions.

These failed efforts had previously led Tracy to feel that the problem was that they were letting him get away with defying them.

She had felt it was time to get tough. However, her journal entries told a different story. She saw for the first time that taking a hardline approach was making the problems worse. When she demanded that Ryan get off the computer and start his homework, or go to bed, and held firm to that line, it often escalated to angry words or even to an occasional physical altercation. She'd end up having to threaten some huge consequence (like not going to the game with Lucas) to get him to back down. In one particularly bad altercation, Ryan ran out of the house and was gone until very late at night.

Tracy also learned from her journal entries that increasing the pressure on him to comply with her demands wasn't leading to more homework being done. Rather it was leading to more undesirable behaviors. Ryan started lying that his homework was done. He was also sneaking his laptop into his room at night and staying up very late playing games.

Tracy was starting to see through her journaling that she wasn't just putting pressure on Ryan to do his work. She was also putting a ton of pressure on herself. She realized that she felt responsible for seeing that he got his homework done. She was losing sleep with worry and during the day she was feeling more tense and irritable. There was more friction with Bob who was less concerned about homework and naively believed that this was just a phase that Ryan was going through. The stress and fighting were negatively impacting Tracy's relationship with Ryan. They had always been close, but now there was a painful distance developing. It all was making her feel like a terrible mother. She remembered from chapter 1 that blame interferes with problem-solving. The journaling helped her let go of a lot of the blame and reduce the pressure.

From her journal entries, Tracy saw more clearly that she was becoming increasingly afraid of Ryan as he grew bigger and reminded her more and more of her brother. She also realized that she was worried that he'd turn out like him—never being able to have a relationship or to consistently hold down a job. Tracy was beginning to see that these feelings about Ryan were based more on her childhood trauma of being bullied by her brother than on who Ryan really is.

With her self-blame and fear about Ryan's future lessened, Tracy could have a more balanced view of her son and see, once again, his many wonderful qualities. Ryan is very smart and is particularly skilled in math and science. He does surprisingly well on tests in spite of the fact that he's usually missing half his assignments by the end of the semester. Ryan is also very loving with the family's pets. He's great with little kids in the neighborhood too. He entertains them in the summer with Rube Goldberg courses that he spends hours building in their backyard. Ryan has a good sense of humor, and not just around inappropriate teenage topics. In the summer, out from under the stress of school, he's basically a happy kid and is great company.

Applying the lessons from chapter 2 to her journaling, Tracy could see how hard Ryan's challenging temperament and executive functioning deficits make school for him. He doesn't have the inhibitory control to filter out distractions to help him keep his attention focused in class. His working memory problems make it challenging for him to understand all the steps in some assignments, and even when he does understand them, he has a hard time keeping them in mind long enough to get them into his notebook. His emotional reactivity causes him to experience a great deal of anxiety and discouragement during the day.

Tracy could see more clearly than ever that Ryan wasn't an oppositional, defiant, or bad kid. He was actually doing his best and, given his challenges, he was doing pretty well. She now understood that Ryan would come home from school psychologically spent. He was mentally tired, and he was full of negative emotion. He didn't get right to his homework because his anxiety was still very high.

The only coping skill that Ryan had for dealing with his bad feelings was avoiding thinking about them. Videos and video games were the best distractions. He found particular comfort in his video games. He was good at them. It helped him feel less like a failure. Unlike social interactions at school or assignments in English class, what was expected of him by the video game was clear. He also knew that if he messed up, he'd get to respawn with a fresh start. The game didn't keep track of past mistakes and hold them against him.

Homework was very anxiety provoking. It required that he stop his impulse to hide away in games (inhibitory control), ignore distractions (inhibitory control), bring to mind what was talked about in class that day (working memory), figure out what his assignments were (working memory), and get started on the work (cognitive flexibility). Sitting down to do homework felt bad. It reminded him that he didn't understand many of his assignments. Further, it taxed his weak higher-order executive functioning skills like planning, organization, and persistence.

Tracy came to understand that stricter limits were only serving to intensify Ryan's anxiety to the point of panic. In fight-or-flight mode he would fight to get his computer back or flee (like running away that night). The limits also became yet another distraction for Ryan. He became consumed with evading his parents' control. Tracy could see that she and her firm limits made him feel trapped. To feel safe, Ryan needed to know he could "flee" from the source of his anxiety if it got too intense.

As is true for many parents, the act of journaling about Ryan's challenging episodes led to positive improvements even before any plans were made for helping Ryan develop new skills. The journaling helped Tracy really take in the lessons from chapters 1 and 2 that Ryan isn't a bad kid, and she isn't a bad mom. In fact, they are both doing their best, and she is a loving and dedicated parent who would do anything for her son. Once she stopped blaming herself, Tracy could see Ryan's temperamental and executive functioning challenges in action in her accounts of his challenging episodes.

In realizing that her own trauma was getting activated, Tracy was able to feel less afraid and see that Ryan's issues weren't nearly as bad as she had feared. A more positive view of him and his many wonderful qualities returned. This lower pressure and increase of positive feelings created space for Tracy and Ryan to once again enjoy spending time together. Their relationship was no longer reduced to fighting about screens and homework. Tracy could also see that the fighting and firm limits weren't producing any positive results but were causing more negative behaviors. Almost immediately there was less tension in the house.

Tracy's question was, "If strict limits don't get Ryan to do his schoolwork, what will?" We will turn to this question in the chapters that follow. We'll discuss the strategies that are effective in teaching boys the skills they need to overcome their problems with challenging behavior. Get your journals out and start recording your son's challenging episodes.

MAKE YOUR EMERGENCY PLAN

Now that you are writing about and reflecting upon your son's challenging behavior, you are ready to make your first plan, an emergency plan. The purpose of the emergency plan is to immediately reduce the frequency and intensity of challenging episodes. You are going to temporarily manage your son's triggers for him. This will decrease challenging episodes while you work on teaching your son the skills he needs to manage himself. Like a firefighter's incident plan, your emergency plan will help you keep your goals clear in your mind, as well as the tactics you'll use to accomplish those goals. You'll know what you should be doing and why. You'll no longer be confused or making things up on the fly when facing challenging behavior. Your confidence will grow, and, like a firefighter, you'll finally be able to remain calm and act effectively.

Here are the elements of your emergency plan:

1. *Make sure all the adults in your son's life understand the true causes of his challenging behavior.*
   Explain to your co-parent, teachers, family members, coaches, and friends that your son is not oppositional, defiant, or bad, but that he has challenges with emotion regulation and executive functioning that make it difficult for him to comply with certain rules and instructions. Tell them that you are actively working on these problems, and you are not asking them to give your son a pass. You are asking for patience. Helping adults have a more positive (and accurate) view of your son and his struggles will make them less likely to be strict and punitive with him—which will lead to less challenging behavior.
2. *Avoid circumstances in which your son is at risk of having a challenging episode.*
   For example, if challenging behavior occurs in the supermarket, leave your son at home. If you must put your child in a situation

where he would be at risk of challenging behavior, have an exit strategy. For example, plan on abandoning your shopping cart and leaving the store if you see signs that he's getting activated.

3. *Reduce the triggering demands and expectations you place on your child.*

For Ethan, his parents temporarily gave up their insistence that he get ready for school on time. Mike, a high school teacher and football coach, hired a former player to come over in the mornings to get Ethan to school. Ethan was in awe of the player, so he was more motivated to get ready. Also, it meant that Mike and Jen and Clara wouldn't have to worry about being late for school or work on days when Ethan was moving slowly. For Tracy, reducing triggering demands meant not pressuring Ryan or taking his devices when he resisted doing homework.

4. *If a challenging episode has started, drop your demand.*

With Ryan, Tracy had several opportunities to de-escalate the challenging episode. She could have refrained from going into his room when he refused to open his door, she could have left his phone with him when he was disrespectful, she could have given his phone back when he took her phone.

Conventional parenting approaches would say that avoiding situations that trigger your son, lowering your expectations, and backing off a limit that has been set all represent bad parenting. It would be argued that these actions teach your son he doesn't have to follow the rules and respect limits. You might also feel like a doormat and that you're letting him get away with bad behavior.

First, it's not a permanent solution. We are *temporarily* managing his triggers for him while we are helping him learn to manage them himself. When we put our son in circumstances where he's likely to become challenging, we are setting him back. A challenging episode results from your child being emotionally flooded. He feels awful and it's a very stressful situation for him as well as you. He feels bad, like a failure, and that he's a problem child.

You might be especially troubled by the idea of giving in to a threat, tantrum, or explosion. We've all been told that this teaches a boy he can get his way by throwing a fit. This is true to some degree, but it is far from the whole story. What if Tracy had said to emotionally flooded Ryan, "I see that you are very upset right now and not in a place to have a productive conversation. I'm going to give you your phone back. We both need some time to cool off." Ryan would learn a lot more from this statement than merely that his opposition "worked." Ryan would learn that his mom cares about his feelings and about their relationship. He would learn that she does not want him to be in a painful flooded state. He would also learn a very valuable lesson about conflict in relationships: it's better to take a break to cool down than to try to deal with a conflict while you are flooded.

After a fire call, when everyone is back at the station and the hoses have been packed carefully on the engines for the next emergency, firefighters conduct an incident debriefing. In the debriefing, the incident plan is evaluated. Now that you have your first plan, you will use your journal to start debriefing. Here are your debriefing questions:

- Is the plan being followed?
- Are there circumstances that are not accounted for by the plan?
- Is the plan working to decrease the frequency and intensity of challenging episodes?
- How can the plan be improved?

Plans are never perfect from the start. As they are put in place, lessons are learned, and the plans are modified to achieve their objectives ever more efficiently and effectively.

There are many benefits to the temporary use of an emergency plan. It will help you keep your cool. You'll no longer be adding fuel to the fire of a challenging episode with regrettable behaviors like yelling, threats, or hurtful words and actions. You'll experience decreased conflict in your house. You'll see almost immediate improvement in the quality of your relationship with your son. There will be more positivity and greater trust. We'll read in chapter 4 about how your relationship with your son is the ultimate foundation for change.

Key Ideas

- Writing about challenging episodes in your parenting journal will help you see them more objectively and it will give you the data you need to solve your son's challenging behavior problems.

- Your journal entries will help you identify triggers (yours and your son's), as well as the patterns his challenging episodes typically follow.

- Your journal entries will help you better understand your feelings and your son's feelings.

- Your journal entries will make it possible for you to create an emergency plan. Your emergency plan will lead to an immediate reduction of challenging episodes.

Parenting Journal Exercise

Look through your journal entries of your son's challenging episodes.

- What are your son's triggers?
- What are your buttons and triggers?
- What are your spouse's buttons and triggers?
- What is the history of your buttons and triggers? What experiences from your past do your buttons and triggers connect to? Think back to times you have had these same feelings in the past. Think especially about your own childhood. Think about who your son reminds you of in his challenging moments.

Create your emergency plan.

- What steps can you take to manage his trigger?
- What situations should you avoid?
- What steps can you take to de-escalate or exit a challenging episode that starts to emerge?

CHAPTER FOUR

Rebuilding Your Relationship with Your Son

The Foundation for Change

After a fire in their home, a family must clean up and repair. Sometimes the damage is mostly on the surface. The house is intact; the cleanup involves removing smoke and soot residue and mopping up the water used to extinguish the blaze. With bigger fires the frame of the building can be compromised, and structural integrity must be restored before the rest of the house can be rebuilt. Often the repaired house (which now meets modern building codes) is stronger and safer than it was before.

Challenging behavior problems can damage trust and connection between parents and their sons. Both sides develop a biased view where they expect the worst from each other. This attitude of suspicion and mistrust reinforces itself because it acts like a filter. Positive actions and positive change are overlooked, problematic behaviors are hyper-focused on, and neutral actions are interpreted in a negative light.

Fortunately, just like a house after a fire, the relationship can be repaired and rebuilt. With care and persistence, it can be stronger than ever. This is a relief because all parents, at one time or another, lose it with their kids. We're all human. We all screw up. This is especially true of parents of challenging boys. Challenging boys are constantly pushing our buttons.

Trust and connection in the parent-child relationship is the foundation upon which parents can help their challenging son build the skills he needs to be happy and successful in his life. A close, trusting parent-child relationship will be the model for healthy relationships in the boy's future. A strong parent-child relationship additionally allows the parents and son to appreciate each other, enjoy time together, and work together as partners in promoting the son's healthy, happy development. Isn't that why we became parents in the first place?

At this point in your journey through this book, you've already taken two huge steps in repairing trust and connection. First, you have a new, more positive way of viewing your son's challenging behavior. You now know it's not opposition, disrespect, or indifference. He just doesn't have the skills he needs to be able to cooperate. You're relieved to know that he's not a bad kid and that you're not to blame for the problems. This new understanding makes it easier to be patient and remain calm in the heat of a challenging episode. Second, in implementing an emergency plan, you have reduced the frequency and intensity of challenging behavior. Challenging episodes erode trust. Preventing them from escalating creates space for trust and connection to take root once again.

Before turning to focus on your relationship with your son, I'd like to ask you to take a moment and check in with yourself. Dealing with challenging behavior problems is extremely stressful. Get out your parenting journal and go through the following questions. Are you OK? Are you experiencing any signs of burnout? Are you having a difficult time focusing on work, your other children, or other responsibilities? Do you feel angry, irritable, volatile, or the opposite—numb, withdrawn, or avoidant? Are you neglecting your health? If you are experiencing any of these issues, please try to take some time to care for yourself. I know being a parent, and especially a parent of a challenging boy, means having virtually no free time. However, the overused metaphor from air travel of putting your air mask on before helping others with theirs is true. You will be best able to help your son with his challenging behavior if you are also caring for yourself. Try to prioritize taking at least a little time to care for your stress—getting more sleep, exercising, meditating, or other healthy activities.

This is even more essential and even harder to do if you are a single parent.

Another area of concern is your relationship with your son's other parent, whether you are married, separated, divorced, or partners. Because opposites attract, parents often have conflicting instincts about how to respond to challenging behavior. Under the stress of ongoing challenging episodes, these differences can expand into a state of polarization where parents pull in opposite directions. To make matters worse, challenging behavior sends us into blame mode (as we learned in chapter 1). When we blame our child's other parent, it increases stress, tension, and conflict, and makes it harder to work together. Challenging episodes often create a snowball effect where challenging behavior causes the parents to blame each other and get into fights. This conflict, in turn, stresses the boy and leads him to be even more challenging.

Going deeper, we also learned in chapter 1 how challenging behavior problems provoke parents' childhood trauma. When we experience our son's challenging episodes through the distortion lens of trauma, our child's other parent can *feel* to us as if they are abusive, neglecting, or abandoning—like someone who mistreated us in the past. When we project our unresolved trauma onto our child's other parent in this way, we feel the urgent need to protect ourselves or our child from them. We mistakenly see the other parent as the problem when the problem is really challenging behavior. Let's return to Andrea from chapter 1. When her husband Chris would walk out during their son Josh's meltdowns, she would experience Chris as if he were her abandoning father from her past and not her vulnerable husband struggling with trauma of his own in the present.

The fighting that can result from experiencing our son or his other parent from a traumatically triggered place is often extremely harmful to family life. We become like the Apollo 13 astronauts, fighting with each other over who is to blame. What we really need to do is to work together if we are going to survive. We need to care for each other and support each other. We need to understand that we're in the same desperate boat (or crippled spacecraft). Both of us are stressed, afraid, and triggered. We're each trying our best and wanting the best for our child. What our child needs most of all is for us to recognize we're in this together.

Ryan's parents, Bob and Tracy, were both traumatically triggered by his challenging behavior. Bob's mother was very volatile. Her outbursts terrified him as a child. In his traumatized view, Bob would experience Tracy as if she were like his mom and felt that he needed to protect Ryan from Tracy's anger. Because he was triggered, he could not see the big picture reality that Ryan and Tracy had a strong relationship. Sure, they had conflict, but Tracy was the first person Ryan would go to if he needed help with anything, and they also enjoyed spending time together. Tracy, for her part, saw Bob as her permissive parents who let her brother get away with mistreating her. She felt alone and unprotected. In fact, because she was triggered, Tracy could not see that Bob was often skillfully de-escalating the fights that she and Ryan got into. Ryan didn't actually need protection from Tracy's anger or Bob's permissiveness. What Ryan really needed protection from was feeling like he was the cause of conflict between his parents; it made him feel even more deeply like a problem child.

Take a moment to check in with yourself about your relationship with your son's other parent. Here are some more questions to reflect upon in your journal. Do you find yourself preoccupied with angry thoughts about your son's other parent? Do you feel they are mistreating you or your son? Do you feel alone and like you can't count on them to work together with you? Do you feel criticized? Is your son's other parent defensive when you try to talk about your son's problems? Do you feel distant? These are signs that stress is impacting your relationship, and that trauma is likely clouding your view of the situation. What situations from your past are being triggered?

The advice given in this book may exacerbate the strain between the parents, especially if your son's other parent is advocating taking a hardline approach to your son's problems, or if they are generally dismissive of the advice found in parenting books. Remind your son's other parent that you both want the same thing. You both want peace, respect, and cooperation in your family, and you want your son to be a person who is respectful, takes responsibility, and is thriving. You just have different ideas about how to reach these goals. Acknowledge that your son's other parent's approach is based on a sincere belief that it is the best way to achieve your shared goals. Try to reassure your son's other parent that the emergency plan is temporary and that the ultimate goal is teaching your son the skills he needs to succeed.

If you can, review with your child's other parent what you are learning from your parenting journal. Help them see how you each get triggered during challenging episodes. Help them understand that when we're triggered, we're like our challenging sons. We're not in our right minds and what we need most is compassion rather than anger. Try to figure out how you can support each other to be the parents you want to be. Try to recognize that tension between the two of you exacerbates challenging behavior and makes the problem harder to solve.

Now let's turn to the important work of building a trusting relationship with your challenging boy.

ACCENTUATE THE POSITIVE

Like the lyrics of the old song, to build a strong relationship with your challenging son, "You got to accentuate the positive. Eliminate the negative." Actually, it turns out that you don't need to totally eliminate the negative. In his marital research, John Gottman found that marriages are strongest when there is a 5:1 ratio of positive-to-negative interactions between the spouses. This "magic ratio" is a valuable rule of thumb for parents to apply in their relationships with their challenging sons.

Children develop best, and parent-child relationships are strongest, when parents predominantly express positive feelings toward their children. Parent-child relationships that are consistently positive form the basis for the development of confidence, healthy self-esteem, and resilience. Relationships that are not experienced by children as clearly positive can lead to anxiety, communication difficulties, and problems with discipline.

Negative behaviors to reduce are criticism, condescension, and defensiveness. *Criticism* is making negative statements about the child's character. For example, calling him selfish, lazy, or irresponsible. Gottman distinguishes criticism from complaint. A complaint focuses on an action: "it upsets me when you leave your dirty socks in the living room," whereas criticism focuses on the person, "you're a slob." *Condescension* refers to the parents putting themselves in a superior position relative to the child: "you're too young to understand," "you'll thank me later," or "don't be so sensitive." It also includes nonverbal expressions of disrespect like mocking, sarcasm, and eye-rolling, as well as dismissive hand gestures (like waving the child away) and scolding the child (especially in public). Finally, *defensiveness* involves denying responsibility, making excuses, or saying that something never happened. Interestingly, Gottman found that expressions of anger were not inherently a negative in the magic ratio. It depended on how the anger was expressed. Anger communicated in non-attacking statements like: "I feel angry when you do _____ (make a mess and don't clean it up, hit your sister, call me names)" are not felt as negative. However, anger expressed as criticism, condescension, defensiveness, or in aggressive gestures (yelling, threats, assuming a physically threatening posture, hitting) are all experienced as extremely negative. Other negative behaviors to avoid are comparing your son to other kids or siblings, blaming, and disregarding your son's feelings or agenda.

It takes effort to maintain a healthy growth-promoting balance of 5:1 positive to negative in all our relationships. In our busy lives the pull is toward a ratio that is closer to 50:50 or even tilted in the negative direction. This is especially true with our challenging sons. Our son's misbehavior grabs our attention, and we address it immediately, regardless of how little time there is. Challenging boys pull for a lot of this type of negative attention. Also, challenging boys are often extremely negative themselves and they engage in a lot of criticism, condescension, defensiveness, and destructive expressions of anger. It's hard not to be pulled down to their level. However, we need to do our best to model being positive and constructive so that our sons have a chance to learn these behaviors.

Negative emotional expressions from parents not only encourage the development of a negative self-image in the child, but also to the development of a negative image of the parent in the boy's mind. A child with a negative image of his parents will be less likely to turn to them for support and comfort. Also, the parents' constructive criticism and good advice are ignored in these circumstances because the parents are experienced as a consistent source of negative noise. Positivity creates conditions in which parents' words (even the occasional necessary complaints) are taken more seriously. In effect, the child thinks "my parents are always on my side and wouldn't say this thing if it wasn't important." As a result, a 5:1 positive-to-negative ratio helps create conditions where kids are more likely to be cooperative and more likely to listen when a parent does have a complaint.

An important factor in maintaining a 5:1 magic ratio in your relationship with your child is remembering that an expression of feeling or an action counts as positive only if the other person experiences it as positive. This is especially true for challenging boys whose temperamental challenges and executive functioning difficulties lead them to be much more likely to experience parents as angry or critical *even when they are not.* Just because something seems positive to you, it doesn't mean that your son will experience it similarly.

Something that surprises many parents about maintaining the positive 5:1 ratio is that what you think about your son matters. If you believe that your son is lazy, selfish, irresponsible, etcetera, it will have a damaging impact on your positive to negative ratio—even if you never call him any of these names. What we think influences what we see. If we think our son is lazy, we can't help but selectively notice the times he acts in lazy ways, and we'll notice fewer of the times that he is hardworking—we'll focus on the missing assignments in English and not recognize that this term he got all his math homework handed in on time for the first time. What we think about our son also influences how we act. If we think our son is irresponsible, we might subtly express it by not giving him opportunities to be responsible—we nag him to pack up his backpack in the morning without giving him a chance to do it without prompting. So, even if you don't verbalize your negative view of your son, the message gets through in these subtle ways.

Here are some positive behaviors to increase to help you move toward a magic 5:1 ratio.

Make Time

I once saw a church sign that read, "How do kids spell love? T-I-M-E." I thought, "Yes, that is how kids spell love!" As I drove on, and reflected more about the sign, I thought, "Well, kids also spell love like Aretha Franklin: R-E-S-P-E-C-T, and probably countless other ways like A-C-C-E-P-T-A-N-C-E or A-F-F-E-C-T-I-O-N." No matter how many ways kids spell love, time is important. Because life is so busy, it's often difficult to find the time to spend with our kids. It's important to prioritize having time to connect every day, even if it's just a few minutes.

Play

Play is a powerful way to build strong relationships. During most of his life, your challenging son is told to do things he doesn't want to do and to follow rules that he didn't make and doesn't like. It's very frustrating! Play is the antidote to your son's constant feeling that he is the square peg being rammed into a round hole. Play is spontaneous and free and doesn't have an agenda. Playing means being silly, laughing and joking (but never at the child's expense), having a playful attitude, having fun. With children it can mean joining in their games or fantasy play. According to Lawrence Cohen, author of *Playful Parenting*, "All you really need to do to be a good playmate for your child . . . is actively observe, listen to [his] stories, support [his] chosen mode of play, and engage in conversation."

Show Interest in Your Son's Interests

With a son who is reluctant to spend time with you, a great place to start is to show active interest in what he is interested in. If he loves playing video games, try watching the game while he plays. Ask questions about the game. Eventually ask if he'll teach you to play. Even if you don't like or approve of video games, it's more important for your relationship with your son to meet him where his interests are than it is to make your point about how video games are too violent or a waste of time. You can also try connecting by listening to, and appreciating, the music that your son is into. Try to learn what he likes about it. Listen to it enough so it has a chance to grow on you. You can also watch the TV shows he likes or ask to see YouTube videos he enjoys.

Showing interest in what your son is interested in will hopefully lead the two of you to develop shared interests. Challenging boys typically aren't big talkers. They often connect best by doing things together. Wonderful activities include fun science experiments (like making a coke and mentos geyser), playing board games, bowling, or going on a bicycle ride. Parents who have the skills can invite their son to tune up a bicycle, do home repairs, or do a building project. If you are feeling unsure of where to start, there are YouTube tutorials describing how to do almost anything. Especially great are hobbies or other activities that last over several weeks. They help create a feeling of continuous connection. If you aren't especially handy, building Lego sets can be a wonderful, shared activity.

Not all boys love sports, but for those who do, sports provide opportunities to connect. You can shoot baskets, play catch, or kick a soccer ball. The exercise is healthy for both of you and the time together is priceless. Rooting for the same teams and attending games are excellent ways of fostering connection. Fantasy sports leagues provide another opportunity to connect around an interest in sports. Studying player stats, drafting a team, making personnel moves, and vying for a league championship are great ways to bond. As with extended building projects, the fantasy season helps create a feeling of connectedness that is more continuous. Other activities that build a sense of continuity in connection are spending many nights reading a chapter book at bedtime or having a TV series that you watch together.

Get Straight A's: Attention, Affection, Affirmation
When thinking about how to build closeness and connection with your son, think about getting straight A's: attention, affection, affirmation.

Pay Attention

All children want their parents' undivided attention. "Hey mom, hey dad, . . . Look what I can do," we frequently hear young children say. In our busy lives it is so easy to get distracted. Our to-do lists are very full. We often don't give our children our full agenda-less attention.

It can be especially challenging to recognize and respond to our challenging son's bids for attention. Some are more straightforward. The boy wants you to be excited about an accomplishment. Often his bids for attention are annoying. He might try to get your attention by interrupting or asking you a million questions. He might invade your personal space. He might tell an inappropriate joke or talk in way too much detail about some topic that he's currently interested in. Your son might be critical of you or another family member. He might complain about aches and pains in his body that seem to have no physical basis. The challenge is to look past the annoyance and see these behaviors as indications that he needs your attention.

Conventional parenting advice suggests we should ignore "attention-seeking behaviors." According to this view, paying attention after the child has sought our attention in an annoying way will reward the behavior and increase its frequency. However, it's not as simple as that. Responding to bids for our attention, even those that are annoying, gives us an opportunity to build connection. If we treat these behaviors as signs that we aren't giving our child enough attention and then make a point of paying more attention proactively (before he needs to be annoying), the behaviors should naturally decrease. Responding to annoying bids by paying attention does indirectly send the message to the child that being annoying is an effective way to get attention. However, it's not the only message that is sent. Responding to his bids for attention (however awkward or annoying they may be) simultaneously conveys the message to our son that we care about his need for our attention and that we want to give it. It tells our child that we want to pay attention, that we want to be connected.

If proactively paying more attention doesn't lead to a reduction of annoying bids for attention, it probably means that our son doesn't know how to seek attention constructively, or he is unable to inhibit the impulses behind the annoying behavior. This circumstance gives us a wonderful opportunity to teach. For example, the parent might say, "I want you to let me know when you need my attention, but when you interrupt my phone call it upsets me. Can we come up with a sign for you to let me know you need me when I'm on the phone?" For younger boys, especially those with inhibitory control problems, a reward chart could be created to reward positive attention seeking (we'll discuss how to create effective reward charts in chapter 8).

When talking about attention, we need to talk about our own computer and phone use around our sons. When we're absorbed with our phones or computers, even if we're doing something important like responding to work emails, we often don't realize that we're sending an unintentional, yet powerful message to our sons about our priorities. They can easily conclude that the email, or text, or social media post, or work deadline that has you focused on your screen is more important to you than they are. It's confusing, especially to younger kids, when we're there but not present. We need to be mindful of being distracted by our devices. If we are working from home, it's important to be clear with our sons about when we can and can't be interrupted and to work out how they are to let us know that they need our attention. In addition to these issues, we need to be aware of modeling: how we handle our devices sets an example for our sons about how they should handle theirs.

Give Affection

Say "I love you." Show that you care with little gestures. Surprise your child with small acts of kindness, such as leaving a surprise treat or loving note in their lunchbox. Kids love hugs, cuddles, and kisses. The quietness of bedtime before sleep is a wonderful time for expressions of affection. As our sons get older, we need to be more respectful of their personal boundaries, but they never grow out of their need for our loving words, our loving gestures, or our hugs.

Express Appreciation

Appreciating who your son is and letting him know how he makes your life better is a powerful antidote to his feeling that he's a problem child. Psychologist Charisse Nixon says that all kids have a need to feel they belong and that they make a positive difference. Challenging boys, however, often instead feel like outsiders in their families. They also, sadly, frequently feel that the only difference they make is to ruin things. Ethan (from chapter 1) felt so bad about himself at times that he believed his parents and his sister would be better off if he'd never been born. Expressing appreciation is an important way to help your son feel that he belongs in your family. Express sincere gratitude for his help with a chore or task. "It was such a pleasant surprise to come down this morning and find that the trash had been emptied. Thank you!" Tell him you are proud of something he worked hard to do or persisted with. Point out to him his genuine strengths. Let him know what you love about him. Let him know how he makes your family better.

UNDERSTAND AND ACCEPT YOUR CHILD'S FEELINGS

Challenging boys, because they struggle with cooperation and have difficulty following the rules, frequently experience criticism and other negative reactions from teachers, peers, and parents. They often feel misunderstood and rejected. Feeling understood and accepted by you helps him feel better and *do* better. Acceptance is the cornerstone of a solid parent-child relationship.

Psychologist Ronald Rohner has found that children everywhere have a basic need for acceptance from their parents and other important caregivers. Children who feel rejected have more behavioral problems, have lower self-esteem, are more pessimistic, are more anxious and depressed, and are more likely to have drug and alcohol problems. In Rohner's words, "parental acceptance-rejection by itself is universally a powerful predictor of psychological and behavioral adjustment."

Like so many things about parenting a challenging boy, understanding and accepting his feelings is challenging. Challenging boys often don't know what they feel, so they can't tell us. We know that part of what predisposes a boy to be challenging is his challenging temperament, which leads him to frequently experience strong negative emotions. The intensity of a challenging boy's bad feelings combined with his executive functioning challenges, make it extremely difficult for him to stop, step back, identify his feelings, and put them into words. Even after the bad feelings pass, a challenging boy doesn't want to go back and think about what he felt. The bad feelings not only felt bad, but they also made him feel that he *is* bad. For a challenging boy, looking back doesn't result in learning. Instead, it forces him to think about what a failure he feels he is. It leads to painful and overwhelming feelings of shame.

On those occasions, when a challenging boy does know what he is feeling, he often doesn't want to express those feelings directly. He can feel ashamed of his feelings of vindictiveness, envy, rage, vulnerability. He's afraid that if he reveals what he is feeling, he's going to be criticized or rejected.

Even if we are able to understand our son's feelings, it can be challenging to accept them. Challenging boys often express their feelings in "unacceptable" ways. Younger boys hit, yell, break things, run away, or refuse to cooperate. Even when challenging boys manage to "use their words," as we frequently tell them to do, the words they use can be difficult to accept. Challenging boys' feelings often reflect biased, distorted, or unproductive ways of seeing other people and themselves. When we hear our son say, "I hate my teacher. She's so unfair" we are immediately anxious that he will say or do something to the teacher that will create even bigger problems for him. It leads us to want to jump in to correct the biased thinking rather than listen to, understand, and accept his feelings.

Challenging boys' feelings can be expressed in ways that put others on the defensive. He criticizes ("You're stupid"), attacks ("I hate you"), or fights ("You can't make me"). Or the words he uses to express his feelings can be intense, even scary: "I hate myself," "I wish I'd never been born," "I should just die." These feelings are hard to hear, let alone understand and accept. Finally, challenging boys can express feelings that go against our family values: rejecting taking responsibility for an offense ("It's not my fault!") or violating principles of kindness and respect by using insults to demean others ("You're an idiot." "Nobody likes you." "You're dumb.").

Here are some ways to help you in the difficult task of understanding and accepting your son's feelings.

Distinguish Feelings from Behaviors

Psychologist Haim Ginott reminds us that all feelings are acceptable even though some behaviors are not. No harm comes to anyone just because we have a feeling or a wish. Feelings are private experiences. There are unacceptable ways of behaving as a result of our feelings (for example, hitting someone as an expression of angry feelings). Parents do need to set limits on unacceptable behaviors. In fact, one of our most important jobs as parents is to teach our challenging sons how to manage and express their feelings in ways that do not harm others.

Understanding and accepting a challenging boy's feelings is not only a powerful step in rebuilding trust in the parent-child relationship, but it also plays an important role in teaching him how to handle his feelings constructively. Feeling understood and accepted helps a boy not feel alone. It helps him feel that he is wanted and valued. Having us work hard to understand and accept his feelings conveys a clear message to the boy that his feelings are worthy of—and capable of—being understood and accepted and that he should work to do it himself.

Unconditionally accepting *all* of your son's feelings—the positive *and* negative ones—helps him accept himself. If he feels that some of his feelings are unacceptable, he will need to reject that part of himself. Not only will this hurt his self-esteem, but rejecting his feelings means that he will need to repress them. You can't constructively manage a feeling that you don't know you are having. These repressed emotions can come out in all sorts of inappropriate ways. None of us choose our emotional reactions to things. They arise in us spontaneously. However, if we know what our feelings are and accept them, then we can choose how to express them and respond to them.

Sometimes the physical or emotional safety of our son or others requires that we act to limit a behavior before trying to understand his feelings. This circumstance occurs much less frequently than we think. I use the guideline "no one gets hurt (body or feelings), nothing gets broken on purpose (accidents do happen)" to determine whether we need to limit behavior before focusing on feelings. If that rule is being followed, then it's safe to focus on the feelings. The rule isn't violated by words that merely express a wish or an intention to harm people or things or to do something self-destructive later such as, "I'm going to beat Steve up," "I'm going to quit baseball," "I'm going to tell my teacher what I think." Of course, if your son is bullying one of your other kids or another child with his words, that *is* hurtful behavior, and it needs to be stopped. So long as nothing harmful is happening or can happen now, it's safe to focus on the feelings first and manage behavior later.

Focus on the Emotional Heart of the Matter

As I noted above, it's often very difficult to know exactly what a challenging boy feels about himself and his world. Most of the time his feelings are hidden behind words and actions that are not, on the surface, about emotions. We need to be emotion detectives looking for clues about the feelings underlying our son's behavior.

There are moments when our sons do express their feelings more directly—in bed just before going to sleep, in the car, or after a challenging episode when everything has blown over. In these special moments we need to turn our full attention to our son. If you are on your phone or computer when they occur, set these distractions aside. Place your phone down on its face and close your laptop. This sends the clear message that you are ready to listen. Tuning in to these quiet moments can be powerful in rebuilding trust and connection. It can be tempting to try to capitalize on these rare moments of openness and ask a lot of questions or try to teach a life lesson. It's best to resist this impulse and focus instead on ending the session on a positive note—especially at bedtime—and leave our child feeling good about the experience of opening up.

When feelings are expressed indirectly (becoming clingy, regressing, tantrums, sarcasm, stomach aches or headaches, cheating at a game, complaining about being treated unfairly) or as attacks on us or another family member, it's much more difficult to stay focused on discovering what's at stake emotionally for our sons. In these moments we need to try to ask ourselves, "What are the feelings behind these words and behind this behavior?" Our journals are a great place to do this work. Some of our very best opportunities to understand a challenging boy's feelings are in those moments when he is angry at us, blaming us, or attacking us. It's difficult, but we need to do our best to be non-defensive, nonjudgmental, not insist on our positive intention, and instead be open to the feelings that lie behind the harsh words. Gottman describes anger as being composed of two things: a goal and something that is blocking the goal. We can learn a lot about what our sons are going through if we can avoid getting caught up in taking the anger personally and instead focus on listening for what our son's goal is and what is blocking him.

Don't Ask Questions, Guess

Because our sons don't tell us directly what they feel, common sense has us believe that we should ask them. Unfortunately, asking our sons what they feel puts them uncomfortably on the spot and under pressure—especially if they are emotionally dysregulated. Our well-meaning questions get interpreted in ways we don't intend. Our sons hear: "What's wrong with you that you don't know your own feelings?" or "You need to confess the shameful thing you are feeling now!" or "I want to bring up the past so I can rub it in your face." Parents are shocked to hear that they are being so dramatically misperceived. Unfortunately, this misperception can't be addressed directly. Our sons won't believe our reassuring words. A change in their view will come with time as a result of our consistent commitment to understanding and acceptance.

It is OK to use questions to make sure that we understand what our son is communicating. For example, we can ask a boy ranting about unfair treatment from a teacher, "So you feel like Ms. Smith doesn't give you a chance?" What works about this question is that it only asks for a "yes" or "no" answer. The boy isn't required to tell us something he doesn't know or doesn't want to talk about.

Since we're mainly limited to asking questions with yes-or-no answers, what do we do? We need to guess. We don't have to worry about being wrong or about putting ideas in our child's head or causing bad feelings that he doesn't actually have. Our sons will correct us when we're wrong. Where do our guesses come from? Watching and listening to our son and connecting what we are observing to our own experiences. *The most important thing is to listen very carefully to how he responds to our guesses.* We often learn the most by tuning in to his responses to our questions and comments.

A devoted mom, Cynthia, was at an occupational therapy (OT) appointment with her six-year-old son, Jackson. She and the OT, Molly, were talking at the end of the session about Jackson's problems with gross motor development. Suddenly Jackson started running around the OT room causing a big disruption to the other OTs and their patients. Cynthia and Molly had to break off their conversation to corral Jackson. His behavior was unacceptable, and they needed to stop it before attending to his feelings. After she got Jackson into the car, Cynthia asked him what happened. Jackson replied, "No talking!" She tried again, "Are you upset about something?" Again, he demanded, "Stop talking!" Then Cynthia remembered about guessing and asking yes-or-no questions. She stopped and thought about what might be upsetting Jackson. She asked, "Were you upset that I was talking to Molly about you?" Jackson replied, "Yes!" After a pause he added, "I'm strong!" Cynthia realized that she unintentionally wasn't being respectful to Jackson by talking with Molly in front of him. Cynthia also learned that Jackson's gross motor problems made him feel weak. As you can see, it is possible to learn a lot in small moments. This happened because Cynthia guessed about Jackson's feelings and then listened carefully to his response.

Validate, Validate, and Validate Some More
As our understanding and acceptance of our son's emotions start to increase, it's tempting to jump in with advice, fixes, or strategies for

dealing with the problems related to the feelings. Before moving on to problem-solving, it's vital to make sure your son feels that you get it. Repeat back to him what you've heard. Ask if you understand correctly. Moving to problem-solving before understanding unintentionally conveys unacceptance, that you see your son's feelings as wrong and needing to be fixed. Instead, validate.

What is validation? It is communicating to your son that his emotions make sense given who he is and how he sees his world. We want to communicate to our son that his experience is valid and he's not wrong for how he feels. A lot of parents confuse validation with agreement. If your son says, "I'm stupid," you can validate the feeling (for example by saying something like "that's a painful way to feel about yourself") without agreeing with him that he is stupid. In fact, if your son is saying something negative about himself you *should* tell him how you feel, but only after demonstrating to him that you understand his experience and have accepted his feelings. At that point you can ask permission to tell him your perspective. You can say, "That's a hard way to feel. I know that's how you are really feeling about yourself right now. Can I tell you how I see things?"

Here are some examples of validating statements. "It's upsetting when _____ (the other kids got together and didn't invite you)." "It's important to you that _____ (the coach treats everyone fairly)." "You're angry that _____ (you got called out at first base when you were sure you were safe)." "It is frustrating when _____ (you try your best and things don't work out)." "It was really embarrassing _____ (for your teacher to call you out in front of the class)." Or even something as simple as, "I'm so sorry that happened to you."

Here are a few things to avoid when it comes to validation. Don't minimize the significance of what is upsetting your child, even if it seems small to you: "You're making a mountain out of a molehill." Don't try to get your son to look at the bright side: "Let's look for the silver lining." Don't say that "life isn't fair." Don't play devil's advocate or take the other person's side: "Isn't it possible that you misunderstood what your friend meant?" Don't tell your son how he created the circumstances that caused his pain (even if he did—now's not the time) or tell him what he should have done.

Once you have checked that your son feels understood and you have validated his experience, you can ask if he wants your help in coming up with a solution for his problem. When your son is caught up in big feelings, he can't listen or think very well. Taking the time to validate your son's emotions helps bring the feelings down to size. It's incredibly comforting to have a parent who gets it and cares.

Many parents worry that understanding, accepting, and validating their son's feelings will make him more locked into his perspective because the acceptance and validation will convince him he's right. These parents are often quite surprised to discover that validating their son's feelings is not only great for strengthening their parent-child relationship, but that it is also one of the most powerful tools for leading their son to be *more* receptive to seeing things from another point of view, *more* likely to see where he's wrong, *more* likely to take responsibility, and *more* likely to accept parental help and influence.

ALWAYS BE ON YOUR CHILD'S SIDE

James Garbarino urges parents to convey consistently to their sons the following message: "No matter what you have done, no matter what has been done to you, I will never stop loving you." It lets your son know that your love isn't conditional. It lets him know that he can always come to you for help. It lets him know that you will be there to support him no matter what.

This might seem confusing at first. Does always being on a child's side mean that we have to believe everything he says or approve of every action he engages in? No, of course not. It does mean that you will be there for him when he needs you. It means that he can count on you to be understanding and accepting. That he can trust you not to criticize or shame him after he's made a mistake—even if he is defensive, not taking responsibility, or seems unconcerned with the fact that he's hurt someone or done something wrong (he almost certainly feels bad about it, even if he is not showing it).

When you have a challenging boy, it's easy to assume that your son is at fault when you hear about trouble at school or about an issue with a peer. Being on his side means giving him an opportunity to tell you his version of events before you draw conclusions. It begins with informing him of what you heard or what you know and asking him to tell you what happened. For example, "Your teacher emailed me about a problem during math today. What's going on?"

The first few times you try this approach, your son might not trust that you genuinely want to hear his side. He might lie or make an excuse. Don't be worried or offended if he does lie. He's probably afraid that you are mad at him or will assume he did something wrong. It's also common for challenging boys to lie impulsively when they are in trouble, even when they are sure to get caught. Accept your son's version of events unless or until you have evidence that things didn't happen the way he said. If you know what your son is telling you isn't true, don't try to catch him in a lie. Instead, just matter-of-factly say that you're confused because what he is saying doesn't match with what you know or what you've heard.

It can be very angering and confusing when our sons lie to us. It feels like disrespect or a betrayal. Why do challenging boys lie? The main reason is that everyone lies. Eventually we learn not to do it most of the time, especially when lying will get us into more trouble. We exercise the executive function of inhibitory control to stop ourselves from impulsive lying. The real question is why challenging boys lie when they are likely to get caught. Why aren't they better liars? We'll often hear our sons complain that other kids were doing the same thing that got him into trouble, but the other kids just didn't get caught. They didn't get caught because they know how to lie and get away with it. Being an effective liar requires having good executive functioning skills. You need to be able to anticipate the future likelihood of your lie being discovered. You also need to be able to remember your lie. Of course, I'm not suggesting that we want to train our sons to be better liars. We want to help them learn how to tell the truth and take responsibility for themselves and their actions. I'm talking about their lying in this way so that we can recognize that, like their other challenging behavior, lying is the result of their executive functioning skill deficits and not a character flaw.

Being on your child's side does not mean letting him off the hook if he has done something wrong. It means being his advocate. If he is at fault, it means supporting him while he takes responsibility and accepts the consequences of his actions. Related to this, it is my view that we should not give consequences at home for our son's misbehavior at school. It is the school's responsibility to administer consequences for actions that occur while our son is there. By staying out of giving consequences, we can be our son's ally. Our role is to help our son reflect on his behavior, face the consequences, and make amends. We also want to make sure that the school understands our son's challenges, not to give him a pass, but to put his behavior in the appropriate context. Additionally, we want to make sure that any consequences are fair, appropriate, and meaningful.

A chapter on trust and connection would not be complete without briefly touching on a child responding to some rule or limit with "why don't you trust me?" I always advise parents to avoid using the word *trust* in talking with their kids, even if the child is using the word himself. Usually, boys complain of not being trusted when parents decide that their son isn't ready to handle a particular freedom or privilege. To kids, *trust* means something very different than what it means to parents, so it almost always leads to miscommunication. When a challenging boy says, "Why don't you trust me?" he's really saying "I need you to believe in me. I need you to have confidence in me. It feels like you just see me as a screw-up. That's painful because I don't have confidence in myself." It's a real dilemma. We don't want to communicate a lack of faith in our son. However, kids do need rules and limits to be safe. What should we do instead of being pulled into an unproductive conversation about "trust"? Validate your son's feelings. Let him know you understand that he doesn't like the situation. Acknowledge that you might be wrong. Let him know that you are open to revisiting the issue later.

APOLOGIZE AND MAKE AMENDS

Knowing how to repair and reconnect after an argument or fight is one of the most important relationship skills that we can learn. We're all human and we all make mistakes. We're not striving for perfection. When we inevitably screw up, it's important to make things right.

Our challenging sons do not expect perfection from us. They do feel things very strongly: hurt, victimization, injustice. When we are insensitive to their feelings, when we say hurtful things, when we don't keep our promises, when we react to their challenging behavior with explosions of our own, it's not the end of the world. It's time to apologize and repair. The goal isn't the elimination of anger, hurt feelings, miscommunication, misunderstanding (that's impossible), but to engage in repair when those things inevitably happen.

I have noticed over the course of my thirty years in practice that we parents aren't very good at apologizing to our children. This might be because our parents didn't apologize to us. It wasn't that long ago when parents felt it was a mistake to apologize to a child. Apologies were believed to encourage the child to feel like an equal to the parents, or to become more demanding. However, we now know that it is important to apologize to our children when we do something wrong. Not only is it the right thing to do, but it also models for our challenging boys how to take responsibility, apologize, and repair things when they've hurt someone else. You might worry that apologizing will reinforce your son's already significant sense of victimhood, but the opposite is true. Apologizing to him and validating his hurt feelings will ultimately increase his openness to examining his own role in causing the conflict.

Because we weren't apologized to, we don't know how to properly apologize. First, we need to consider what is the goal of a successful apology? One goal is to affirm the worth of the injured person, that they matter and their feelings matter, that they did not deserve to be injured. Another goal is to repair damage. This could be to an object, but mostly it refers to repairing the damage done to the relationship.

Typically, the past mistake can't be "fixed." Repair usually is a promise made to take steps to avoid causing this injury in the future.

What are the steps of a good apology? A helpful mnemonic is the four Rs of apology: Recognition, Responsibility, Remorse, and Repair. In the Recognition stage, the person who caused the hurt takes steps to understand (i.e., "recognize") what the other person feels upset about. This involves listening carefully to our son's account of why he feels wronged. The recognition phase is not a time to offer explanations for our behavior, which might be experienced as us making excuses. The recognition phase is also not a time to argue that the facts our son presented are not correct. It is further not a time to lodge your own complaint or defend your actions. The recognition phase is complete when our son feels that we satisfactorily understand why he's upset.

Many people, especially those who were blamed by their parents growing up, can have a very hard time with this step. It can feel like groveling or giving your child license to mistreat you. Usually, when there is conflict in a relationship, both people bear some responsibility—although it might not be equal—for the problem that has transpired. If you feel in need of repair for your own hurt feelings, it generally works best if you wait to talk about your feelings until after you have completed the four Rs to your son's satisfaction. Then it's your turn to have your son go through the four Rs.

In the Responsibility stage, we need to acknowledge that our actions have caused hurt. We do not minimize the hurt, make excuses, blame circumstances, or blame the victim. Be careful of the "but." "I shouldn't have done x, y, z, *but* you did a, b, c which led me to do it."

In the Remorse or Regret phase, we need to express our feelings about having hurt or upset our son. It's important to be open and vulnerable when you convey your sadness and regret at having caused suffering. Your son needs to feel that his hurt feelings matter. He will recognize how important his feelings are to you in the heartfelt expression of the pain you experience at having hurt him.

The final step is Repair or Resolve. Usually there isn't an opportunity to actually repair the injury. Occasionally you're able to do something like buy a replacement of a toy that has been accidentally thrown out. The repair might be some gesture of making amends. It might be a gift or other token to symbolize the desire for repair. The most important type of repair is a promise to change in some way. You pledge to do your best not to hurt your son in this way again. You commit to working on whatever factors led to you causing the hurt. Again, your son gets to decide whether he is satisfied with the repair.

Some other thoughts to help make your apologies and repairs go more smoothly. Allow time for healing. It can be hard to wait while your son takes the time he needs to feel better. He might need time even if our apology has been great. Also, be prepared that your apology might initially be responded to with more anger or upset feelings. Your son might take your apology as an invitation to tell you how he really feels and with greater intensity. As difficult as it is, try to be receptive and appreciate this as greater openness. Don't say you're sorry for how your son feels. "I'm sorry I hurt you" is an apology. It is taking responsibility for causing suffering. "I'm sorry you feel hurt by what I did" is at best sympathy. You are regretting that he suffers, but not owning your role in causing it.

Be cautious about explanations. They are tricky. Sometimes your son will want an explanation, but usually not. If not asked for, explanations can sound like defensiveness or excuses. Often, we want to emphasize that the hurt we caused wasn't intentional. This is usually OK, but be careful that it doesn't feel like you are taking away the need for an apology. Also, it can be tempting to skip past apologizing by immediately trying to fix things or asking for a do-over. Finally, what do you do if your son feels hurt and expects an apology, but you feel that you didn't do anything that needs to be apologized for? Listen carefully to your son and put yourself in his shoes and see if there's anything that you feel comfortable taking responsibility for and saying you are sorry for. Try to validate his feelings and then say you're sorry and that you'll try to be more sensitive next time.

In this chapter, we've learned ways to rebuild trust and connection in our relationship with our son. We're working to establish a more peaceful and more collaborative dynamic in our homes. This will be the foundation from which we'll be able to teach our son the skills he needs to have a less challenging life. Trust and connection in our parent-child relationship feels better and it creates space for our son to be receptive to the interventions that will be discussed in the remaining chapters.

Key Ideas

- Trust and connection in the parent-child relationship is the foundation from which parents can help their son learn the skills he needs to overcome his problems with challenging behavior.

- Establishing a 5:1 "magic ratio" of positive to negative interactions in the parent-child relationship is key to rebuilding trust and connection.

- Negative parental behaviors to eliminate are criticism, condescension, and defensiveness.

- Positive parental behaviors to accentuate are attention, affirmation, affection, understanding, acceptance, and validation.

- When parents inevitably screw up, it is important to apologize and repair.

Parenting Journal Exercise

- What self-care practices can I implement in my life to reduce my stress level?

- What are some ways that I can engage in more positive interactions with my son? Where can I find more time for him? More play? More investment in his interests? More attention, affection, and affirmation? Make a list.

- Think over the past week, especially any challenging episodes. What do I think are the feelings behind the challenging behavior? If he was angry during the episode, what was his goal and what was blocking the goal? Where do I need to take responsibility, apologize, and make amends for my part in the conflicts?

- What changes have I noticed so far in my son's challenging behavior and in our family life as a result of implementing the lessons I've learned from this book?

Chapter Five

Communication
When to Talk, How to Talk, and When to Listen

Communication on the fire scene is vital for safely coordinating the firefighting efforts of all fire companies and crew present. As a result, communication is practiced during training like all critical firefighting skills. Effective communication is also essential to a healthy parent-child relationship. Communicating with challenging boys, however, is frequently a very frustrating experience. They don't talk. They don't listen. They get angry, explode, and run away. Trying to talk with them always seems to ultimately lead to conflict. As in the fire service, effective communication takes practice.

In this chapter you will learn how to communicate more effectively with your son. You will learn how to talk, when to talk, what to say, and when to remain silent in order to increase your chances of being heard. More importantly, you will learn how to listen carefully to what your son says, because even when challenging boys refuse to speak, they are often saying a lot indirectly or in disguise. One of the most important forms of communication in the fire service does not involve words, it is the sirens and lights on the vehicles that announce, "Make way, there's an emergency we need to get to!"

When communicating with a challenging boy, it is helpful to think about it as two separate, but related, conversations. First, we want our sons to *talk*—that is, open up to us. We want to be closer to them. We want to know what their thoughts and dreams and hopes and worries are. We want to know who they are and how they experience the world. We want to enjoy our time with them, and we want to support and nurture them.

Listening carefully to your son helps you create an increasingly more accurate understanding of how he thinks and feels, what Gottman calls a "love map." Your love map is an invaluable guide for navigating conversations with him. It helps you know what to ask when you want your son to open up and shows you the best ways to communicate when you need him to listen.

Second, we want our sons to *listen* to us. As parents we have many roles. It is our job to keep our sons safe. It is our responsibility to keep them nourished physically and emotionally. And it is our duty to teach them. It has been pointed out many times in parenting books that the word *discipline* means "teach." We can't teach our child, if he won't listen to us, if he's ignoring our words, if he's rejecting our influence. We can't help our son learn the skills he needs to overcome challenging behavior if he rejects our guidance.

As parents we need to be able to teach our sons. This is especially true for challenging boys who cannot solve their problems with challenging behavior on their own. It's important to recognize, though, that trying to talk to our sons can be highly stressful for them. We can relate. We've all felt that surge of anxiety when someone says, "We need to talk." Just like us in these moments, he assumes "talking" means he's going to be told something upsetting. Even if you never say "we need to talk" to your challenging boy, he feels stressed by heavy conversations. This is especially true when you want to discuss a problem he's having, or you need to deal with a conflict between the two of you.

We'll have more success in communication with our son if we don't try to accomplish these two goals (the goal of getting him to open up and *talk* to us and the goal of getting him to *listen* to us) in the same conversation. So, when communicating with our son, it is important to be clear with ourselves about what type of conversation we are having: are we focused on getting him to talk, or on getting him to listen?

I often see parents spoil a wonderful conversation where their son is being vulnerable and *talking* openly about his feelings by seizing it as an opportunity to teach a lesson or to get him to listen to advice. It is easy to make this mistake. When your son is confiding in you, it can feel like the intimacy creates a natural opportunity for him to listen also. If your son is opening up, it means he feels safe enough to let his guard down. When he's sharing, shifting the conversation to your teaching agenda can feel blindsiding to him. His sense of safety is shattered. It makes him less likely to open up again in the future.

In chapter 4, you began the vital process of rebuilding trust and connection with your son. This foundation is key for effective communication. Your efforts to understand and accept your child's feelings and experiences without judgment make it more likely that he will feel safe opening up. Similarly, by respecting and validating his perspective, he'll be increasingly more receptive to yours.

There are two keys to improving communication with your challenging boy. First, prioritize, above all else, making talking with you a positive experience for him. With challenging boys, it's tempting to try to milk as much as you can out of any windows of openness because they are so rare. However, it's better to keep conversations brief. Kids are more likely to open up if they feel assured that they won't be dragged into a long conversation or pressured to talk. It's much better to make the opening up feel good to your child, than to try to get as much information as you can or to make your point.

Second, *listen carefully to how your son responds. It's even more important than what you say to him.* A frequent conversation I have with parents of challenging boys goes like this: I suggest something for them to say to their son, to which they reply, "We already said that." When I ask, "Great! How did he respond?" they're often unsure. Unfortunately, many parents don't pay careful attention to their son's responses, failing to see their significance. However, your son's reactions, whether it's remaining silent, disagreeing, or saying something seemingly off-topic, are important communications. This information is a key part of building your "love map," which will guide you in how to engage with him in the future.

ENCOURAGING YOUR SON TO TALK

Getting a challenging boy to share his inner world is a formidable task. Even if they want to do it, they often don't know where to begin. As we discussed in chapter 4, challenging boys frequently don't know what they are feeling, let alone have the words to express it. One of the most important reasons we want to encourage them to open up is that it gives them practice paying attention to their feelings and putting them into words. The ability to identify and verbalize our feelings is an important emotion regulation skill. Putting bad feelings into words doesn't just share them, it reduces their intensity. As Mr. Rogers said, "Anything that is mentionable can be more manageable." Knowing our feelings is also the basis of empathy, the ability to understand the thoughts and feelings of others, which is one of the most important aspects of emotional intelligence.

Challenging boys also often resist opening up when they are struggling, not to be difficult or to shut us out, but because they expect that "talking about their feelings" will make them feel worse. It can be hard for those of us who find relief in getting things off our chests to understand that not everyone feels this way. Challenging boys typically deal with negative emotions by trying not to feel them at all. They push their bad feelings away and distract themselves, often with videos or video games. Asking a challenging boy to talk about his feelings means asking him to bring those painful feelings back to mind. It works directly against how he is trying to cope. The whole process of talking about their feelings can be deeply unpleasant for them, from the discomfort of dredging things up, to the stress of being pressured to talk.

Another reason our challenging sons hold back from sharing their thoughts and feelings is that they fear we will respond in a way that will be upsetting. Our son needs to feel safe that we won't overreact, criticize, or reject him for what he feels. He needs to feel safe that we won't take over and handle the situation in a way that he's not comfortable with. For example, if a boy is being bullied at school, he might already feel powerless and out of control. If his parents, with the best of intentions, take action and contact the other kid's parents, the boy might fear retaliation and feel that even more control has been taken away from him. This type of experience will lead the boy to be more hesitant to share his problems in the future. He needs to feel secure that we'll handle his concerns with care, respect his feelings about the situation, and not take action without discussing it first.

How to Make Opening Up Feel Good

The first step in getting him to open up to us more is cultivating those rare moments when he chooses to share, rather than us asking probing questions. We can increase the opportunity for these spontaneous moments of openness by being around doing our thing (chores, cooking, not something where we can't be interrupted), on the lookout for signs that he has something on his mind. If he starts to talk, stop what you are doing and quietly turn your full attention to him. Don't make a big deal of it (not "oh my God, I've been waiting for this moment when you finally share your feelings with me!"). Just make it clear with your behavior that you are fully present.

Be especially ready during times when sharing is likely to occur——like bedtime or in the car. Bedtime encourages openness. Once the boy has settled, the frantic activities of the day give way to quiet. His thoughts and feelings come forward and may be expressed to you. The car is another wonderful time because you're together, but not looking at each other. We're told that it is important to make eye contact. But with challenging boys, eye contact can be overwhelming, and the car provides a great space to talk with no demand of looking at each other. Challenging boys also are often more open and vulnerable about their painful feelings after a challenging episode. In these moments you might hear how bad or worthless he feels. He also may swear he won't do it again. Even though you know he probably won't be able to keep this promise, don't correct him. Focus on accepting and validating his wish to do better.

When your son is talking, less is more. Haim Ginott says that talking is strong medicine for all kids, especially challenging boys. Resist the urge to push him to open up more than he's comfortable with. His tolerance for talking is probably far less than you think it is.

Less is more also applies to your responses when he's opening up. Adele Faber and Elaine Mazlish, authors of the parenting classic *How to Talk So Kids Will Listen*, suggest using simple responses to a child's openness like "Oh?" or "Mmmm" or "I see." These comments convey your interest and attention without making a big demand on him for an elaborate response. Try experimenting with brief, empathic words like these and notice how it goes.

It's crucial to not confirm his negative expectations. Apply the lessons of chapter 4. Be attentive and affirming. Accept his feelings without judgment or criticism and validate his experience. Don't shift the conversation to your agenda. Don't teach, lecture, give advice, or problem solve. Stay focused on his feelings. Don't push him to share more than he's ready to. Listen and reflect back to him what you understand. And remember the number one priority is to give him a positive experience.

Here are some other things to keep in mind to help make the experience of opening up positive. Keep the conversation brief. Long, emotional conversations (even ones that seem short to you) are draining for challenging boys. Do your best to remain calm, even if what he brings up is upsetting. Like the flight attendants casually serving drinks on a bumpy flight signaling that everything is fine, your calm response will help him feel more confident that he can get through whatever problem he might be bringing up. Pay careful attention to his emotions during the conversation. If he's getting overwhelmed or feeling bad or ashamed, check in with him and let him know that it's OK to take a break. "This is big stuff to be talking about. Should we take a break and come back to it later?" Similarly, if he starts getting defensive, that means he's feeling criticized or under attack. If he starts to shut down, that's a sign he's getting overwhelmed. Tell him how much you appreciate him letting you know how he feels; then shift to doing something that is positive for him (watch TV, play a game, play with the dog). This way, even if the talking got overwhelming, things end with something positive.

When a challenging boy opens up about his difficult feelings, we need to remember he's taking a big risk. In our culture, boys are taught to keep their feelings to themselves and that feelings like sadness or fear are signs of weakness. In addition, a challenging boy generally experiences himself to be a problem child, that something is wrong with him and how he feels. He expects to be criticized, rejected and humiliated. Be prepared, as a result, for him to be sensitive, prickly, and prone to shut down or run away. Don't take it personally or lose your cool.

Approach your son with the care you would give to an injured animal. He needs your help, but he's afraid and might "bite." Take things slowly and gently. Listen closely to what he says directly and indirectly. Imagine yourself in his shoes and tell him what you think he might be feeling (refer to the list of challenging feelings from chapter 3 to guide you). As we learned in chapter 4, this approach makes it easier for him to recognize and articulate his emotions, rather than feeling pressured to figure them out on his own.

Validate frequently. Your validation helps him not feel weak for turning to you for help with his feelings: "Those are big feelings to be all alone with." Your validation also helps him feel that he's not weird or bad for feeling the way he does: "It makes total sense that you feel this way." These are things we all want when we open up: to feel understood (not judged), to feel accepted (not alone), to feel normal (not crazy), and to have our feelings make sense (not feel confused). To experience this relief of opening up about our feelings, we need to feel safe and relaxed. This is why the hard work of building trust that we started in chapter 4 is so vital.

Sometimes it is helpful to share your own experiences, but remember it's important to ask his permission before doing so. Here are a couple of examples of things you might say: "Would you like to hear about a similar struggle that I have?" or "Would you like to hear about a time I felt that way?" By asking for his permission to share, you're letting him know that you're not trying to take over the conversation, but rather, you're there to empathize. Your story might help him to feel less defective for having the struggles he's having. Keep an eye on how he responds. If it seems like he doesn't relate to your sharing, then shift your attention back to him.

Nine-year-old Mason was overwhelmed by intrusive fears about something happening to one of his parents, and this was leading to explosions. His dad, Jonathan, had similar struggles with intrusive thoughts. I suggested to Jonathan that he share this with Mason. At first, Jonathan was reluctant. He worried that Mason would feel even more upset if he was told that he might still have the same problem even as an adult. I convinced Jonathan that Mason would have the opposite reaction. I explained that his worries make him feel like a problem child. Hearing about his dad's similar struggles will help Mason see himself instead as a child with a problem. He'll think, "If someone I respect as much as my dad can struggle with this, I must not be so messed up."

With my coaching, Jonathan ended up saying to Mason, "I'm the same way. Sometimes, I have thoughts that get stuck in my head." Mason was astonished, "Really?" Jonathan said, "Yes. We all have a part of our brain that tries to keep us safe. But sometimes ours works overtime and can't tell the difference between real and make-believe dangers. When I have a worry, I ask myself, 'Is this something I can do anything about?' If I can, I work on that problem. If I can't, I get busy doing something else. It takes my mind off the worries." Hearing this was a big relief to Mason.

What happens if, in opening up, your son tells you about a problem that he's having that does need solving? In the example above, a boy was getting bullied at school. That is a problem that calls for a response. In these circumstances, is it OK to switch to a problem-solving conversation? Yes, if your son feels you understand what his concerns are. Again, ask his permission. "Would you like my help in dealing with this situation?" Often, when they are opening up about challenging feelings, challenging boys want more than validation. They don't want to be left holding all their bad feelings alone and not knowing what to do. They don't want you to take control, however. They want to have a say in any actions that might be taken.

What if your son doesn't want help with solving a problem, but you think he needs it? Generally, most problems don't need to be solved right this minute. Don't rush to action. You risk him feeling overwhelmed and out of control. It will increase his anxiety, and he'll regret opening up. Give him time to process your conversation (remember that challenging boys have big emotional reactions that take a long time to dissipate). Of course, as a parent, you do need to take actions sometimes that he might not agree with. His fear might be leading him to want to avoid doing anything, but you know the problem will only get worse. Let him know that you understand that he doesn't agree with your plan and that you are open to thinking about alternatives, but you need to do something, and this is the best thing you can think of now.

How to Get Our Sons to Talk

We don't want to always have to wait around for our son to initiate a conversation. However, it can be very difficult to get him to talk, especially in the beginning. Ultimately, we want talking with each other to feel easy and comfortable. We want to be able to check in with him, hear about his day, bring things up, or just connect without it feeling like a big deal.

Timing is important. Right after school isn't the best time to try to get a boy talking. He's probably stressed from his day and needs to relax and unwind. During or immediately after a conflict isn't a good time either. Generally, it's best to talk when our son is calm; the worst time is when he's flooded with bad feelings.

Getting a challenging boy comfortable talking is a process that takes time. At first, he will do almost anything he can to avoid conversation. He'll ignore questions. He'll give one-word answers. He'll bury his face in his phone. He'll tell us we're being annoying. He'll yell. He'll run off.

We want to begin by focusing on getting to know our son better and adding to our love map. What is he interested in? What does he do during the day? Who does he hang out with? It is best at this initial stage to limit our efforts to asking questions about his interests and to keep conversations brief. I have a mantra when it comes to talking with challenging boys: *"It's better to have twenty-five one-minute conversations than one twenty-five-minute conversation."* Instead of trying to accomplish everything in a single sitting, it's preferrable to break a longer talk down into several shorter ones. The goal of each brief conversation is to learn something that can be built upon in the next. This series of short talks helps establish momentum in opening up. The conversations don't all have to literally be limited to one minute in length; they just need to end before the boy gets overwhelmed and he has yet another negative experience of talking with us. I use the rule of twenty-five one-minute conversations to highlight how parents generally try to talk too much and for too long when speaking with their challenging sons.

For example, if you notice that he's playing a new video game, you might ask: "That looks like a pretty cool game. What is it?" If he tells you, don't inundate him with questions about the game. Ask, at most, one or two and pay careful attention to his response. If he gets annoyed, stop asking questions. Instead, do some research on your own later to learn more about the game. Your research will help facilitate future one-minute conversations. You might also ask if you can watch him play. If he agrees, watch quietly, and be sure to celebrate any wins with a cheer or high five. Again, file away your observations and questions for future conversations. At this beginning phase, be prepared for him to reject your efforts. He wants to make sure you are really interested. Don't take it personally. Don't get provoked into a fight. Stay calm. Be gentle but persistent.

Over time, and across many of these brief conversations, your son will start to notice that something different is going on: you are listening better, you seem genuinely interested, you aren't expecting lengthy conversations. You are also no longer taking the bait and reacting when he shuts you out. He also has noticed the work you've done to improve your relationship with him. He might not be able to describe it, but he feels a change. Eventually you can start asking him questions that are a little more personal.

As you progress, your son will start being more open, but he'll also be on guard for any signs of criticism or judgment. He might test you to make sure the changes are here to stay. As he expresses himself more, the feelings will often be very hard to hear. He'll be angry with you. He'll be critical and blaming. He'll be activated emotionally and might even be yelling. It's important that you survive these tests and not get provoked to react.

This testing phase is like a backdraft in firefighting. Sometimes with a building fire, the blaze runs out of oxygen and goes out, but the structure is still filled with smoke and superheated gases. If you open a door, the oxygen rushes in and it can cause an explosion as the fire suddenly reignites. Your son's feelings are like this. They've been closed off and deprived of oxygen. When he starts opening up, the first feeling that comes out is often anger. Sharing one's feelings is a vulnerable thing to do, but expressing anger feels strong. It's a safer way for him to begin. Be prepared for this possibility of an emotional "backdraft." It makes it easier to stay calm, nonreactive, and focused on the fact that things are actually getting better.

Remember, even after you get through the testing phase, putting feelings into words will still be a challenge for your son and avoiding his feelings may remain his preferred way of coping with them. He'll be more open to answering questions about how he's doing, but talking is still stressful for him. In chapter 4, I recommended not asking questions like "what are you feeling?" Instead, I suggested guessing based on your observations. If your son is talking about getting made fun of at school by a friend, you could say, "That sounds upsetting" or "I could imagine that making a person feel mad (or sad or confused)." You can also invite opening up by observing behavior and speculating on the feelings behind it. If your son comes home from school and noisily dumps all of his belongings on the floor, instead of saying "pick up your things right now!" you could try putting words to the feelings: "looks like it was one of those days."

Questions can be useful in helping our sons talk, but they need to be questions that are easy to answer. Questions that are very open ended are too stressful. "How was school today?" is too big a question. He doesn't really know what type of answer you are looking for. It encourages responses like "fine," "OK," or "boring." Yes-or-no questions work very well if you are checking in with your son to confirm that you understand his point of view correctly. However, yes-or-no questions generally don't help you gather any new information. "Did you learn anything interesting at school today?" invites the answer "no." Here's an example of a question that is not too open-ended but also yields some information: "On a scale of one to ten, how was school today?" Follow this question by giving him some reference points: "One is the worst school day ever, like taking standardized tests all day, and ten is the best day ever, like last color day." This is a way of asking how school was that is much easier to answer.

Sometimes asking a multiple-choice question can be helpful if there is something you want to learn about. For example, your son said he wanted to play soccer, so you signed him up. Then on the day of the first practice he refused to go. You might ask, "Help me understand. You said you wanted to play soccer, but now you don't. Are you afraid that the coach will be mean, the other kids won't like you, you won't be good at soccer, or something else?"

As I said above, when trying to get a conversation going, the easiest questions for a boy to answer are about his interests. "Who are you starting at quarterback for your fantasy team this Sunday?" Or "I watched this video on Fortnite strategy, have you ever heard of DrLupo (a Fortnite streamer)?" It also generally works well to ask questions following up on things you already know about. For example, your son is attending a baseball camp, but he's frustrated with it even though he loves baseball. You know from a previous conversation that he feels that the coach talks down to them and treats them like little kids. After the day's camp session, following up, you could ask: "How was it? Did the coach talk to you again like you didn't know anything about baseball?"

Below are some examples of questions that are open ended enough that they might lead to a bit of talking but not so much that they'll shut down conversation. I've organized them into groups. Boys are generally more comfortable answering the "interests and preferences" questions. "Imagination" questions are a little more challenging. They aren't particularly personal, but they ask him to think. Finally, "what happened at school" questions start treading into more personal territory. Don't pepper him with questions about multiple topics.

Interests and Preferences
Who's your favorite YouTuber or Tik Tok personality?
What's your favorite video on the internet right now?
Who is your favorite athlete?
Who's your favorite musical artist?
What's your favorite app or game on your phone or tablet?
(With these questions you can follow up and ask him
    to show you the YouTuber, video, athlete, artist, or
    game on his phone or computer. You'll learn a lot,
    and it won't demand that he do a lot of talking.)

Imagination
If you could have any superpower, what would it be?
If you could be any animal for a day, what would you choose?
If you could have any pet, real or imaginary, what would it be?
If you were the principal for a day, what would you do?
If you could change one rule at home or school, what would it be?

What Happened at School
What special classes did you have today? Art, music, or gym?
What was the best thing that happened to you today?
What was the worst thing that happened to you today?
Who did you talk to (or play with) today?
Did anyone get in trouble today?

Carefully note how your son responds. Which questions does he easily answer and answer follow-up questions about? Which questions go nowhere? Don't push it if you get no answer or silence. We want his experience of talking to you to be positive, not awkward or pressured. You can say, "It looks like you don't feel like talking. That's OK." As you get more familiar with what types of questions your son is likely to answer, you can evolve into asking more personal questions about what is going on in his life and what he's feeling. "Is there anything that scares or worries you?" "Is there anything that you are looking forward to?" "How well do you feel that you fit in with your friends at school?"

Be sure to respond positively to the sharing, even if the information shared is upsetting. We don't want to punish honesty either directly (by punishing the misdeeds we are told about) or indirectly (by being judgmental or getting upset about what we hear). Our child might tell us about something he has done wrong or some risky behavior he has engaged in. We want our sons to feel safe opening up. Remember the message Garbarino says we all should convey to our sons: "No matter what you have done, no matter what has been done to you, I will never stop loving you." We want our sons to turn to us when they need help. It's very important to not overreact, especially about smaller things our sons tell us. Not making a big deal about small things helps our sons come to us with big things.

As our boys become older and more independent, they will have less and less adult supervision. If they don't tell us what they are doing, we won't have any way of knowing. If we don't know what's happening in their lives, we can't guide them, support them, and help them figure out how to handle their problems.

There is an exception to the rule of not mixing conversations where you want him to talk and conversations where you want him to listen. If your son attributes thoughts or feelings to you that are not true, you get to speak for yourself. You need to because if you don't, he might conclude that he's correct. If he says things like: "You hate me," "You wish I was never born," "You think I'm stupid (lazy, no good, etc.)," you should validate *his* feelings but correct his statement about yours. "You believe that I think you are stupid. I'm sorry you feel that way. That's a painful way to feel. I'd like to tell you how I actually feel. I don't think you're stupid at all. I know you are smart. What about that English paper you wrote that Mr. Jones said was the best one he'd read all year?"

Similarly, if he says something critical or contemptuous about himself, you can validate that he feels badly and ask if you can tell him how you feel. "I hear that you feel lazy. I get that's how you really feel and it's upsetting. I don't think you're lazy. That Lego set you put together had almost two thousand pieces and took you three weeks to build. That doesn't sound like a lazy person to me." Such a response not only validates his feelings, but it also demonstrates to him a way of thinking about himself that isn't so negative.

Getting Your Son to Listen

At the heart of the Challenging Boys approach to solving challenging behavior problems is helping you to create a relationship with your son where he is open to your guidance. Too often a pattern of challenging behavior leads to circumstances where our son tunes us out. He assumes when we talk to him that we don't care about his feelings, we won't understand where he is coming from, and we will criticize him and make him feel bad about himself. Given that, why would he listen?

As you have worked your way through the book so far, your efforts have been focused on turning this unfortunate situation around. You have worked to reduce conflict and increase feelings of acceptance. Your son's default assumption about you is shifting from suspicion to trust.

Now how do we get our son to listen? What if you want to talk with him about your concern that he's not doing his homework and it's impacting his grades? What if you are frustrated that he's not getting off his video games and it's keeping him up late? What if you want to bring up an email you received from his fifth-grade teacher that he's refusing to do classroom work?

Most of us believe the best way to get our son to listen is to make our point very clearly. We even get him to repeat back to us what we've said. If we face resistance, we reword and rephrase our point, assuming that if we find the right words he'll finally get it. It turns out that focusing on making our point actually interferes with being heard. Instead, the harder we push our point, the firmer his resistance to it becomes. Kids generally feel that parents talk too much. They resent being lectured at. All they hear is that we think they need to be fixed or controlled.

Steven Covey said about influence: "Seek first to understand, then to be understood." It's easy for us as parents to assume we understand what our child is going through because we were all children once.

Understanding a child is actually quite difficult. I spend a lot of my time talking with kids and I am impressed by how differently they see the world. The difference is not simply based on the fact that they don't have as much life experience as we do or that they are living at a different time in history. Their brains are also very different from ours. They experience the future and assess risk differently than we do because of the lack of development of certain brain structures. We can't really remember what it is like to be a child with a child's brain because we're remembering our childhoods with our adult brains. Our starting place should be to assume that we don't understand, even if it feels like we do. From there we need to work hard to understand our son's perspective and validate it.

Validation is one of the most powerful tools for increasing your son's receptivity. In research I conducted during graduate school, I studied how validation and influence are related. Validating another person increases their receptivity, but only if you do it a lot. If you try to move from a single instance of validation to trying to get someone to take in your point of view, it won't be effective. In my research, I found that people were most receptive to new ideas about themselves when their existing view was validated an average of nine times. This 9-to-1 ratio of validation to influence makes sense if we stop and think about it. When we're consistently validated, we feel that the other person really understands us. We don't need to keep insisting on our point of view because they get it. In this circumstance, when the other person has something to say that's different from what we think, we believe it's probably worth listening to. If we're validated once and then the person immediately moves on to trying to change how we think, the validation is discounted. It feels like lip service or manipulation.

The clearest sign that we are trying too hard to make our point is our son getting defensive. Resistance and defensiveness indicate that he feels criticized or threatened. Continuing to push will only increase his feelings of threat. We must avoid the natural urge to press harder in the face of resistance. Instead, we need to pivot to trying to understand what is causing it. We might be failing to grasp that our son feels our agenda is in conflict with his. He might feel we are putting him down or that we are encroaching on his autonomy. Perhaps he believes that we are suggesting he do something that he is sure to fail at. He might mistrust our advice because he thinks we've given him bad advice in the past. When facing resistance and defensiveness, we need to shift to listening. To paraphrase Covey, being receptive to another person makes them more receptive to us. Pushing, forcing, arguing, coercing all intensify opposition.

I mentioned my rule of thumb above that it's better to have twenty-five one-minute conversations than one twenty-five-minute conversation. This is an easy way to remember that we do best when we don't try to accomplish everything in one long talk. It rarely works. Talking with kids, especially when we want them to listen, is stressful for them. It's a lot easier if we break the big conversation up into a series of brief ones. These short conversations have two goals: the first is to not overwhelm our son with too much talking. If we do, he'll tune us out. The second goal is to learn something in the current brief conversation that we can use to start the next one. We are much more likely to succeed in getting our point across when we spread it out over the course of several short conversations where each subsequent one builds upon things we learned in the previous one. Most kids can only handle three to five minutes of talking before tuning out. This means that twenty-plus minutes of our twenty-five-minute-long conversation will be at best a waste of time and at worst will get him to shut us out more.

It's not necessary to have the perfect answer to everything our son says at the tip of our tongue. It's even OK to say the wrong thing sometimes. We can go back to it in the next conversation by saying, "I've been thinking about what we were talking about (or what you said, or what I said)." This gently reintroduces the topic and gives us a chance to respond in the way we weren't able to in the moment. It also models for our son reflecting on our relationships. It teaches him that it's OK to take time to work through thoughts and feelings, and that conversations are an ongoing process.

A particularly crucial time to get our sons to listen is when there is an important problem that needs to be solved. Often this means resolving a conflict between us. One of the most important life skills we can teach our sons is the ability to resolve conflicts constructively. Skilled conflict resolvers have happier marriages, better friendships, and generally more successful careers. The most powerful way for your child to learn healthy conflict resolution is for you to model these problem-solving skills in your parent-child relationship.

How to Problem Solve
Authors John Gottman, Ross Greene, Adele Faber, and Elaine Mazlish all outline similar ways to problem solve when there is a conflict. The approach described below is based on Greene's, Faber and Mazlish's, and Gottman's methods of problem-solving, but it relies most heavily on the Gottman approach. problem-solving conversations should not happen in the heat of the moment, but after everyone has had time to cool down. If, in the problem-solving conversation, you or your son start to get heated again, it's time to take a break.

Step 1: Gentle Start-up
The research of John Gottman says that the best way to bring up difficult topics is with what he calls a "gentle start-up." Too often we're mad or upset when we try to get our son to listen to us. We lead with intense feelings, we lead with critical words, we lead with a disapproving tone. According to Gottman, these types of harsh start-ups create negative emotional arousal in our son, which makes it practically impossible for him to listen to us.

Use "*I*" statements instead of "*you*" statements. When I talk about what *I* feel, it's about me. When I start with what *you* did, it's easy to feel it to be a criticism or an accusation. Talk about feelings rather than "facts." Here are some gentle ways to start a conversation where you want your son to listen. *I feel worried when I see that you have several assignments missing."* Instead of *"How do you expect to do well in school if you never do any work?"* Greene suggests asking a "what's up" question as a form of gentle start-up. Greene's what's up question begins with an observation and concludes with "what's up?" "*I see that you have several assignments that haven't been turned in; what's up?*"

In addition to these approaches, you can try to inject playfulness and humor into your start-up. If we see our son on his phone and not getting to homework that needs to be done, you might say "permission to nag?" By asking if you can nag, it gives your son the opportunity to say no. When presented with "nagging" as something he can choose to accept or not, versus having it imposed on him, you'll be surprised how often he'll say yes. Another approach that starts things up gently with humor is to say, "I'm here as a representative of future you. He will feel better if he's not stressed out, scrambling to get his homework done at the last minute. He's hoping you'll get started now."

Criticizing your son's character ("you're lazy"), being condescending or sarcastic ("When you're an adult, you'll understand what I mean" or "really looks like you're working hard"), or with yelling, threats, or an angry tone are examples of a harsh start-up. Learning what start-ups work for your son comes from trying different approaches and noting carefully how he responds.

Step 2: Understanding His Perspective

In this step, we apply the skills we've learned about understanding, accepting, and validating our son's point of view. It's best if your son goes first to explain his perspective. Gottman suggests the listener have pencil and paper to write down the key points. It helps us focus on what the other person is saying.

Sometimes parents don't believe that their son is telling the truth. They feel he's trying to deflect or make excuses. Accept and validate anyway. If he's not telling the truth, it means that he doesn't feel safe doing so. Your acceptance and validation help create that safety. Communicate back to him your understanding and ask if you have it correct. If he says "no," ask him to tell you what else you need to know to understand better. If he says yes, then ask if you can tell him your perspective. If he's not ready to hear your point of view, take a break. Begin your conversation about your feelings with a gentle start-up.

Step 3: Brainstorming

Once everyone's feelings are understood, it's time to brainstorm possible solutions. Faber and Mazlish stress that in the brainstorming phase, none of the ideas are evaluated. They are just written down, no matter how ridiculous they are. Ethan and his parents (from chapter 1) were having a conflict over bedtime. When they got to the brainstorming part of their conversation, Ethan's first brainstorming suggestion was that his parents let him go to bed whenever he wants to. His mom just calmly wrote it down. Then she playfully suggested, "How about you just go to bed when we ask whether you feel like it or not?" Of course, neither of these initial suggestions reflect solutions that both sides can accept. The brainstorming session lasts until some ideas have been generated that you and your son can agree to. Sometimes challenging boys have difficulty with brainstorming. Be prepared that you might be the only one suggesting ideas, especially the first few times you try problem-solving.

Step 4: Agree to a Plan

Hopefully, at least one of the ideas will satisfy both of you and seem realistic. An agreement is made, and the plan is written down. It is important for me to stress here that in my experience the first plan never works. *Expect failure.* The point of the first plan is to start a process of trying things, learning from them, and trying new things. Don't get mad when it fails or accuse him of not keeping his promise. Although do apologize if you didn't hold up your end of the plan. Problem-solving is almost always a work in progress.

Step 5: Evaluate the Plan and Make a New One

It's not a big deal if a plan doesn't work; it's just time for another problem-solving conversation where you go over what you've learned and brainstorm some new possible solutions.

In this chapter we've learned strategies for helping our sons open up and talk to us so that we can know them better and they can know themselves better. We've also learned strategies for talking to them so that they are more likely to accept our influence. Finally, we learned that it's generally best to keep these two types of conversations separate in order to have the greatest likelihood of success.

Talking is one way to influence your son, but not the only one, or even the best in all circumstances. Other tools can be more effective, especially early on in working with a challenging boy. In the chapters that follow, we'll continue to learn other techniques and strategies for teaching your son the skills he needs to put challenging behavior problems behind him.

KEY IDEAS

- Communication with your son has two aspects: getting him to open up and talk and getting him to listen to influence. It's usually best not to try to accomplish both goals in the same conversation.

- Generally, it's not a good idea to try to get too much information out of our son during a listening conversation nor to use his opening up as an opportunity to get him to listen to our agenda.

- The most important thing when having a conversation with your challenging boy is to make it a positive experience for him.

- Always listen carefully to what he says and doesn't say.

- Attention, understanding, acceptance, validation, and keeping the conversations brief are your key tools in making communication positive.

PARENTING JOURNAL EXERCISES

- Love Map.

    Start building your love map. Your love map is built up of what you know about your son's feelings, preferences, interests, friends, and activities. You can begin by finding out the answers to the following questions.

    - What is his favorite activity? What does he love about that activity?
    - What's his favorite food?
    - Who's his favorite influencer?
    - What's his favorite subject in school? What's his least favorite?

- Who's his favorite teacher?
- What does he do during his school day?
- Who are his friends?
- What present would he want?
- What does he feel he is good at?
- What is he worried or stressed about?
- What is he sad about?
- Is there something he's looking forward to?
- Who does he admire?

(go to challengingboys.com/book for more love map questions)

- Write about a recent attempt to talk to your son, what went well, what went badly? What can you do differently next time?

- What do you really want to get your son to talk about or get him to listen to? How might you break this topic down into one-minute conversations?

- What times does your son spontaneously open up to you? How can you be more available during those moments?

CHAPTER SIX

Co-regulation

Laying the Groundwork for Self-Regulation

It's time to start teaching our sons the skills they need to no longer be challenging, but before that I want to take you back to my first experience fighting a real fire. As I told you in the introduction, on that day our crew worked calmly and efficiently to put the fire out in just a few minutes, preventing it from spreading from the bedroom where it started to the rest of the house. My role, along with another new member, was to connect the fire engine to the hydrant. We were a long way from being ready to perform more dangerous jobs: leading an interior attack on a fire or conducting search and rescue for possible victims.

After the fire was safely extinguished, a lieutenant called me and my fellow newbie over. He told us to put on air packs because he wanted to take us into the house while it was still smokey to give us experience working in those conditions. Adrenaline was surging through my body. My heart was pounding, and my breathing was fast as I followed the lieutenant into the dark smoke-filled building.

Like a SCUBA tank, a firefighter's SCBA tank (there's no "U" because they aren't used underwater, it's just a Self-Contained Breathing Apparatus) has a finite volume of air. Although they are rated as thirty- or forty-five-minute tanks based on the amount of air they contain, the amount of time your tank lasts is determined in large part by your respiration rate. In my state of hyperarousal, I was breathing so hard that it was barely ten minutes before the low-air alarm went off on my thirty-minute tank. Experienced firefighters know how to manage their emotional arousal to keep their breathing slow so that their air supply lasts as long as possible.

Managing emotional arousal is vital for firefighters to be able to preserve their lifesaving air in the dangers of a burning building. Managing our emotional arousal is necessary as a parent to keep our cool in the heat of the flames of a challenging behavior episode. In fact, according to psychologist Desiree Murray and colleagues, the capacity to regulate one's emotional arousal is essential for success across almost all areas of life: promoting physical and emotional health, excelling academically and professionally, and maintaining fulfilling relationships. We need to be emotionally regulated to be motivated, to be able to focus, to concentrate, to think. If we're unregulated emotionally, we can't learn and we can't perform. When our emotions are well-regulated we are better able to complete tasks, organize our behavior, control our impulses, and solve problems effectively. Emotion regulation is the most important skill that we need to teach our challenging boys to help them to not be challenging.

What is emotion regulation and why is it important? For an answer to that question, we must go back to 1908 and look at the work of psychologists Robert Yerkes and John Dodson. Their research led them to formulate what has come to be known as the "Yerkes-Dodson Law" which says there is an inverted U-shaped relationship between emotional arousal and performance (figure 6.1). Looking at the figure, we see that at low levels of emotional arousal—boredom, disinterest, apathy—performance on tasks is poor. We don't do well when we don't have energy and motivation. Following the curve to the right, we see that as emotional arousal increases, performance improves but only up to a point. When arousal gets too high—like me that first time in a smokey building—performance starts to deteriorate. Eventually, arousal increases to the point where the individual is activated into full fight-or-flight mode. The optimal level of emotional arousal for performance has been called the "Goldilocks Zone." In the Goldilocks Zone arousal is not too low, it's not too high, it's just right (see figure 6.1).

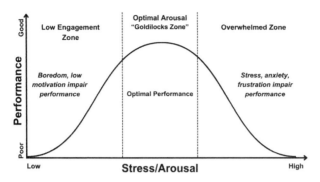

Figure 6.1. Yerkes-Dodson Law

Challenging boys have a much harder time keeping their arousal in the Goldilocks Zone than typical kids do. Their challenging temperament means they frequently experience intense negative emotions (anger, frustration, anxiety) that push their arousal into the Overwhelmed Zone. For challenging boys, these strong emotions also dissipate more slowly than they do for kids with easy temperaments, keeping the boy in the Overwhelmed Zone longer. Additionally, challenging boys frequently experience motivation-sapping negative emotions, like hopelessness and helplessness, which lower their arousal into the Low-Engagement Zone (think of how often we hear our challenging boys say "I'm bored").

Making matters worse still for our challenging sons is the impact of skill and practice. Individuals who are highly skilled and practiced at a task experience less stress while performing the task as compared to less skilled individuals. We see this in action when comparing the veteran firefighters in my department to me at my first fire call. As a novice firefighter, entering a smoke-filled building for the first time was very stressful, leading to high emotional arousal. For the seasoned firefighters, the call was routine, so their arousal stayed in the Goldilocks Zone.

Highly skilled and practiced individuals can also tolerate much more emotional arousal before their performance starts to suffer (think of star athletes in the final seconds of a big game). After emotion regulation, the most important skills a child needs to have to not be challenging are executive functioning skills. Challenging boys have poorer executive functioning skills so that many tasks that are easy for typical kids cause them more stress. Additionally, challenging boys can tolerate less stress before their executive functioning breaks down. Both factors combine to make them highly vulnerable to getting emotionally overwhelmed. This, in turn, leads them to behave in a challenging manner.

There is good news. Parents can help challenging boys develop better emotion regulation skills. The primary method by which our challenging sons will learn better self-regulation is through our consistent, warm, and responsive efforts to help them regulate themselves. This developmental process through which all of us learn to self-regulate is referred to as "co-regulation." Challenging boys won't learn emotion-regulation through rules, limits, consequences, or punishments. These things govern *behavior*, not *emotions*.

The term *co-regulation* initially referred to the role of parents in soothing their infant's distress. Parents help the baby regulate his emotional arousal through several means: by regulating the environment (making sure that it is safe and not overstimulating), by helping the baby regulate his body (ensuring he is fed, dry, dressed appropriately for the temperature, gets enough sleep), and by supporting the baby's efforts to soothe himself through warmth and affection (holding, rocking, singing).

Co-regulation occurs throughout the life span. Even as adults we turn to our partners, family members, friends, therapists, and clergy to comfort us when we're upset. What co-regulation looks like—and when and how often it is needed—changes as the baby grows to toddlerhood, childhood, adolescence, and beyond. As a child develops, two more forms of co-regulation are possible: modeling and coaching. In modeling, our child learns self-regulation skills through observing us regulate ourselves. In coaching, we use encouraging words; help him identify his feelings; and offer guidance, motivation, and support for his efforts to regulate himself: "I know you're scared, but you can do this, just take one step at a time." Finally, as coaches, we can teach self-regulation skills directly. For example, teaching our son a breathing technique that he can use to lower his arousal.

Through the experience of responsive co-regulation from parents, the child develops expectations, motivations, and skills that assist him to regulate his own emotions. When parents create an environment that is reliable, secure, and not overwhelming, it instills in the boy a belief that the world is safe and manageable. When we feel safe and secure, our emotional arousal naturally settles in the Goldilocks Zone. When we feel threatened, we're much more likely to tip into fight-or-flight mode (the Overwhelmed Zone in figure 6.1).

Assisting our son to regulate his physiological arousal helps build a positive relationship between the boy and his body. He learns that his body can play an important role in emotion regulation. The boy can discover that exercise is a powerful tool for self-regulation, teaching him that physical activity can calm his feelings by calming his body. A boy experiencing his body to be a vehicle for emotion regulation lays the groundwork for him being open to learning body-based self-regulation techniques such as deep breathing or progressive muscle relaxation. A body that is experienced solely as a cause of emotional dysregulation must be dissociated from, placing the boy at future risk of using alcohol and other substances to numb himself.

By providing emotional support and soothing, we show our son that negative emotional arousal is temporary and manageable. He trusts that others care when he's upset and will assist him in calming down. He knows to seek out help and to be open to it when it is offered. He learns that bad feelings don't last forever and he's not helpless when they arise. This makes them easier to tolerate. Repeated experiences of parental co-regulation (of environment, body, and emotions) change the boy's developing nervous system. He becomes less reactive to stress and quicker to calm down.

In coaching our son through emotionally arousing situations, his motivation to regulate himself is developed, his emotion regulation skills are enhanced, and his confidence in his ability to face difficult feelings is bolstered. With respect to modeling, when we as parents actively and intentionally work to regulate our own emotions, we set an example for our challenging son to follow. From this he internalizes the idea that negative emotional arousal requires intentional, effortful regulation, and he learns skills to manage his emotions effectively. Finally, direct instruction in self-regulation skills further equips our son with practical strategies and methods for managing his emotional states.

Conversely, if a child doesn't receive attuned co-regulation and is often left drowning in emotional dysregulation, he will come to believe that others do not care when he is distressed. Initially, he will intensify and escalate his expressions of distress—that is, throw a tantrum—in order to get the attention he needs. This is ultimately self-defeating because it contributes to the boy's self-image as a problem child, and it contributes to others seeing him that way too. Eventually he will become hopeless and untrusting. He'll be on guard and shut down when distressed, and not open to connection and help from others. This mindset keeps him aroused and vigilant, constantly on the verge of tipping into the Overwhelmed Zone. In this stressful context, his nervous system becomes more reactive and slower to soothe.

HOW TO CO-REGULATE

To review, emotional self-regulation is the most important skill that we can teach our son to help him overcome his problem with challenging behavior. As he learns to be increasingly more aware of his level of emotional arousal and has growing skills for bringing his arousal into the Goldilocks Zone, he'll be able to face ever more challenging situations without becoming challenging. Remember, developing improved self-regulation comes primarily through our co-regulation efforts. I'll discuss how to co-regulate our sons below.

One final point before we turn to this topic. Not only does co-regulation promote the development of this crucial life skill, but it sets the stage for all the teaching that we'll be doing throughout the rest of this book. Our sons can't learn new skills unless they are in the Goldilocks Zone. For all of the teaching that follows, the first step will be to ensure that he's in a well-regulated state and ready to learn. Trying to teach a dysregulated child will result in little learning, a lot of frustration, and the potential for further dysregulation.

Tuning In

The first step in co-regulating your son is to tune in to what he's feeling and where his arousal is (low engagement, optimal, or overwhelmed). As you tune in, one of the first things you'll realize is that challenging behavior, above all else, is a signal that your son needs help regulating himself. Challenging behavior occurs when your son is facing a demand that he doesn't have the emotion regulation and executive skills to handle. This leads to the experience of painful negative emotions—anxiety, fear, anger, frustration—that start to overwhelm him and eventually escalate him into fight-or-flight mode (the extreme end of the Overwhelmed Zone). The resulting challenging behavior is actually a maladaptive effort on your son's part to regulate this painful emotional arousal. Fight-or-flight is focused on eliminating the overwhelming demand—getting away from it (flight) or getting it to go away (fight)—so that the boy can feel safe and return to calm.

Tuning in, as we get better at it, will expand to include noticing our son's feelings and arousal before he enters the Overwhelmed Zone. We will be aware of whether he seems content, happy, sad, lonely, angry, frustrated, scared, or anxious. We will also be aware of his arousal. Is he becoming bored, disengaged, apathetic—approaching the Low-Engagement Zone? Or becoming agitated, stressed, overstimulated—heading to the Overwhelmed Zone? Tuning in to his feelings and arousal as he's becoming dysregulated, enables us to co-regulate him before a challenging episode begins. Tuning in also means anticipating how situations are likely to impact him so that you can avoid them or modify them. This is facilitated by the work you did in chapter 3 to learn his triggers and is part of your emergency plan.

Tuning In to Yourself

Tuning in to your child's emotions and arousal is a challenging task. Often you have to search for subtle clues. Other times you are facing the emotional heat of a challenging episode. To perform well at this difficult task, your emotions and arousal must be in the Goldilocks Zone. To keep your own arousal well regulated, you must tune in to what you are feeling and your stress level so that you can self-regulate as needed. In fact, John Gottman, in groundbreaking studies of co-regulation, found that parents' ability to tune in to their children depended largely on their ability to tune in to themselves.

What makes it difficult to tune in to ourselves? For one thing, because we're constantly dealing with the fires that our son is setting, it can feel like there is no time or space to check in with ourselves (although we learned above that effective firefighting requires being aware of and regulating one's own arousal). Gottman found that the biggest obstacle parents face in tuning in to their emotions and their kid's emotions was the attitudes, feelings, and reactions that the parents have about emotional arousal. (Gottman uses the term *meta-emotion*—that is, "feelings about feelings"—to describe this.) We all have attitudes, feelings, and reactions to emotions. Some of them we are aware of, many of them are unconscious, just part of the fabric of our emotional experience.

Common examples of meta-emotion are feeling weak when one feels scared. Feeling worried about losing control when one feels angry. Feeling afraid of falling into depression when one feels sad.

We learn our attitudes, feelings, and reactions to emotions primarily in our families growing up, but we also absorb them from our culture and our peers. For example, in the United States we tend to see certain emotions as undesirable. The very fact that we talk about anger, sadness, fear as *negative* emotions demonstrates our cultural bias against these feelings. Our attitudes are also influenced by gender. There is, for example, more tolerance of girls being sad or scared and of boys being angry, but much less acceptance of anger in girls and sadness or fear in boys.

In his research, Gottman identified two main meta-emotional styles that interfere with tuning in to kids' feelings. He called them *dismissive* and *disapproving*. If you were raised by parents who fell into one of these categories, it is probably harder for you to tune in to your own feelings and those of your son. The good news is you can learn to take a different approach.

In dismissive families, emotions are ignored, minimized, seen as unimportant, and dismissed as irrational. Parents in these families tend to say things like: "you're too sensitive," "you're not upset, you're just tired," "you're overreacting," and "there's nothing to be upset about." Many dismissive parents are actually interested in co-regulating their children, they just believe that the way to do it is to treat emotional upset as something to try to move their child's attention away from with humor, with urging him to look at the bright side, with distraction, or with helping him see the situation in a different way. These parents believe that paying attention to negative feelings causes those feelings to grow.

Being dismissive isn't always a bad thing. In my own research on resilience I found that a dismissive attitude toward emotion helps people survive childhood trauma. If anger is perceived to be the cause of an alcoholic father's violence, or sadness the cause of a depressed mother's incapacity, then negative emotions are not safe to feel. Furthermore, paying attention to your own bad feelings about the abuse or neglect in your home growing up—where no one was present to help you process it—only threatened to flood you. Shutting down these overwhelming emotions makes it possible to focus on school work or other positive activities that promote future success.

Disapproving parents, like dismissive parents, have a negative view of emotional reactions. These parents, however, don't just see emotional arousal as counterproductive, they are actively critical of negative emotions and see them as needing to be controlled. Parents in these families often respond to tantrums with a spanking, and to tears with threats or humiliation: "I'll give you something to cry about" or "stop acting like a baby." Stoicism and toughness are prized, and emotional expression is seen as manipulation. A friend of mine told me a very painful story that illustrates disapproving parenting. Once as a child, he was crying because he was being bullied by a kid at school. Instead of providing help, support, or comfort, his mother spanked him because she believed he needed to be "toughened up."

Dismissive and disapproving parents don't necessarily love their children any less than other parents. They believe what they are doing is the best way to keep their child safe and to teach him to be well behaved. They also don't know how to tune in to their child's feelings because they were raised by dismissive or disapproving parents or were victims of abuse or neglect. Gottman found that the children of these parents were more likely to have problems with emotion regulation.

In the parent journal exercises at the end of the chapter, we'll examine your parents' attitudes toward emotional experience and expression. We'll reflect on how your experiences growing up created your unique set of attitudes, feelings, and reactions about emotions. As we raise our awareness of our meta-emotional responses, we'll be able to begin the work of learning to tune in to ourselves and our feelings.

Our goal is to come to see emotions as a fundamental and helpful aspect of human experience. In the words of Haim Ginott, "Birds fly, fish swim, and people feel." Our emotional reactions tell us what we want and help us make decisions. They give us energy and motivation to do difficult things. They alert us to danger and injustice, and they help us stand up for ourselves and others. A parent with this type of accepting and affirming view of emotional expression sees anger, fear, or sadness in their child as, in Gottman's words, "an opportunity for intimacy and teaching," not a threat. It's also seen as an opportunity for co-regulation.

Now that we know the importance of tuning in to ourselves and our sons to be able to co-regulate them, let's turn to a discussion of the ways in which we can co-regulate.

Managing the Environment

Co-regulating through managing your son's environment involves avoiding situations where he's likely to become dysregulated. It also includes leaving places if you see him starting to get overwhelmed (ideally before a challenging episode starts). In general, it means not asking him to do things he doesn't yet have the skills to do, and withdrawing requests that you see are starting to dysregulate him. How much you need to manage his environment isn't constant; it depends on where his emotional and physical arousal is in a given situation or on a given day.

By way of illustration, like many families during the pandemic, we got a dog. We saw an adorable puppy photo on a rescue website. One thing led to another and a week later we adopted a 30-pound, four-ish-month-old dog, Milo. A friend jokingly called him "Clifford" after the Big Red Dog because Milo just kept growing and growing until now, three years later, he is tall enough to steal food from the counter while standing on all fours and weighs over 110 pounds!

Luckily, Milo is gentle and sweet tempered and likes all people and dogs. However, the problems started on walks around the neighborhood. When he's on a leash and sees another dog he exhibits what I have learned is called "leash reactivity." He goes into the Overwhelmed Zone and growls and lunges at the other dog. He's very strong so it's hard to manage him. It is upsetting to the other dog owners to have a giant dog act in a menacing way toward them. It's bad for Milo because it's stressful for him, and each episode reinforces this undesirable behavior.

I had a co-regulation challenge on my hands. The first way I managed it was by managing the environment. When we're walking, I'm on alert, looking down the road and up side streets for the presence of other dogs. I need to see them before he does. When I do see another dog, I turn the other way or cross the street in order to avoid him getting triggered. This is an example of co-regulation through managing the environment. I manage his trigger (close encounters with other dogs) to keep him regulated.

In the exercises in chapter 3 you learned about your son's triggers. In your emergency plan you applied this knowledge and made plans to manage or avoid, whenever possible, the situations that would trigger your son. This part of the emergency plan is co-regulating your son by managing his environmental triggers—avoiding them or modifying them.

Like with a challenging boy, Milo's temperament is a big cause of the problem. He is a mix of three guard dog breeds (Anatolian Shepherd, German Shepherd, and Great Pyrenees) so it is in his DNA to "protect" me from these other dogs. However, to get along in the neighborhood, Milo needs to learn how to not be reactive on his walks. The first step in teaching him has been to co-regulate him by managing his environment so that he stays in the optimal arousal zone. The next step is teaching him a skill to help him manage these environments. I have been working with him on the skill of heeling so that he's paying attention to me rather than to the dogs we encounter. He can only learn this alternative behavior when he's well regulated, so I always try to make sure that we don't get too near other dogs as we're practicing our heeling. As his heeling skills have improved, we gradually have moved closer and closer to the dogs we pass. This way we have a pattern of success that we can build upon. The goal is to be able to walk through the neighborhood without worry. If I don't manage his environment, he experiences stressful encounter after stressful encounter and his reactivity grows. A pattern of failure is reinforced. Using this co-regulation approach, Milo's behavior has gotten much better.

The plan is similar for challenging boys. We'll flesh out the details in the following chapters. First, we need to co-regulate our son so that he is in the Goldilocks Zone and can learn the executive functioning skills that he needs to succeed. Managing his environment means not putting him in situations where he'll fail. We'll gradually introduce him to increasingly stressful contexts as his skills improve, thereby creating a pattern of success and growth. Every time a boy gets dys-regulated and has a challenging episode his nervous system becomes a little more reactive, he feels more like a failure, and he increasingly believes that it's impossible for him to succeed.

Managing His Body

Twenty years ago, when I would meet with parents of kids with ADHD or autism, I would hear about the special diets that they had their kids on. Full of compassion, I would think to myself something like, "Of course they are doing this pointless thing. They are desperate to find something that works." I learned later that I was completely wrong. Nutrition does matter. Emerging research on the microbiome has found that it impacts our mood, anxiety, symptoms of ADHD and autism, as well as many other aspects of emotional and physical health. One important way to improve the microbiome is through diet.

Before I lose you, I want to be clear that the items in this section are aspirational goals. If you can get your son to eat a healthy, well-balanced diet, that will be better for his health and will help with his physiological arousal. But anyone with a challenging boy knows that most of them only want to eat pizza, chicken nuggets, pasta, and dessert. Even getting a typical child to eat a healthy diet is practically impossible.

One thing you can do that will help your son regulate his body and avoid challenging episodes is to always be sure that you have food he likes at hand. Often challenging boys won't eat their lunches and will be starving after school. Have a snack he'll eat ready to have in the car if you have to go straight to another activity. Also, always have an "emergency snack" with you. An emergency snack is something you know he likes that you can give him if you see signs that hunger is leading to his behavior breaking down. When I would go on longer flights with my family, I'd always have a big bag of snacks with me to head off anyone melting down because they were hungry. If you have a challenging boy, you need to have the snack bag with you at all times. Hydration is important too, so keep water handy.

Another aspirational goal is to make sure that your son gets enough sleep. Tired boys are more susceptible to being challenging. As we saw in the story about Ethan and his family, getting a challenging boy to go to bed can be a very difficult proposition. Things to try are having a consistent bedtime schedule that includes regulating activities like turning off screens, taking a bath, and reading to the child. Avoid caffeinated beverages like colas and teas. Create a sleep-promoting bedroom with white noise and blackout curtains; additionally, some children find weighted blankets to be calming. Melatonin and sleep medications are sometimes prescribed but are controversial and should only be used in consultation with your doctor. Getting physical exercise is also very important for sleep.

A novel approach that you might try is having a bedtime alarm or timer. When we tell a challenging boy to do something, it risks causing a power struggle. This is the case with telling him that it's bedtime. If you have an alarm or timer that is in a common space like the kitchen, family room, or playroom (not on your phone) that announces that it's bedtime, it might be easier for your son to accept. It's not *you* telling him to go to bed, it's the timer letting him know it's bedtime. In addition to removing the opportunity for a power struggle, the alarm, if he accepts it, will become a conditioned stimulus for him feeling sleepy like Pavlov's dogs salivating when the bell announced that dinner was coming.

Finally, we can help co-regulate his bodily arousal by trying to make sure he gets exercise and movement breaks. It's great when challenging boys love sports. Practices and games ensure that he gets lots of exercise. When challenging boys aren't into competitive sports, swimming, martial arts, and rock climbing are forms of exercise that they will often participate in. In addition to the exercise, swimming can be particularly helpful to challenging boys because the sensory experience of feeling the water passing over one's skin can be soothing. Martial arts programs are great because they emphasize teaching discipline and self-regulation in their classes, and they are generally led by instructors who can tolerate a lot of unregulated behavior in their students.

Movement breaks are another way to help a boy regulate his bodily arousal. Sedentary activities such as doing homework tend to shift a challenging boy into the Low-Engagement Zone, of the Yerkes-Dodson curve, where he has a difficult time maintaining his attention and motivation. Getting your son to take regular movement breaks where he engages in some vigorous physical activity (shooting baskets or kicking a soccer ball with you, doing calisthenics together) is essential to his staying regulated and on task. You may have heard of the Pomodoro Technique, which prescribes five-minute breaks after every twenty-five minutes of work. This method of time-limited work periods followed by scheduled breaks is designed to manage procrastination, distraction, and mental fatigue. Recent research has found that when those breaks involve movement, say five minutes on a treadmill, the restorative impact is even larger.

By aspirational, I mean that we try to get our sons to eat well, sleep enough, and exercise, but they often resist these efforts. It is crucial to not let these aspirations turn into power struggles and triggers for challenging behavior. We're going to do our best to find ways to improve their diet, sleep, and exercise that don't require more than a little bit of coaxing. If things start to escalate or turn into a fight, we'll relax our demands for now.

Soothing

With our crying infant, we instinctively move in to soothe his distress. We tune in and try to identify the cause of the upset—hunger, wet diaper, tiredness, overstimulation, needing a cuddle —and remove it. If we try one thing and it doesn't work, we move on to try something else. We also aim to be a calming soothing presence for our baby: cuddle him, swaddle him, sing a soothing song.

The steps are essentially the same for a child of any age (or adult for that matter). We need to recognize that the behavior (infant's cries or a challenging episode) is a communication: "I'm in distress. I need soothing." We want also to see this request for soothing as an opportunity to deepen our connection with our son and to help him develop his capacity for self-regulation through the co-regulation that we provide.

I know this isn't easy to do. It's very difficult to hold on to the fact that challenging behavior is a request for comfort when we're being embarrassed by a public meltdown or infuriated by hurtful behavior directed toward us or another member of the family. It's similar to exhausted parents in the middle of the night with a colicky baby struggling to maintain compassion and to stay calm and soothing (this analogy might bring back memories because many challenging boys were colicky babies).

After recognizing the need for soothing and regulation that lies behind challenging behavior, we need to tune in. We use our eyes to observe his body language, our ears to listen to what he says. Also we need to tune in to our own feelings to keep ourselves regulated and to see what feelings are present in us. Upset children often act in ways to make us feel what they feel: misery loves company. But this means that even *our* distress can be a clue to what is going on for our son.

In a challenging episode we tune in to his distress, and we work to help our son regulate himself—*before* teaching or consequences. In the words of psychologist, Jane Nelson, "connection before correction." Remember, our son can't learn if he's emotionally overwhelmed. So, our first step in responding to challenging behavior is to identify the source of the distress in order to remove it, or remove our child from it, or at least acknowledge its presence. This is a major aspect of our emergency plan. We keep trying until we identify the trigger, deal with it, and help our son return to the Goldilocks Zone.

Hugs can be helpful (especially with little kids and especially with sad feelings), but often boys need space. Your empathy and validation are often your most powerful tools for soothing. In his video, *Happiest Toddler on the Block*, pediatrician Harvy Karp demonstrates the power of validation to soothe even very little children. In example after example, Karp regulates tantrumming toddlers by getting on the ground, kicking his arms and legs, and passionately saying over and over whatever the kid is upset about. "You want a cookie! You want it now!" It's amazing to watch. These little children almost immediately stop melting down and focus on Dr. Karp. It's as if they're saying, "finally someone gets it!"

What is Dr. Karp doing and how do we apply it more generally? First, he is naming the feeling. Using language to describe what is happening emotionally helps bring the child's rational mind back online. Second, Dr. Karp is resonating with the child's emotions using his words, tone, and body. He's not remaining detached. In doing so, Dr. Karp is demonstrating that he understands the feelings, accepts them, and most importantly that he cares. Once, when one of my daughters was in elementary school, she was angry with me for something. I remember saying, "It's OK that you're mad at me." I thought I was being a great dad by accepting her feelings. "It's not OK!" my daughter responded through tears. She wanted me to feel badly that I had upset her. I did of course, but my tone and words did not convey it. Reflect the emotion, don't counter it. It's not "oh you're angry with me, well I'm angry with you too!" It's "oh no! I'm so sorry I upset you!" Third, Dr. Karp is validating the child's feelings in a way that helps the child to feel heard. Remember from chapter 4, effective validation requires that the child feels that you understand and accept his feelings.

It works the same with older boys. Validating and empathizing with their feelings and mirroring some of their emotional intensity helps them feel understood, accepted, and cared about. You're letting them know that they are not alone. With repeated experiences of being responded to with caring, validation, and acceptance, the child develops the expectation that when he's upset there will be people around who care and who can help. Just believing that help is available calms the child even before any help is received. Conversely, a child who isn't responded to in a soothing way, learns that being upset and overwhelmed means also being alone and helpless. This negative expectation intensifies the distress, and it snowballs into overwhelm and meltdown.

After a challenging episode is over, and the dust has settled, it's time to take your journal out and record what happened. What did you say or do that seemed to help your son regulate himself? What words or actions on your part made things worse? This data will help us to know what to do and not do in future episodes.

To review, co-regulating our son involves the following steps:

1. Understand challenging behavior as a need for co-regulation.
2. View it as an opportunity to help our son develop the vital skill of self-regulation and as an opportunity to deepen our connection.
3. Tune in to our own emotions and arousal and regulate ourselves.
4. Tune in to his emotions and arousal.
5. Try to identify and remove the trigger.
6. Mirror his emotional intensity.
7. Help him put his feelings into words, validate, and empathize.
8. Observe his response and adjust your actions.

What to Do When Nothing Works

Sometimes we won't be able to prevent a challenging episode, and we won't be able to help our son calm down once it has started; removing the trigger doesn't help him regulate, and our validating words don't reach him. In these very stressful circumstances you can try the following things. First, as with all challenging episodes, make sure your son and others are safe. This creates space for the episode to run its course. Second, make sure that you are well regulated. Focus especially on your breathing. People tend to unconsciously mirror each other's cardiac and respiration rates. If you can slow your breathing down, it might help your son to slow his. Begin your self-regulation efforts by taking a few especially deep and visible inhalations and exhalations. This can signal to your son to slow his breathing. If validation hasn't been working, it's probably best to shift to using fewer words and simpler phrases like: "I want to help." You can try simple requests: "I need you to come with me"; or present a choice: "We can go outside and cool down or we can go home." You can offer soothing activities: a cold drink, some chewing gum, or to go take a walk. Your body language can help. Get down to his level. Don't tower over a dysregulated child. Don't touch without permission; instead, ask, "Can I give you a hug?" Generally, we want to reduce the level of stimulation and get him to come with us to a quieter spot. Record in your journal what you try and how well it works.

Modeling

As social animals, one of the ways that humans learn is by imitating others. This is called "modeling" or "observational learning." Children learn by imitating teachers, peers, athletes, and people they follow on social media. They also learn from observing what their parents do. This is the idea behind the concept of role model.

We model self-regulation when we take steps to keep ourselves well regulated. The steps are similar to those involved in co-regulating our son. First, tune in to yourself, your emotions and your arousal. Second, manage your environment. If the news is a source of stress, limit your consumption. If your commute is taxing, try listening to soothing music or an audiobook. Third, regulate your body. Get sleep, exercise, and try to eat a healthy diet. As with our sons, these are aspirational goals. Try also to avoid unhealthy coping like alcohol, tobacco, and other substances. Fourth, when you're upset, take steps to soothe yourself. Breathe deeply, take a break, write in your journal, use a relaxation technique, listen to music, say encouraging things to yourself, allow others to help. Fifth, have a regular mindfulness practice: meditate, do yoga, garden, get involved with your religious community. When our sons observe us regulating ourselves in these ways—especially when they see the impact it has on our ability to remain calm—it provides a model of self-regulation for them to imitate.

We can enhance the impact of our modeling by being explicit about efforts to self-regulate. If you and your son are having a conflict, you can say, "I'm starting to feel upset, I need a break so I can calm down. Let's try talking again in ten minutes." Or, if you are getting stressed about something, you can say, "I'm feeling stressed. I need to remember to breathe deeply." These statements set an example of checking in with your arousal and taking constructive steps to manage it. If you have a regular meditation or relaxation practice, do it in full view. Also, let him know what you are doing. "I'll be in the family room for the next ten minutes meditating, in case you need me." If he asks why you meditate, you can tell him what it does for you. "I meditate because it helps me feel better and it helps me not get so upset when something frustrating or disappointing happens."

Your work to increase trust and connection in your relationship makes you a better model for your child. He's more likely to look to you as an example to emulate if he respects you, likes you, and feels that you like and respect him.

Coaching

Coaching a boy through the ways that he can regulate himself relies heavily on a strong parent-child relationship. There needs to be a warm connection, a high degree of trust, and good communication for the boy to be receptive to being coached. Coaching also requires that the two of you are on the same page. Your son needs to see regulating himself as an important goal.

Many parents try to coach their kids in emotion regulation even though the preconditions for coaching have not been met. I frequently hear parents telling their dysregulated son to "breathe," which unfortunately usually results in an escalation of challenging behaviors. The boy doesn't believe that breathing will help him. He perceives it merely as a dismissal of his distress. In chapter 9, we'll discuss how to create a coaching relationship with your son.

CHALLENGING BEHAVIOR ACADEMY

Congratulations! Just like cadets go through training in the fire academy before they are placed on active duty, you've made it through the "challenging behavior academy." You've learned what causes challenging behavior: temperament and executive functioning deficits. You have developed an emergency plan for dealing with challenging behavior that is built on knowing your son's triggers. Your plan prepares you to avoid your son's triggers when you can and to manage them when present. Your emergency plan also includes the steps you will take to de-escalate and quench the flames of challenging behavior when it does arise. This plan will help you remain calm and effective during challenging episodes.

You have been working on team building with your son, and you have been taking important steps toward developing trust and connection. You've also been working on communication and problem-solving. These actions are strengthening the bond between you and your son. He increasingly sees you as someone who is helpful and can be trusted to help when things run hot.

Things are definitely better. Because of your plan, you're experiencing fewer challenging episodes and the ones that do happen are briefer, less intense, and more easily redirected. You feel more connected to your son and your house is a happier and more peaceful place. He feels happier and he finally feels accepted, validated and understood. It's such a relief. Some families even stop here. Eliminating the negative dynamic of escalating power struggles and accentuating the positives in the parent-child relationship has so dramatically changed family life that things feel solidly back on track.

Most families feel grateful for the changes, but they know there is more work to do. Up to this point, you have reduced your son's challenging moments primarily by changing yourself and how you relate to your son. There's a Zen proverb about a man with very tender feet. He set out to cover the world with leather so that his feet wouldn't hurt. The Zen story ends with the man making some sandals. By covering his feet with leather-soled sandals, he transforms the impossible task of covering the world with leather into a possible one: placing the layer of leather protection on his feet so it's always between them and the hard edges of the world. Up until this point, you've been learning how to cover some of the world with leather for your son. We've modified our responses to him and the situations he's in so that he has to face the pain of being triggered less often. In the next chapter we will focus on teaching him skills, the skills he needs to place a layer of protection between the challenges of the world and his emotional sensitivities.

Key Ideas

- The capacity to regulate one's emotional arousal is essential for success across almost all areas of life: promoting physical and emotional health, excelling academically and professionally, and maintaining fulfilling relationships.

- Parents help challenging boys develop better emotion regulation skills through consistent, warm, and responsive efforts to help them regulate themselves; this is referred to as "co-regulation."

- We co-regulate by helping our sons manage triggers in their environments, helping them regulate their bodies, and by helping soothe their emotional pain.

- Co-regulation necessitates tuning in to our son's emotional state and into our own. It also requires that we work to keep ourselves regulated. This can be especially difficult to do if we were raised in houses that were dismissive or disapproving of emotions.

- Our goal is to experience challenging behavior as a nonverbal communication from our son that he needs co-regulation. And to see challenging behavior as an opportunity to deepen our connection with our son and to help him develop his capacity for self-regulation through the co-regulation that we provide.

PARENTING JOURNAL EXERCISES

How the families we grew up in dealt with emotions led us to develop attitudes, feelings, and reactions to emotions that are largely automatic and out of awareness. These "meta-emotions" typically go unnoticed by us, like the air we breathe. An important part of tuning in to our sons and ourselves is becoming aware of the attitudes about emotions that we absorbed growing up.

- When you experience sadness, anger, fear, or loneliness, write down what "meta" thoughts and feelings go with those emotions? Do you experience feelings of shame or weakness? What critical thoughts accompany these emotions?

- How do you deal with negative emotions when they arise? Do you try to distract yourself? Do you try to numb them with food or alcohol? Do you accept them and wait for them to pass? Do you try to understand them?

- What was your family's attitude toward emotions growing up? Was the expression of emotion permitted or even encouraged (accepted)? Or were emotions seen as unimportant, irrational, not worthy of attention (dismissed)? Or were they regarded as the root of bad behavior (anger leads to aggression, sadness leads to passivity) that needs to be controlled (disapproved of)?

- How do you feel about emotions now? Do you feel uncomfortable with, afraid of, or critical of strong emotions?

- What's your view of anger? Does it feel dangerous and on a slippery slope that leads to aggression and violence? Does sadness feel like a bottomless pit that needs to be avoided?

- How do you feel about emotional expression?

- When your challenging son experiences strong emotions, what happens in you? Do you feel emotionally activated yourself? Do you feel scared? Do you feel the impulse to criticize or fix his emotions? Cheer him up? Fix the situation? Distract him? Do you feel like ignoring his emotions?

- Does your son's expression of emotions feel like a demand? Do you feel like you have to do something? Does it feel like manipulation?

- When your son is upset, do you feel upset or agitated also? Do you shut down? Do you try to manage him? Are you able to turn toward him, while keeping your own feelings regulated?

- Write about the most recent challenging episode, or a time when your son was really upset. Reflect on the emotions you felt and how they relate to the attitude toward emotion that was present in your family growing up.

- In thinking back on that challenging episode, what did you say or do that seemed to help your son regulate himself? What words or actions on your part made things worse?

CHAPTER SEVEN

Punishments, Consequences, and Rules

In the fire service we don't just plan and prepare for emergencies, we also work to prevent them. Fire officials enforce building codes that make structures more fire resistant. We educate at schools about fire safety. We do campaigns to remind people to change their smoke detector batteries. Helping your son develop the skills he needs to not be challenging—emotion-regulation and executive functioning skills—is your prevention plan. We will accomplish this by teaching him how to successfully handle the situations that currently trigger him. Up until now in this book we've been focused on helping you understand, accommodate to, and manage his challenging nature. Now it's time for him to start taking responsibility for his challenging behavior and his life.

In working through this book and implementing its lessons, you've already been doing a lot of teaching. From your hard work to identify, reflect upon, and accept his feelings, he is learning to understand and accept them more himself. From your efforts to shift the dynamic of your relationship to focus more on positivity, acceptance, and validation, he is developing improved self-esteem. From your co-regulation he is having fewer challenging episodes—that is, fewer moments of emotional and behavioral "failure"—and he is starting to let go of his identity as a "problem child." Your co-regulation is also teaching him that he's not alone and helpless when bad feelings overtake him; he is discovering that you care and are available to assist him in navigating overwhelming emotions. From your modeling of empathy, he is learning to be empathic with himself and others. Now it's time to turn our efforts to teaching him skills directly.

If we take seriously the idea that discipline means *teaching* and not *punishment*, then there's a difficult truth that we must face here: *effective discipline takes discipline*. It means having a proactive plan and sticking to it. When it comes to discipline, most of us are winging it. We're doing some mishmash of what our parents did, as well as the opposite of what they did that we think was wrong. We also add in things we hear from friends, experts, and parenting influencers. Mostly we're operating based on instinct.

On top of that, we're not proactive. Instead of keeping an eye on the long game, we react to the negative thing that is happening now. When our son's behavior is bad, we focus on it, punish it, and brood about it. Instead of having a lesson plan like a real teacher, we seize on "teachable moments" (where whatever wisdom we hope to impart is certain to be ignored). When things temporarily quiet down, our attention drifts to the things we've been neglecting in our lives. We need to be proactively focused on the behaviors we want to see more of (and not just the ones we want to see less of) and have a systematic plan for bringing about these changes.

The first step in teaching your son the skills he needs is to make sure he's regulated. Remember that your son can't learn well when his emotional and physiological arousal aren't in the Goldilocks Zone. You've learned from your journaling how to tune in to him and read his arousal level. If he's in the Low Engagement Zone or the Overwhelmed Zone, the teaching isn't going to land. Also, good teaching requires that you be well regulated, so check in with yourself.

Next, we need to identify the skill you will be teaching in your plan. When I work with parents, I ask the following question: "What is the one thing we can improve that would have the biggest positive impact on your family life?" It might be getting ready for school on time, doing homework, getting off screens, going to bed on time, not fighting with siblings, not refusing to go on family outings, or poor hygiene. We can only effectively work on one problem at a time so our first prevention plan should focus on teaching the skill that will have the biggest impact. The rest will have to wait for now.

Once we know what behaviors we'll be addressing, we'll next identify what tools we'll use to teach the skills. As parents we have three types of discipline tools at our disposal: punishments, rewards, and coaching. Punishments and rewards are based on the principle that behaviors that result in negative consequences (punishments) will decrease, and behaviors that result in positive consequences (rewards or reinforcements) will increase. It's how animals are taught, but it's also how the world works for humans. We incur fees for paying bills late or fines for speeding (punishments), and we receive free beverages for being in the loyalty program at the coffee shop and paid for going to work (rewards). Punishments and rewards are powerful teaching tools, but most of us use them inappropriately. We yell, we threaten, we coerce, we bribe, we unintentionally reward behaviors we want to eliminate. I'll cover the effective use of punishment in this chapter. Chapter 8 will focus on the use of rewards and chapter 9 will cover coaching.

PUNISHMENTS

Psychologist Alan Kazdin calls punishment the most "widely misunderstood, chronically misused, and wildly overused method for changing behavior." I hope to convince you, in this section, to use punishments proactively, with a plan, and only in very limited circumstances. Remember, punishing a child or using some other consequence when he's overwhelmed does not teach and will likely lead to an escalation of challenging behavior.

Let's separate the two common meanings of the word *punishment*. First, a punishment is a penalty imposed for committing an offense. In this meaning the purpose of punishment has more to do with retribution or vengeance than it does teaching. It is commonly believed that the threat of punishment deters people from breaking rules, but this is almost never the case. The second meaning is based on principles of learning theory set out by psychologist B. F. Skinner. In this meaning, punishment is not punitive. It is a communication about what behaviors are unacceptable.

Most parents use punishments routinely. One typical way we apply them is to stop misbehavior in the moment. We don't have a plan. We're just reacting with reprimands, scolding, threats, time-outs, taking away phones or privileges. This often puts an immediate end to the misbehavior—provided that the pain of the punishment is sufficiently severe—creating a false impression that these types of punishments are effective. However, punishments given out in this unsystematic way generally only work in the short term. The misbehavior is likely to return because punishments don't teach our son how to behave, only how not to behave. This reactive use of punishments is especially ineffective with challenging boys. When a challenging boy is misbehaving, it's likely he's in the Overwhelmed Zone. He can't stop himself. He'll say things like "go ahead and punish me, I don't care!" In these circumstances you risk getting sucked into an escalating fight where you have to keep raising the intensity of the punishment to try to make an impact. This is a dangerous place to be and can lead to a physical altercation.

When things get physical with our sons, we can be flooded with strong feelings of guilt, shame, and fear. While extremely upsetting, physical conflicts do occur at one time or another in almost every family. It doesn't make you a terrible parent or your son a terrible child. However, it does need to be a top priority of your emergency plan to keep challenging episodes from escalating to the point where things get physical. We must commit to not putting our hands on our son in anger or to punish—to not hit, spank, force into a time-out, or physically coerce in any other way.

Spanking and other physical punishments are not only ineffective, but they are associated with many bad outcomes for children, including increases in aggression, antisocial behavior, and mental health problems. Corporal punishment can also lead to escalating physical struggles between parents and children that spiral out of control. According to psychologist Elizabeth Gershoff, "physical punishment doesn't work to get kids to comply, so parents think they have to keep escalating it. That is why it is so dangerous." Many people believe that spanking teaches kids right from wrong, but it actually does the opposite. It models for kids problematic lessons like "might makes right" and that physical aggression is an appropriate way to solve conflicts between people. These punishments should never be used. In the words of Alan Kazdin, in giving up physical punishment we are "not giving up an effective technique. We are saying this is a horrible thing that does not work." If you are having physical fights with your son, it's time to get help. If the fights are happening with more frequency or intensity, or if family members are being hurt or intimidated, this is a crisis and requires immediate professional attention.

The other common way we use punishments is as a "consequence" for some relatively large misbehavior: getting in trouble at school, lying, or sneaking out. In these circumstances—either with anger and vengeance or calmly meting out "justice"—we decide on a punishment to fit the crime. Punishments of this type rarely lead to desirable changes in behavior. They don't teach skills and, despite what is commonly believed, they don't teach "a lesson." Punishments do not encourage a boy to reflect on his actions. If anything, they build resentment and reinforce a challenging boy's sense that he is always treated unfairly. The threat of punishment as a deterrent is especially ineffective for challenging boys because they have a difficult time anticipating the consequences of their actions. If punishments teach anything, they teach a challenging boy that he needs to get better at covering his tracks—to hide better, to be sneakier, to be a better liar.

As I hope you can see, punishment as a discipline tool can backfire if used improperly. As part of a systematic plan to teach, punishments can give feedback to our sons about what behavior is unacceptable. When paired with rewards, they can also help motivate him to learn a new skill. Reactive punishments like yelling, threats, and scolding only train our sons to ignore us.

One of the simplest and most effective forms of punishment is ignoring misbehavior. The most powerful reward to a child is your attention. Your child craves your positive attention, but your negative attention is generally preferred to being ignored. This is especially true if bad behavior pulls your attention away from a sibling. Often, we fall into the trap of unintentionally rewarding negative behaviors by responding to them with our angry, upset attention. Try ignoring them instead.

Here are some guidelines for making an effective behavior plan that includes punishments. This list is significantly based on ideas presented in the excellent book *The Kazdin Method* by Alan Kazdin.

1. Rules and punishments should be clear, decided on in advance, and communicated to the child before the program is started.

Your son should know what to expect. "If you hit your sister, you will get a four-minute time-out." Ideally, the rules should be written down and posted. Sometimes, as a program is implemented, parents will realize the existing rules and punishments aren't working. Do not change rules on the fly. This erodes trust. Modify the rules and punishments and then inform your son of the new plan going forward. Vague rules prevent learning and create feelings of frustration and defeat. A boy can't really know if he's complied with rules like "Use your good judgment," "Be a good person," "Do the right thing."

2. Pair the punishment program with a reward program.

Because punishments don't teach what to do once misbehavior has stopped, pair your program with a rewards plan that teaches your son what behavior you want him to do instead. We'll learn about how to make an effective rewards program in the next chapter.

3. Punishments should be respectful to the child.

Punishments that are humiliating should be avoided. Punishments should be administered without anger, shame, blame, or lectures, like a referee in a game. Referees don't call penalties in anger or scold a player for breaking a rule. It's just cause and effect; you broke the rule, here's the penalty. Referees also don't threaten penalties. In some sports, like a yellow card in soccer, you get one warning, but no threats.

4. Punishments should be "mild and brief."

Kazdin stresses that parents typically choose punishments that are too harsh and that last too long. Remember our goal is to build new skills. We want to accomplish this with the least amount of negativity. It turns out that mild, brief punishments are the most effective. According to Kazdin, the effect of a punishment comes from the taking away of something, not from the duration that it's away. A boy sitting with a punishment for a long time (a week of being grounded or losing his phone) doesn't reflect on his misbehavior. Instead, he broods on his anger and resentment. One day would be a more effective punishment. In general, I recommend against taking away a child's phone as a punishment because it violates this rule of mild and brief.

5. Punishments should be immediate and consistent.

To produce behavior change, a strong association needs to be built between an undesirable behavior and its punishment. The strongest association is formed when a punishment is immediate (while the unacceptable behavior is occurring) and consistent (every time the unacceptable behavior occurs). When time passes between a behavior and its consequence (think poor diet and later ill health), the power of the negative consequence to modify behavior is reduced. Also, when there is inconsistency in the link between a behavior and the punishment (think of speeding, mostly we get away with it, so we keep doing it) the effect is weakened. This is one of the reasons why I recommend parents not punish misbehavior at school. Your punishment occurs after so much time has passed from the infraction that it is unlikely to have much of an effect. It also comes with a big cost. The punishment will undermine your ability to be a trusted source of support and guidance to your son as he deals with the consequences that the school administers.

6. Make sure you can enforce the punishment.

Parents sometimes threaten punishments that they don't have the power to enforce. They give time-outs to a boy who refuses to go into time-out, they threaten to take the phone away from a boy who won't surrender it. These situations risk becoming physical fights, which, as I have already said, should be avoided at all costs. The only time you should be physically restraining a child is when there is the imminent threat of significant physical harm to the child or others, or that the child will do significant damage to property. If these situations are occurring, it is a sign that you need professional help.

7. Don't use punishments that punish you or others.

Often parents choose punishments that make life worse for them-selves or others. They cancel a family outing that the parent or another child would have enjoyed going on, or one parent must stay home with the boy to enforce the punishment. Another example of a pun-ishment that punishes you is taking away screen time when you could really use the break it provides.

8. Don't take away things that you want your child to be doing.

Sometimes parents will take away some activity from their son, like sports practice, as a punishment. However, being on a team does all kinds of good things for a boy. He gets exercise and he gets to be part of a group. Sometimes taking away video game time or his phone means isolating a boy from his social connections. He can't text his friends or meet up with them online.

9. If you do not see immediate positive effects of your punishment program, modify it or abandon it.

If you find that your punishments are not reducing the unwanted behavior, or if your punishments are leading to an escalation of defiant behavior, scrap your plan and go back to the drawing board (or better yet, switch to a reward plan). Do not fall into the trap of ramping up your punishments to try to get an effect. This is counterproductive and potentially dangerous.

Two Examples of Effective Punishment Programs
Example 1: Time-out for Hitting

All children need to learn to not hit or bite or otherwise be violent when frustrated. With young children, a time-out can be a useful way to modify this undesirable behavior. The first step in the program is to inform the boy of Rule Number 1: "Nobody gets hurt, and nothing gets broken on purpose" (I'll discuss rules later in this chapter). Rule 1 is then posted in a visible place (even if the boy can't read). He is also informed that breaking rule number 1 will lead to a time-out. This is the setup for the program.

Going forward, if your son starts getting frustrated and you anticipate him acting aggressively, you can give one reminder, "remember Rule Number 1: nobody gets hurt, and nothing gets broken." If he breaks Rule 1, he is given a time-out. The time-out should be brief (the general rule is one minute per year of age of the child) and accompanied by no lectures or reprimands. After the time-out, the boy has "paid his debt" and is allowed to return with a clean slate. This system works with little kids because you or a surrogate are there with them all the time, so the time-out can be administered immediately and consistently.

Kazdin recommends praising a child for complying with the time-out. It might seem crazy to you to reward a child immediately after misbehaving, but time-outs only work if the child accepts the punishment. We want to reinforce that behavior. If your son does not comply with the time-out, Kazdin recommends adding time to the time-out up to double. If he still doesn't comply, have a backup punishment determined ahead of time (for example, no screentime that evening). Administer that punishment and then walk away. Never physically force a child into a time-out.

An alternate approach, suggested by Adele Faber and Elaine Mazlish, is to ignore the child who hits and instead focus lavish attention and comfort on the child who has been struck. This evens things by giving the injured child something extra, while it indirectly punishes the challenging boy. In this plan the boy is not unintentionally rewarded for being aggressive by getting your attention. Additionally, his behavior is "punished" because it has led to his sibling getting your attention instead.

A plan I often recommend when there is a problem with aggression between a challenging boy and his siblings is to put the children in charge of their relationship. This program works in situations where they like to play together but sometimes physically fight. As with all punishment plans, the terms of it are explained to the children in advance. They are informed of Rule Number 1 and that if they physically fight, they will be separated (usually for five to ten minutes, the exact amount of time determined by their ages). After the break they are allowed to resume playing together. If a fight starts up again, the procedure is repeated. I like this plan because it makes the kids responsible for getting along. Another advantage of this approach is that it doesn't single out your challenging son as *the* problem. Often non-challenging siblings become skilled at setting their challenging brother off to get him in trouble and to pay him back for being a pain.

All three of these plans can be highly effective. However, even the best plans can have unintended consequences that we need to be on the lookout for. Here are some examples. When giving time-outs for aggression (as in the first plan) it runs the risk, as I mentioned, of non-challenging siblings provoking their challenging brother into being aggressive so he'll get into trouble. With the Faber-Mazlish approach, you might be unintentionally communicating to the aggressed-upon child that they aren't resilient, that they need to be babied. With the last approach, your non-challenging child might just stop complaining about your challenging son's aggression because they don't want their play to be interrupted with a time-out. The possibility of a plan not working is not a reason to not make plans. We need plans to keep us on track. We just need to pay careful attention to how well a plan is working and revise or abandon it if necessary.

Example 2: Getting off Screens When Time Is Up

If getting off the phone, video games, YouTube, or other screen activities when time is up is a problem, you might try a program like the following. If, for example, your son is entitled to an hour of screen time per day, every minute he goes over the hour is deducted from the next day's sixty (the punishment for going over time today is losing time tomorrow). This is an example of how good punishments are mild. Many parents wouldn't consider losing an equivalent amount of time to be a real punishment. They would think it'd be better to lose two or three minutes tomorrow for every minute over today, but that actually would be less effective. The goal is teaching, not retribution. I recommend pairing this plan with a reward plan. For example, the child could receive a bonus for ending when asked (ten minutes or so to start) along with the opportunity to bank time if he ends before sixty minutes. This pairing of punishments and rewards teaches him what to do: end on time without a conflict.

All behavior plans ideally start with a problem-solving conversation. You: "I've noticed that there's been a lot of fighting around getting off screens lately. I'd like us to figure out something to do about that." In the conversation propose the plan and get his input to tweak the details. The procedure goes like this: he gets a digital timer that will show him exactly how much time he has remaining in his sixty-minute screen session. Your son gets at least two warnings that his time is about up (say at fifteen minutes and five minutes, you can experiment with when you give the warnings to find out what works best). The warnings are to give your son a chance to prepare for the transition and to not start a new game or a new video. The banking of time is important. We don't want to punish him with lost time for following our rule. If the child chooses to not start a new game with five minutes to go, he gets the five minutes that he's giving up plus a ten-minute reward for ending on time added to the following night's session. The ten minutes added on to tomorrow is an example of pairing a rewards plan with a punishment plan. He gets punished by loss of time tomorrow for *not* doing what we want, and he gets rewarded for doing what we want (getting off screens without a fight).

The disadvantages of punishments are numerous. As we've discussed, punishments do not teach any positive skills or behaviors. They just teach what not to do. What to do is not guided. Punishments build anger and resentment and erode trust and connection. They pit you and your child against each other. Rather than being on the same team in facing the challenges that life presents, punishments put parents and children on opposite sides of a struggle over who is in control of the child's behavior. You do something bad to him because he has done something you don't want him to do. Punishments, further, don't teach a lesson. If anything, they motivate children to get better at not getting caught. Instead of reflecting on how hurtful his behavior was, punishments focus a boy's attention on how he has been treated unfairly or on how he will get even.

Natural and Logical Consequences

Because of the inherent problems with punishments, child development experts like Rudolf Dreikurs and Haim Ginott began discouraging parents from using punishments as a part of child discipline. They both believed, however, that it is important for a child to experience the consequences of his behavior: if I do this, then that will occur. For example, a boy has a tantrum and breaks his favorite toy. The natural effect or consequence of the action is that he doesn't have that toy anymore.

Natural consequences occur without parental intervention. In this example, the boy's parents didn't need to do anything to create the consequence of no toy. Other natural consequences include getting bad grades for not doing homework or getting detention for misbehaving at school. When a natural consequence occurs, because they didn't give it, parents can be on the child's side in helping him cope constructively (consoling the child about the loss of his toy or guiding the child in how to respond to trouble at school). A child needs to be protected from the natural consequences of his behavior if his actions will endanger or harm him or another person. In these cases, his behavior needs to be stopped.

Logical consequences are different from natural consequences in that they result from parental intervention. A logical consequence is just another name for a punishment. It is a punishment that is logically connected to the misbehavior being punished. A teen who misuses his phone faces the logical consequence of losing use of the phone for some period of time. Losing the phone for fighting with a sibling is not a logical consequence because fighting with the sibling and the phone are not logically connected. It is argued that logical consequences are preferable because they feel less arbitrary and fairer. However, logical consequences typically fall prey to the problems associated with other types of punishments.

Justice

Some parents view punishments not merely as a teaching tool but as a means of upholding justice within the family. When a challenging boy acts out, such as by hurting a sibling, damaging their belongings, breaking significant house rules, or undermining core family values, issuing a punishment can seem essential for restoring moral order. To not punish a behavior can feel like we are condoning it. This perspective is reinforced when our other children demand accountability. Parents may feel that punishment is necessary to demonstrate the seriousness of these violations to all members of the family and to maintain a sense of justice in the household.

Here are some alternative ideas about how to deal with these situations. If you absolutely feel that a punishment is necessary, ask the boy what he thinks his punishment should be. Initially this might seem like a bad idea because you probably imagine that your son will choose a very lenient punishment. In my experience, the opposite is true. Most challenging boys do feel that they deserve to be punished for certain infractions and, in fact, often offer suggestions of punishments that are way too harsh. In these cases, work out a punishment with him that is less severe and implement it. Often your son will feel that you have been lenient, and he will feel less resentful.

Consider restorative justice instead. Restorative justice combines the needs of the victim for repair, the need of the offender to take responsibility, and the need of the family to have a safe and healthy home environment. If your son has hurt one of his siblings, involve the other child in deciding how repair should be made. If your son gets an allowance, his allowance can be garnished until there is enough saved to pay for the broken item. If the damage can't be fixed, he can do something for the sibling: buy a present, make a card, do some work for them. The apology or repair can't be forced. If it is, the challenging boy won't learn any positive moral lesson and his sibling won't feel that there has been a genuine repair. Consider leading your son gently through the four *R*s of apology that we discussed in chapter 4 to help him connect with his sincere remorse and desire to make amends.

Before moving on to discuss rewards in the next chapter, it's important to point out that there are times when punishments may be your only option in dealing with your challenging boy's behavior problems. To be effective, reward programs—and it is even truer with coaching—require that there be trust and positive connection in the parent-child relationship. If your son is engaging in behaviors that are unsafe to himself or to members of your family or others—like drugs, delinquent behavior, being violent, bullying members of the family—and there is no trust in the parent-child relationship, then punishments and other coercive measures may be necessary. If this is the case in your family, it is a crisis and absolutely a time to seek professional help. Trying to manage a situation like this without guidance from a qualified behavioral health professional is dangerous.

RULES

In families, the standards for behavior are generally clear and do not need to be explicitly stated. House rules become important when there are specific problems that need to be addressed. With young kids, rules are often created regarding aggression, unsafe behavior, and screens. With teens, the rules frequently apply to things like computers, phones, social media, video games, curfew, and driving. Parents shouldn't try to cover everything; usually having three to four house rules is best. Too many rules dilute all the rules. Create rules that address the main struggles in the house. Here are my "rules" for rule setting.

1. Rule Number 1 is always: "Nobody gets hurt. Nothing gets broken on purpose."

The most important rule for every household is that the home be an emotionally and physically safe place for all family members. In families with younger children, I have parents use these words to convey the safety rule: "Nobody gets hurt. Nothing gets broken on purpose." This rule prohibits physical aggression and intentional destructiveness, while allowing that sometimes people get hurt or things get broken accidentally. In my experience, younger kids find this phrasing of the safety rule clear and easy to understand.

As children become preadolescents and adolescents, feeling safe at home is as important as ever. Rather than having a posted house rule about nobody getting hurt, nothing getting broken, we need to talk to our sons about how it's a core family value that all family members feel emotionally and physically safe at home. If this is a rule that you are unable to establish in your home, seek professional help.

2. "Everyone has a right to a life."

Having a challenging boy can dominate family life. He can demand a tremendous amount of parental attention. And parents often feel compelled to do everything and spend everything it takes to get their son what he needs. It's a noble impulse, but it comes at the expense of their own needs and the needs of their other children. "Everyone has a right to a life" means that meeting the needs of one family member cannot be allowed to unduly impinge on the ability of other family members to live their lives and be happy. Rule 2 is just for the parents to help guide them in running the family. It is not posted anywhere or stated as a family value. It's a mantra for parents to keep in mind to help establish priorities.

3. Rules should be simple, clear, and concrete.

There should be no doubt about what is required to comply with a rule. As I've said, rules like "be a good person" "be respectful" "have a good attitude" are too vague. It's difficult to know whether you are following the rule or not. The child might attempt to follow what he understands the rule to be, only to have the parent administer a consequence. As a result, unclear rules can increase mistrust in the parent-child relationship. A rule like "put your phone on the hall table by 9 p.m.," leaves little room for misunderstanding.

4. Give children a say in what the rules are and in what the consequences are for rule infractions.

Ultimately, parents want to get to the place where their challenging boys are trusted partners who work together with them to make life better for everyone in the family. Challenging boys resist this type of collaboration initially because they mistrust authority. However, they care deeply about justice (I should point out that challenging boys often have a biased view of justice, usually feeling that the scales of justice are tilted against them). Fortunately, this strong interest in justice means that they are generally more open to working collaboratively around setting rules and consequences than they are about almost any other problem to be solved. It's a foot in the door to working on solving problems together.

All children, but especially challenging boys, are more likely to follow rules that they help create and to accept punishments that they had a say in establishing. This is essential with teenagers; they generally have the power to get away with doing what they want. Teach them to collaborate or you will be unintentionally teaching them to get good at breaking rules while not getting caught. Haim Ginott recommends giving them "a choice and a voice."

Parents sometimes resist including their sons in the rule-making process because they worry that it will erode their parental authority. They fear that giving their son a say in the creation of rules and consequences means letting him decide what the rules will be. What rules are eventually set is ultimately the parents' decision, even if the boy's opinion is taken into account. If the boy refuses to participate constructively in rule making, parents have the right and responsibility to set the rules themselves.

Younger kids have a harder time coming up with rules, but it's good practice for them to be involved in setting them anyway. The process of soliciting input from children on rules and consequences helps develop their thinking about norms for behavior. The more that rule making and rule enforcement are top-down, the less our sons will be encouraged to think ethically and the less they will internalize family values and feel responsible for upholding them. As I said before, we don't want to turn our challenging boys into compliant boys. We want them to be self-governing, self-regulating individuals who can collaborate with others, but also stand up for important values.

5. The rules apply to everyone in the family.
Challenging boys are exquisitely sensitive to unfairness and double standards. Making rules that apply to everyone dramatically increases

the boy's buy-in. Making rules that apply to everyone also helps keep the focus on creating rules that are relevant to the family culture you want to create and to the life skills you want to teach. Finally, by following household rules, a parent models for the challenging boy being an accountable member of the family.

Of course there are standards of behavior, responsibilities, and authority that are different for parents and children. I am talking about the issues that have become significant enough to be turned into house rules. If phone use is a problem and the rule is no phones in the bedroom, then the parents should not have their phones in the bedroom either. If the problem is yelling, then the parents should be expected to not yell also. If the issue is the boy not letting his parents know where he is, then they should be expected to let him know where they are. As a family, we want to work together to help each other to be accountable.

6. Post written rules.

House rules should be visibly posted (this rule applies only to families with children ages ten or so and younger). When a parent tells their son to stop doing something, it quickly becomes a power struggle over the parent trying to control the boy and him resisting parental authority. Something magical happens, however, when rules are written down and posted. When I work with families where a challenging boy is aggressive with parents or siblings, I first recommend posting Rule Number 1. Parents are usually highly skeptical that this will accomplish anything, but in most cases, this simple act solves the problem. After Rule Number 1 is posted, when a boy is being aggressive, the parents point to the displayed rule and say, "remember rule number 1, nobody gets hurt, nothing gets broken on purpose." It's amazing how often this stops the behavior without causing a fight. Posted rules become separate from the people who created them. It's similar to how laws don't feel connected to the people who wrote them. For example, when motorists get pulled over for speeding, they don't feel mad at the legislators who passed the speed limit laws.

When children become preteens and teens, posted rules feel childish and embarrassing. Also, at these ages we want to move away from externalized rules toward internalized values. We want to make statements like: "in this family we believe in . . . (helping each other live happier lives, education, serving others, etc.)." With older kids we want to encourage discussions about what our family values are.

In the next chapter, we'll move on to a discussion of rewards as a discipline tool.

KEY IDEAS

- Punishments don't teach a child how to behave. They also don't teach moral lessons. Punishments only teach what not to do.

- Punishments should only be used in limited circumstances, with a plan, and following the guidelines described in this chapter.

- Physical punishment should never be used.

- One of the best forms of punishments is to ignore misbehavior so as to not reward it with your attention.

- Rules need to be simple and clear and apply to everyone in the family.

CHAPTER EIGHT

The Effective Use of Rewards

A second discipline tool for gaining your child's cooperation and teaching him the skills he needs to not be challenging is positive reinforcement (rewards). Rewards are another behavioral learning strategy. Just as punishments decrease the frequency of a behavior, rewards (giving the child something he wants when he performs a desired behavior) increase the likelihood that a behavior will occur.

We all routinely fail to use a powerful reward strategy that is right at our fingertips. Instead of knee-jerk negative reactions to our son's misbehavior, we should pivot toward looking for opportunities to, in Kazdin's words, "catch him being good" and praise him. Our sons crave our positive attention and praise, but we don't give it to them nearly enough. Being on the lookout for moments when he's acting in non-challenging ways (he gets ready for school on time, gets off his video game when asked, does his homework) and rewarding it with our praise, will improve his behavior *and* our relationship with him. When using praise, it's very important to be as specific as possible in your praise and to praise your son's actions, not qualities of his character or person. ("I'm proud of how hard you worked studying for your math test" rather than "you're so smart.")

Adopting this positive outlook is immensely beneficial. It helps us increase the ratio of positive to negative interactions (remember the 5:1 magic ratio) by actively searching for and celebrating moments of good behavior. It's demoralizing to a child when we focus solely on his undesirable behavior (where he's falling short) rather than emphasizing his successes. Ryan, for example, was discouraged because he felt that his mom only paid attention to what he was doing wrong—missing homework assignments or playing video games after his screen time is over. He wanted her to see that he's a "good kid"—he doesn't drink or do drugs, he's involved in sports, and at least he tries to do well in school even if he doesn't always succeed.

Rewards have several other clear advantages over punishments. As I've previously pointed out, rewards can be used to teach your son skills that you want him to acquire. Punishments only teach what you don't want your son to do. It's up to him what he does instead. If you punish your son for hitting his sister, he might go and break something of hers.

Rewards can be used to teach new behaviors in steps. This is called "shaping." If you want your son to sit down and do homework for thirty minutes before dinner, you could first set up a reward program where he earns points for a ten-minute homework session. Once he can successfully do ten minutes then you can start gradually lengthening the sessions over time until you reach your ultimate goal of thirty minutes.

Rewards also can be used to help bolster a child's motivation to do something that is difficult to do because he is anxious (try out for a team, go to the dentist, go to a birthday party). It's important to explain to your son that you are offering the reward to help him with *his* challenge of tolerating his anxiety. "I know this is hard for you. It's scary. I'm going to help you get through it by giving you something to look forward to. What can we do afterward that would help make this more bearable?"

Most importantly, rewards are "win-win." Challenging boys and their parents are frequently locked in win-lose power struggles. With reward charts you're working together. Parents get the behaviors that they want, and the boy gets the rewards he wants. When we work together with our challenging sons on a reward program, we make life better for both of us. It helps us in our goal of rebuilding trust.

REWARD CHARTS

A systematic approach to positive reinforcement takes the form of reward charts. Reward charts have a mixed reputation. I often hear from parents who say that they tried reward charts and they don't work. In my experience this is usually because the reward program hasn't been properly designed. For example, the rewards are too hard to earn, or the point system is too much for busy parents to keep track of. However, when correctly set up, incentive programs and reward charts are very powerful tools for teaching kids new skills. They are used widely in schools with great success.

Just like punishments, rewards are most effective when implemented as part of a plan. As I mentioned above, all plans should begin by answering: "What is the one thing that you can improve that would have the biggest positive impact on your family life?" Once you have an answer to that question, you can use the steps outlined below to create an effective reward program to address the problem. The discussion of reward charts below draws upon the work of Alan Kazdin.

1. Identify the behaviors to reward.

When creating a rewards program, we need to identify what behaviors we are wanting to cultivate. The first step in this is to understand what issues underlie the problem being addressed. For example, if fights over homework are causing the most distress in the family, we need to figure out why the boy is having difficulty getting homework completed. He might be struggling with keeping track of what homework is due. Or he might be emotionally exhausted at the end of the school day and has a hard time sitting down and focusing on work. Or the boy might resent homework as an unreasonable intrusion by the school into his personal time. Each of these causes of homework problems requires a different focus for a behavior plan. If the main problem is keeping track of the homework due, the plan might be to reward him for using an academic planner notebook. If the main problem is fatigue, you might reward your son for taking an exercise break after school followed by sitting down to work for ten minutes. If he is opposed to doing homework, the plan might involve him earning his screen time by completing the assignments he has due.

Often the purpose of your program is to eliminate some undesirable behavior. In the example above, it's avoiding doing homework. In these cases, rewarding your son for performing a positive behavior that is incompatible with the unwanted behavior is usually more effective than rewarding him for not doing the negative behavior. Kazdin calls these incompatible behaviors, the "positive opposite." Examples of positive opposites include expressing disappointment calmly (rather than throwing a tantrum when denied something) and getting out of bed and dressed right away (rather than being late for school).

Many reward programs fail because the initial behavioral goals are too ambitious. The principle is to pick objectives that challenge your son enough so that he will grow but that are not so difficult that he will be unable to meet them. When parents set goals for their son's behavior that do not accurately reflect what he is capable of, everyone involved is going to be frustrated and the reward chart abandoned. Selecting modest initial goals helps increase the likelihood of success and builds momentum for tackling larger goals later.

2. Determine your rewards.

In my experience, reward programs work best when there is an ultimate big prize that the boy is highly motivated to work toward. We want the time needed to get the reward to be around two to five weeks—depending on the value of the reward and the age of the boy. If it takes too long to earn the prize, the big reward will lose its motivational power.

Typically, one big prize alone is not sufficient to keep the boy motivated to stick with the reward program. To help maintain engagement we also want to have smaller rewards that can be earned along the way, every day or so. Rewards that are priced to require more than a couple of days to earn are less effective at maintaining motivation because of the time that passes between behavior and reward. Take, for example, ten-year-old Jacob who is working on getting into bed on time. The big prize at the end of the program is a sports jersey that has his favorite baseball player's name and number on the back. Jacob is also an avid Pokémon player. His small rewards are Pokémon cards that he can earn several times a week. Earning small rewards along the way helps build positive feelings of success, excitement, and cooperation that give the plan momentum while the point total slowly builds toward the amount needed for the big prize.

As an alternative to these small rewards, Kazdin recommends having a prize store. The prize store has several small to medium rewards in it—trading cards, going out for ice cream, special time with a parent, extra screen time, etcetera. Each reward has a point value associated with it. The boy can spend points that he's earned in the program on things in the store. The points spent in the prize store still count toward the total being earned for the final prize. The prize store can be more motivating for some boys because of the variety of rewards. You'll need to experiment to see which works best for you.

3. Involve your child in the creation of the incentive plan.
Your child will be more likely to participate in the rewards program if he is involved in creating it, particularly what rewards he will earn. For older kids, it also helps to get their input about what behaviors are being reinforced. It works best when we begin these conversations with a general plan in mind—what behavior is being trained, what the rewards will be, and how long it will take to earn the rewards.

Begin the conversation with a statement like: "We've noticed that bedtime has been a struggle lately, and we think it's time to work together on a plan to make it smoother for everyone." Listen to any thoughts or objections he has and then suggest your program (in the example of Jacob, an 8:00 p.m. bedtime and working toward earning the sports jersey he's been wanting). If the big reward is enticing enough to your son, he'll want to talk about the program. Have ideas ready about what the small rewards might be, but also encourage him to suggest some others. You might want to be flexible on the goal of the plan. In this case, the boy might suggest 8:30 p.m. as the bedtime. If this is acceptable to you as a starting place, agree to it (remember, after 8:30 p.m. is successfully established as a bedtime, you can always make a new program to move the bedtime to 8:00 p.m. if it feels necessary). The older the child, the more important it is to be open to negotiating the terms of the program.

4. Don't take away points.
Rewards programs work best if the boy can only earn points, but not lose them. If the boy is inconsistently following the program, it will mean that it will take him longer to earn his big prize. There's no need to increase his incentive by docking points for noncompliance. Taking away points is discouraging. It leads boys to lose faith that they could earn the big reward and, as a result, they lose their investment in the plan. If the boy isn't consistently following the program, it's best to reevaluate the behaviors being rewarded (maybe they represent too big a change) and the rewards themselves, rather than adding punishments.

5. Make it manageable.
One of the biggest reasons that rewards programs fail is that they require too much work on the part of parents to keep track of the points, so the program isn't stuck to and eventually is abandoned. Here are some ideas to make the rewards program less of an administrative burden. Make sure that what it takes to earn points is very clear in order to minimize disputes. Make keeping track of points a joint project. When a program is proceeding well, the ritual of tallying up the points together is a positive experience and promotes the development of trust and connection. Even consider awarding points to your son for reminding you to update the chart. Kazdin suggests taking days off from the program (for example, only doing it on weekdays) to help make it easier to stick with.

6. Document the terms of the rewards program and the points progress where everyone can see it.
For younger kids, create a big chart and post it on the refrigerator or somewhere else that everyone can see. The poster documents the behaviors to be rewarded, point values, and a grid to keep track of the

points earned per day with stickers or checkmarks. The poster will also have a visual way of tracking the total progress toward the big reward (a thermometer, a road, Kazdin recommends "a rocket ship to the moon"). You might want to add a picture of the big reward. Making the poster together can be a fun activity and help build excitement about the program.

For older kids, tweens and above, publicly tracking of an incentive program can be embarrassing. A google doc or a paper notebook can be used to record the terms of the program and to keep track of the points.

7. Practice.

To jump-start rewards programs, it often helps to practice. The practice involves the child performing the behavior that is being rewarded in the program and giving points for correct practice. This is similar in the fire service. In training, firefighters practice using the Jaws of Life on unoccupied junked cars, they practice search and rescue in buildings filled with non-toxic smoke, they practice active firefighting in specially constructed burn buildings. This allows them to master the skills in low stress simulated conditions. In the example below, Aiden's reward program is designed to help him get ready for school on time in the morning. To familiarize him with the program, its steps, and rewards before officially beginning it, his parents did practice sessions on Saturday and Sunday morning. Aiden did each step of the program and was praised and awarded points for successful completion. He was then able to exchange these points earned during the simulation for a reward; his points earned this way also started off his progress to his big reward. As with firefighting training, practice sessions help the child learn the desired behaviors when tension is low (Aiden's parents aren't stressed about him being late for school on the weekend). If the boy can't (or won't) successfully perform the program's behaviors during practice, it is likely that the program will need to be revised because it's too difficult or the rewards aren't appealing enough to him.

8. Evaluate and revise.

Frequently the first reward chart program we create will not be successful. It's also common for a particular rewards program that once worked, to lose effectiveness over time. These are not reasons to not use incentive programs. They are powerful tools. With all programs it's important to monitor how well they are working and revise them accordingly. Let your child know in advance of any changes you intend to make to the plan. Kazdin recommends changing up rewards, adding bonuses for streaks, or double-point days to help keep things fresh.

Example 1: Getting ready for school on time

Nine-year-old Aiden has difficulty getting out the door for school in the morning. His parents have to constantly nag to keep him moving through his morning routine. From their work in their parent journal, they think that the main underlying problems are attention and working memory. They made a list of all of the tasks Aiden needs to do to get ready in the morning and set a time for completing each activity: out of bed 7:15, get dressed 7:25, eat breakfast 7:45, brush teeth 7:55, pack bag 8:10, get in the car 8:20. Aiden gets one point for each activity he does on time and five points for being in the car by 8:20. Because of his working memory problems, Aiden's parents created a checklist of these activities to help him remember everything he needs to do. Aiden can earn an additional two points for marking completed items off on his checklist. His parents also decided, because of his attentional challenges, that in the beginning of the program they will help him stay on track. Rather than nag him, if they see him getting distracted, they will remind him to check his list.

Generally, small rewards are priced at the number of points earned during a perfect day. In this case twelve. It was not expected that Aiden would have perfect days, especially in the beginning, so his parents anticipated that the small rewards would be earned every two days on average. They decided that the price of the big reward should be equivalent to three weeks of perfect performance: twelve possible points per day multiplied by five school days per week for three weeks, equaling 180 points. Aiden is a huge Lego fan, so his parents proposed that the big reward for the program would be a Star Wars Lego set that he has been wanting. His small rewards will be Lego action figures.

This plan was discussed with Aiden and his input was gathered. He was excited by the program, but wanted a different Lego set from the one his parents originally had in mind. The sets were similarly priced, so his parents agreed.

Aiden and his dad made the poster to track the plan. They decorated it with pictures of Lego Star Wars sets and Lego action figures. The total points toward the plan's big reward was tallied by coloring in segments on a light saber. (Go to challengingboys.com/book to see a picture of Aiden's chart.)

Example 2: Swearing

Sometimes there's not really a positive opposite behavior to reinforce so what you end up needing to reward is the absence of a behavior. This can get a little tricky. Ten-year-old Dylan's parents were faced with this challenge when they wanted to create a program to eliminate his swearing. The behavior was triggered by frustration, but it didn't always occur when he was frustrated, so it was hard to predict.

Given the concerns about punishments raised in chapter 7, his parents decided to not use punishments. Instead, they decided on a program of rewarding him for not swearing. Many of us use this type of rewards approach in an ad hoc way. "If you behave yourself in the supermarket while I'm shopping, I'll buy you some gum when we check out." The absence of misbehavior during shopping trips leads to a reward. Anyone who has tried this knows that it can seriously backfire. This occurs when your child misbehaves in the first aisle and loses his reward (along with the incentive to behave) with thirty minutes of shopping to go. Suddenly you have nothing to motivate your son with for the rest of the shopping trip.

To address this problem, Dylan's parents decided to divide the time from when he got home from his afterschool program at 5 p.m. until his bedtime at 8 p.m. into thirty-minute blocks. He could get one point for each thirty-minute period with no swearing with a ten-point bonus for completing all six periods successfully. When he slipped up and swore, his parents would calmly say, "OK, too bad, but a new chance to earn a point will start at 6:30." Using smaller blocks of time means that Dylan will be motivated to not swear through the entire evening. Even if he slips up and does not earn his point for one of the thirty-minute periods, he can still earn points in later periods.

Once Dylan reached 15 points, he could trade it in for fifteen extra minutes of Xbox time. Given that he could earn up to 16 points per day, it fits the rule of the small reward being about the equivalent of a perfect day. His parents decided during the weekend they would do the program from 5 p.m. to 8 p.m. and take a break from the program for the rest of the day. For his big reward, Dylan wanted to buy a new game he'd heard of. A perfect week would earn Dylan $16 \times 7 = 112$ points. His parents decided on 350 points as the total for the final reward, which is a little more than three weeks of perfect performance $(3 \times 112 = 336)$.

Fading

Some critics of rewards programs argue that you are bribing or paying your child to behave appropriately. This might be true if you had to indefinitely give rewards to get the desired behavior. Fading is the process by which the rewards for a behavior are gradually phased out until they are no longer needed.

In the case of Dylan, it is entirely possible that fading won't be needed at all. The program described above might be sufficient to resolve the issue. It's not uncommon for a reward program like his to establish a behavior as a stable habit. If it reduced the frequency of the behavior, but didn't eliminate it entirely, his parents could make a new program. In this new program the rewards would be harder to earn and so would occur with less frequency. For example, in the new program there could be three one-hour periods instead of six thirty-minute periods. Each subsequent phase of the program would have less and less frequent rewards until the behavior occurred without reward.

Sometimes fading can be a more complicated process, as in the case of Aiden. Several aspects of his program would need to be faded, and it would be best to do one at a time. The rewards would need to be consolidated until Aiden was just rewarded for being out the door on time. His parents' reminders would need to be gradually eliminated also. Eventually Aiden would be on time with no reward at all except for his satisfaction at helping his mom. The goal of rewards programs is to teach habits and skills that eventually become self-reinforcing and persistent.

Preadolescents and Adolescents

As your son grows into preadolescence and adolescence, how you use punishments and rewards needs to be modified to fit this new phase of his life. Time-outs, rewards charts, and point systems, which work well for younger children, become increasingly less effective for older kids who may view them as childish. This shift necessitates a change in approach for managing challenging behavior with preteens and teenagers.

Interestingly, the challenging behaviors that concern us most in preadolescence and adolescence are not that different from those of childhood: doing chores, getting off screens, completing homework, participating in family activities, not fighting with you or his siblings, and being respectful. Adolescence does introduce additional concerns like leaving the house without telling you where he's going, breaking curfew, and engaging in risky behaviors like alcohol, drugs, and sexual activity. Alcohol, drugs, and sex are behaviors of concern for all teenagers. Experimentation in these areas is normal for teens, but definitely anxiety provoking for parents, and can develop into serious problems.

In my experience, problematic substance use and risky sexual behavior are not frequent problems for challenging boys. Although their lack of impulse control places them at risk for these behaviors, their overall immaturity and social struggles mean that they are generally not in groups with "fast" kids who would pull them toward these behaviors. Challenging boys are far more likely to get into trouble with their phones, computers, and video games.

With all kids the biggest protection from risky substance use or sexual behavior is a close trusting relationship with their parents. Children who feel safe confiding in and getting guidance from parents have far fewer problems in these areas. A discussion of how to handle these risky behaviors is beyond the scope of this book. If you have concerns about your son, please consult an appropriate professional.

Another normal, but frustrating aspect of teenagerhood is "attitude." It's normal for teens to be impatient, condescending, or just plain rude in dealing with their parents. It's also normal for teens to feel entitled to your services as a maid, cook, and chauffeur without expressing the slightest bit of gratitude. Attitude is an abstract concept. It's like art, we all know it when we see it, but because it's so vague, it's difficult to use punishments or rewards to shape it. Mostly I'd advise "punishing" it by ignoring it. However, if there are some aspects of your son's attitude that are over the line or really get your goat, do your best to identify discrete behaviors that can be addressed (for example, swearing, yelling, telling you to "shut up," or calling you "stupid" or an "idiot").

With preadolescents and adolescents, it's more important than ever to negotiate about behavior plans. Imposing a behavior change plan on them is more difficult to do as compared with a younger child. You have less control over rewards and punishments, and he has much greater power to refuse your plan. If you try to take away screen time, he might sneak it, or it might lead to physical fights over equipment. If you tell him he can't go out with his friends, he might go anyway. If you tell him he can't have the car, he might search to find where you hid the keys.

Teens tend to ignore rules that parents impose on them. They may not overtly oppose the rule, they just may choose to not follow it. I frequently have parents express dismay that their son didn't follow a rule like "no phones in rooms at night." A boy not following a rule is reason to be curious. The first step is to have a "what's up?" conversation with your son to find out why. "I thought we agreed, no phones in bedrooms at night, what's up?" Usually, you will hear something like, "I never agreed to that." When you were "talking" with him about the rule, he remained silent. This wasn't agreement with the rule, he was just trying to end an annoying conversation. When teens have a say in the making of rules, and if the rules also apply to the parents, you have your greatest chance of compliance.

For example, if curfew is a problem. Find out what is difficult for him about keeping his curfew. Maybe he loses track of time (remember "time blindness" is a common problem for challenging boys), maybe he's doing something really fun and is having a hard time leaving, or maybe he's embarrassed at how early his curfew is compared to his friends. You also need to know what your no-compromise line is. Is a specific curfew time what matters most to you, or are you flexible about when he comes home provided that he satisfies some other condition: he lets you know where he is, he texts or calls when he's going to be late, he answers your texts or calls promptly when he's out? Once you understand what the primary issue is for you, and what the main obstacle is for him, you can set up a program. If his problem is keeping track of time, the program can involve you calling or texting him to remind him to come home. In this case, your son can earn time added on to his curfew the next time he goes out if he answers your text or call and makes it home before his curfew. Also, this program might include a big goal of him earning a permanent later curfew if he establishes a pattern of coming home on time.

Often with teens and preteens, their desire to meet up with their friends online or to go out with them can be a useful incentive. You can set the expectation that chores, homework, or room cleaning must be done before he goes out or takes the car. Points systems also do have a place with preadolescents and adolescents. If your son wants something (a new video game, headphones, cool new shoes), you can set up a point system for him to earn the item in exchange for doing things that you want: doing chores, speaking to you respect-fully, going over homework assignments with you each day. The only difference from plans with younger boys is that you would place even greater emphasis on including his input in the creation of the program and the points would be tracked discreetly.

Generally, boys at this age want greater independence. Prominent examples are to be left alone about homework and screen time and to go out with their friends or take the car when they want it. Simple if-then situations can be set up. They shouldn't be made up on the spot. There should be clear expectations established ahead of time. You can play video games after your homework and chores are done. You can have the car after you walk the dog. You can do homework in your room if you show us the completed work when you are done.

FINAL THOUGHTS

It's very important to start with small, realistic goals. The objectives for the child need to not be overly ambitious, to prevent failure and discouragement. Likewise, the program should be manageable for the parents. Their busy lives and their own executive functioning challenges might make a formal rewards program too difficult to keep up with. In these cases, it might make more sense for the parents to shift to focusing on increasing their praise for the child when he behaves well ("catching him being good"), and to "punishing" misbehavior by ignoring it. This can be a more feasible approach in busy households.

Proper use of rewards is crucial to the success of a program. Avoid rewarding outcomes that the child doesn't control (like grades). In these cases, focus instead on rewarding process and effort (for example, using an organizer, or time spent in homework sessions). Additionally, rewards should only be given after the desired behavior has been performed. Premature rewards based on your son's promises to complete the program later can undermine the system. Once you have given the reward, his incentive for completing the program goes away. Also, don't ad lib or turn the points into bribes. For example, in a program working on bedtime, don't offer points on the spur of the moment for some unrelated behavior. "I'll give you two bonus points if you empty the dishwasher." Finally, avoid threats and nagging. These will not increase the success of the program and will actually train your child to ignore and avoid you.

Siblings can become jealous of their challenging brother's reward chart. This can actually be beneficial. You can use it as an opportunity to create a program to help that child with some challenge they might be having. This is a lot of extra work, so it might not be feasible. In that case, Kazdin suggests rewarding both kids for the challenging boy's success in his program. When this approach works well, the sibling helps the boy stick to the program by providing reminders and encouragement. This can backfire and lead to increased conflict between siblings, so be alert and change the program as necessary.

Behavior change is not a linear process. A child may show improvement one day and revert to old behaviors the next. However, if the targeted behavior is not improving overall, it's time to revise or even abandon the plan. Behavior plans are powerful tools for modifying challenging behavior. Sometimes the complexity of the situation you are in would benefit from consulting a behavior therapist to help you build a successful plan.

The big goal behind every reward program is to create a positive experience for the challenging boy and his parents of working together, being on the same team, and having their efforts lead to everyone's lives being better. This starts to build a foundation for a coaching approach to discipline that I'll discuss in the next chapter.

KEY IDEAS

- We all have an overlooked reward strategy right at our fingertips: "catch him being good." We need to shift our focus from correcting misbehavior to looking for opportunities to praise our sons for behaving well.

- Parents underutilize praise as a reward. Praise effort and improvement, not qualities of the boy or outcomes that he doesn't control (like grades).

- Reward charts are powerful tools for teaching skills. They have the added benefit of being win-win arrangements that build trust and connection in the parent-child relationship.

- Two keys to success in creating an effective rewards program are (1) involve your son in developing it, and (2) make it as easy as possible for you to administer.

PARENTING JOURNAL EXERCISES

- Where are opportunities to catch your son being good? What techniques can you use to remember to be on the lookout for good behavior to praise?

- Are there annoying behaviors that your son does that don't really cause harm and you'd be best off "punishing" by ignoring them?

- Think about your current challenges with your son. If you could change one thing that would have the biggest positive impact on family life, what would it be? This should be the focus of your first reward chart.

- What are the issues that underlie this problem? Are there behaviors that you could target with a rewards program?

- Brainstorm some ideas for small rewards and big rewards that you can use with your son.

CHAPTER NINE

Coaching

The fire department operates with a chain-of-command structure, where the chief is at the top and orders flow downward through the ranks. As parents, it is not our goal to be the chief of our challenging son. Our ultimate aim is for him to learn the skills he needs to be able to take responsibility for himself and his challenging nature—to become the chief of his own life.

Because of its hierarchical structure, I needed to look outside the fire service to come up with a metaphor to describe this third tool, or approach, to discipline that emphasizes empowering a child to take ownership over his life. John Gottman suggests that parents need to be "emotion coaches." This seemed like a perfect fit. Unlike a fire chief exercising final authority, a coach guides, mentors, and supports players as they strive to achieve *their* goals. Additionally, understanding, regulating, and appropriately expressing his emotions are the areas where a challenging boy needs the most "coaching."

There are many definitions of coaching, one of my favorites comes from Wayne Goldsmith: "Coaching is the art of inspiring change through emotional connection." Even if we were never an athlete or a sports coach, this idea of inspiring growth through connection resonates deeply with our hopes as parents. No parent dreams about fighting with their child, of being constantly at odds, or of being a strict disciplinarian. No one dreams of constantly issuing reprimands, warnings, and punishments. No one even dreams of learning to be a skilled behaviorist who gets model behavior from their child through the expert application of the principles of punishment and reinforcement.

What we dream of instead is of passing along our wisdom, of teaching, and of guiding our child to have a happy life, to be a good person, and to be successful and fulfilled in work and relationships. We aspire to help our children dream their own dreams and to aid them in fulfilling those dreams. We also dream of building a family culture where we share values, care for each other, and work together to make each other's lives better. Coaching is an approach to discipline that is fun and rewarding and not just hard work. So much of parenting a challenging boy can feel like a grind.

Because a coaching approach embodies our parental aspirations, many of us instinctively try coaching our challenging sons. Unfortunately, things usually go wrong. We give inspirational talks, but the boy feels lectured to. We teach, but the boy doesn't learn. We make "game plans" for dealing with problems, but the plans are for a game the boy refuses to play. We encourage our son to breathe when he's dysregulated so he can calm down, but he doesn't want to calm down—he wants the world to stop upsetting him. The reason that these well-meaning coaching interventions often fail is that the necessary conditions for successful coaching haven't yet been met.

Fire engines carry many tools—ladders, saws, prybars for forcible entry, the jaws of life, etcetera. Which one to use depends on the needs of the situation. In parenting, which discipline tool to use in addressing a particular behavior problem—punishments, rewards, or coaching—depends on the status of the parent-child relationship. Which tool is appropriate is based upon how much you and your son agree on what your goals are, and whether you have sufficient trust and connection in your relationship to be able to work together.

Discipline tools exist on a continuum regarding these factors. Punishments are at one end. They require little or no agreement between parent and child on what the goals should be. Punishments also require little in the way of a positive parent-child relationship and no buy-in from the child. The child's only motivation is to avoid the punishment—he's not trying to be "good" or to please us. Punishments are win-lose coercive arrangements. "I'll do something to you that you won't like because you did something that I don't like." As a result, punishments further erode trust and connection. If you are in a place with your son where punishment is your only tool, it's best to refocus your attention on taking the steps described in chapters 1 to 6 for rebuilding your relationship with him rather than by trying to control his challenging behavior with punishments. This also might be a good time to consider getting professional help.

Reward programs are in the middle. Generally, reward programs are chosen when there is low agreement on goals, but there is some willingness to work together. This allows you and your son to come up with rewards that are sufficiently enticing to get him to perform the desired behavior. With rewards you aren't working together to achieve a shared goal, but you are working together to each get something you want. It's win-win. "I'll give you something you want for you doing what I want." Both sides end up better off. In this way, reward programs are practice at collaboration. Successfully completed reward programs make everyone feel good, and as a result, they help build trust and connection.

At the other end is coaching. For coaching to work, there needs to be high agreement on what the goals are and a high agreement on how to achieve those goals. Coaching also requires a strong parent-child relationship that includes trust, respect, and good communication. The parent-coach and the child work together because they are on the same team and share the same goals and values.

THE NECESSARY CONDITIONS FOR COACHING
1. Trust and connection in the parent-child relationship
It takes courage for anyone to change and grow. It's a risk to try to do things differently. Our fears tell us, "What you're doing now might not be working that great, but trying to do things a new way might be even worse."

A trusting relationship with a parent helps create a safe and secure base from which a boy can draw the courage he needs to take the risk to change. If he trusts that his parents have his best interest at heart, if he trusts them to be reliable guides who wouldn't lead him astray, if he trusts them to be true to their word and follow through on their promises, if he trusts them not to criticize or shame him for making mistakes, if he trusts them to be there to support him—especially if he stumbles—then a boy can have the courage to change.

As I described in chapter 4, challenging behavior problems erode trust and connection between parents and their sons. Work must be done to rebuild the parent-child relationship for coaching to be effective.

2. A regulated parent and a regulated child

A coach who isn't well regulated can't regulate others, can't teach effectively, and can't be a role model for coolness under pressure. A boy who isn't regulated can't listen, can't learn, and can't be coached. He needs to be regulated first. Review chapter 6 on co-regulation for suggestions on how to satisfy this important condition for coaching.

The experience of being coached can itself be anxiety provoking. Coaches nudge athletes to challenge themselves. When we push for our son to talk to his teacher, to go on a playdate, to study for a test, we might not realize that we are unintentionally dysregulating him, that our demands are asking more of him than he is ready for, and we are pushing him into the Overwhelmed Zone.

After I graduated from college, I traveled to Europe. My first stop was in Paris. I was staying with the friend of a friend. This young man lived in an apartment that was on the top floor of a building that had access to the roof and a beautiful view of Paris. There was a flat area where he and his friends had set up chairs; there they could sip wine and enjoy the view. They invited me to join them. The problem for me was that there was no railing. Even more of a problem was that you had to walk across the flat narrow ridge cap of the roof for some distance to get to this area.

My new friends all walked comfortably out to the "patio" to enjoy the evening. I was frozen. I was flooded with images of falling off the ridge cap and sliding down the steep metal roof grasping in vain for a handhold before plummeting six stories to my death. They tried to encourage and coax and reassure me that it would be fine, but all I could feel was terror. They gestured to the magical sunset view of Paris. I resisted their encouragement and would have fought them (i.e., had a challenging episode) if they'd tried to force me.

This is how it is with challenging boys when we try to show them a different way. They can become dysregulated by our nudging, and it can trigger a challenging episode. They use their defiance to try to gain some control because they feel so out of control.

When we venture down the path of coaching, we need to pay consistent and careful attention to our son's level of arousal. While it's important for coaches to push athletes outside their comfort zones, the athlete's relationship with the coach also needs to be a zone of comfort and support as he faces the hard emotions that go with striving to grow and improve.

3. Shared goals

Coaching is about an emotional connection that inspires us to work together to reach a shared goal. For a coaching approach to be effective, we must be on the same page with our son about what the goal is. If a boy isn't completing his homework, the parents' goal is that he consistently finishes it. If the boy shares that goal, then a coaching approach might be appropriate. He and his parents could brainstorm about a plan—get a tutor, learn some organizational strategies, or even try a rewards program to help increase motivation. However, if the boy does not share the goal of doing his homework—perhaps his goal is to have his parents stop nagging him—a coaching approach wouldn't work.

Up to now in this book, parents have owned the goal of ending their son's problem with challenging behavior. The reduction in challenging behavior that has come so far is due to changes the parents have made in their ability to anticipate triggers, manage their own reactions, and respond more effectively to challenging moments. Even in the teaching of skills through rewards, the parents own the goal of what skills will be learned. The boy has not yet begun to take responsibility for his behavior.

For coaching to work, it ultimately should be the parents and the boy working together to pursue *his* goals: *his* goal of getting to school on time, *his* goal of getting homework done, *his* goal of doing better in math, *his* goal to not say hurtful things when angry, and so on. In coaching it is the parent's role to help make a plan for how the boy might reach his goal, and to support and encourage him to stick with the plan so he can achieve it.

We need to be absolutely sure that our son is fully onboard with a goal before coaching. Frequently when we try to coach our son, we think we are on the same page when we are not. Challenging boys will often imply (or even explicitly say) that they agree to a plan, when they don't. They give this false agreement because they are focused in the moment on getting us to stop talking and leave them alone. It's important to be attentive to this possibility of false agreement on goals. If we find out that it has occurred, it's important not to overreact. Rather than getting upset and criticizing our son for breaking his promise, we should seek to listen and learn about what got in the way of his letting us know that we weren't on the same page.

4. Openness to influence

Coaches can do a lot to help players achieve. Likewise, parent-coaches can offer a great deal of support and assistance to a challenging boy as he pursues his goals. Parents can teach him skills if he is open to learning. Parents can provide emotional support—motivation and encouragement, consolation and co-regulation—if he is open to receiving help. Parents can brainstorm plans and then later problem solve when adjustments need to be made. The boy needs to be able to accept the parents' help and guidance. Coaching cannot be forced on another person. We need to be sure that we have our son's permission before proceeding with a coaching approach. Coaching cannot happen if he isn't open to influence.

Parents also need to be open to influence. We need to be aware of, and receptive to, our son's emotional state. Parents need to listen to his feedback on their teaching and accept his input.

Challenging boys can struggle with accepting help even when there is a trusting parent-child relationship. This difficulty taking in help is present in many areas of a boy's life. Often there are teachers, special educators, and school counselors there to support him, but he won't/can't take them up on their availability to help.

As we have previously discussed, challenging boys often see themselves as "problem children" and getting help can feel like a painful reminder of this defectiveness. They experience the help as a sign they need to be "fixed." They have to reject the help out of pride, or out of a mistaken belief that the only way they can be redeemed is to do it totally on their own. This rejection of help can be compounded by adolescence, which is a developmental stage marked by a push for greater independence. Challenging boys don't realize that we all need help to get where we want to go. Working on acceptance and validation in our relationship with our son will create conditions where he's more open to influence and help.

We do not need to have all of these four conditions perfectly met in every area of our relationship with our son to try coaching on a particular problem. They just need to be met more or less well, regarding the problem being addressed. Before taking a coaching approach, ask yourself: "Do we have sufficient trust and connection?" "Are we both regulated?" "Do we have the same goal?" "Are we open to each other's influence?"

A COACHING MINDSET

Now that we know the conditions that allow for a coaching approach to be used, let's discuss some of the qualities of a coaching mindset that will enable you to use this powerful and rewarding approach to discipline effectively.

1. Great coaches understand that emotional connection is the foundation of coaching.

Jay Martin, the winningest men's soccer coach in NCAA history, says that a coach's most important work happens during the twenty-two hours of each day that the team isn't on the field. This is the time coaches put into the work of developing their relationship with a player, building trust, respect, communication, and emotional connection. This relationship building is what makes the player receptive to learning during practice and being guided during games.

The same is true for working with our challenging son to solve his problem with challenging behavior. Our effectiveness as a coach is built upon the quality of the emotional connection between us. Therefore, we must take on the mindset that the majority of our efforts need to be applied to building trust and connection in our relationship with him (the work described in the first six chapters in this book). This relationship building will lead him to be open to our efforts to teach him the skills he needs to no longer be challenging. The ultimate goal is to build our relationship to the point where all of our discipline comes in the form of coaching.

2. Great coaches are gentle.

John Wooden, widely considered to be one of the greatest coaches of all time, stressed the importance of being gentle. For him, gentleness was the foundation of influence. Many of us confuse gentleness with weakness. Our raised voices and stern tones are not signs of power; they are indications that we are losing control. To Coach Wooden, "there is nothing stronger than gentleness."

Gentleness is calm and calming. It is patient and respectful. These are enormously co-regulating qualities, and we need to be well regulated ourselves to embody them. I mentioned that Gottman recommends a "gentle start-up" to problem-solving conversations. This concept was based on a study of newly married couples he conducted with Sybil Carrère. They found that couples who were gentle with each other during conflicts were significantly less likely to divorce within the first six years of marriage. Similarly, Wooden advised that "gentleness can fix in a moment what an hour of shouting fails to achieve."

Gentleness is especially important when engaging with challenging boys. Their reactive temperaments make them extremely prone to having strong emotional reactions when parents are even a little bit harsh or impatient. It's important to do our best to approach our coaching efforts with gentle energy.

3. Great coaches get buy-in first.

First and foremost, coaches get buy-in from their players. Getting buy-in is crucial to successful coaching because, as Lindsay Kibler says, "no one can motivate you without your consent." Trying to motivate and push someone who hasn't consented is just nagging and pressure.

The era of the "my way or the highway" authoritarian coach is long over. We should stop trying to raise challenging boys in this way also (although it may have been the way you were raised). These coaches (and these parents) got compliance through fear of pain, punishment, and humiliation. In spite of what many people think, it didn't work then, and it doesn't work now. I've heard too many horrific stories from adults about how their parents' attempts to hold a hard line with them, or a challenging sibling, led to violence, abuse, or other terrible outcomes.

Coaches take the time to explain the "why" behind goals and plans in the player's terms. Players can't take ownership of a goal that they don't understand. An important part of the "why" comes from core values. As trusted and respected leaders, coaches are in a position to teach values like the importance of hard work, integrity, enthusiasm, honesty, and loving a challenge.

Similarly, in families, shared values contribute to a culture of cohesion and collaboration. Parents can say things like, "We Smiths believe in perseverance." Then when they see their son sticking with something, they can praise him by saying, "There's that Smith perseverance!"

Getting a player's buy-in doesn't mean that the coach accepts the player's initial idea of what is possible. Often coaches can see the player's potential more clearly and think bigger than the athlete can. In goal setting, the coach's job is to inspire the athlete to set and believe in a bigger goal.

The first thing to establish before trying to coach a challenging boy is that he has bought into the goals that you are trying to pursue. Establishing shared goals takes patience, listening, and problem-solving.

4. Great coaches are great listeners.

One of the ways coaches get buy-in is by being great listeners. Great coaches listen with full attention. They know that listening carefully builds trust and connection. It is a sign of respect. Listening makes people feel valued and validated. Coaches also know that the surest way to get listened to is to listen first. They don't assume that they know all the answers.

Listening is also key to getting buy-in with a challenging boy. Often our sons process things in ways that would surprise us and, as I said above, they frequently pretend to agree with our agenda when they really don't. You won't know that you are on the same page if you don't listen carefully to what your son says and does.

Great coaches know the difference between teaching and learning. Just because you *teach* a child something, it doesn't mean that he *learns* what you are trying to teach. Coaches ask for opinions and elicit feedback. They listen carefully in order to find out how their coaching is landing. This ensures that coaches are responsive to the unique needs and feelings of their athletes.

Great coaches further reflect on how it feels to be coached by them. They think about whether the way they are coaching is the way they would want to be coached themselves. They also ask their players how it feels to be coached by them and are prepared to engage with whatever feedback they receive. Get your journal out and ask yourself: "How does it feel for my son to be parented by me?" "How would I feel if someone interacted with me the way I treat him?" Maybe you also want to ask him: "How am I doing as a parent? What is going well? What needs to change?" He might see this as a trick or a trap. He might not take it seriously at first, but once he sees you are serious, listen very carefully to what he says. Be prepared for the possibility that he might be critical, so you'll be sure not to get defensive.

5. Great coaches empower players.

Another strategy that coaches use to get buy-in is that they share power. They don't impose values and goals. They work collaboratively with players to create them. This helps the players feel ownership over the process.

Coaches empower players to think, solve problems, and make decisions. This shows respect for the player as a partner, and it conveys the coach's belief in the player's ability to think for himself and make good decisions. The coach's belief in the player strengthens the player's belief in himself. It helps the athlete develop self-efficacy and confidence in their abilities.

Coaches don't immediately jump in and offer players solutions to problems, even when they believe they have the right answers. Instead, they create an environment that supports players to think independently. By posing questions and allowing time for thought, coaches support their players in solving their own problems. Coaches know that ultimately players are the ones who make the decisions on the field. The more practice they have in making decisions, the better those on-field decisions will be.

When coaching challenging boys, we want to help them learn to be good decision makers. We need to ask them what they think, not hand them answers. We don't do the thinking for them. Instead, we give them the support they need to think things through for themselves.

When I was in graduate school trying to learn how to work with pre-adolescents and adolescents in psychotherapy, I had a teacher who was very skilled at encouraging kids to think for themselves. When they would ask him for advice on how to handle a problem, he would scratch his head and say something like, "Wow, that's a tricky one. I wonder what someone does in a situation like that." Then he'd let some silence fall to convey that he was thinking hard about the problem. Eventually he'd ask, "Do you have any ideas?" What was so effective about this approach was that the kids didn't feel that their request for help was being rejected. They felt respected and taken seriously. They thought something like: "I guess there's not something wrong with me for not being able to figure this out, even an adult doesn't know what to do."

Often when we ask kids to come up with their own ideas, they feel like we have an answer in mind, but we're just making them work to figure out what it is. It feels condescending. In contrast, my teacher's patients felt that he was there to help. Encouraging them to think didn't mean leaving them alone to flounder. He was very present. He facilitated their thinking process with his questions and brainstorming.

6. Great coaches make things fun.

One of the most powerful ways that coaches get buy-in from players is by making things fun. Coaches are constantly trying to learn new ways to make practice an ever more enlivening and enjoyable experience for players. They know that people are the most motivated, learn the best, and work the hardest when they are having fun. They understand the power of play and spend a lot of time figuring out how to "gamify" drills to make them fun instead of tedious and boring. While some people think that fun and hard work are opposites, in actuality, the more fun players have and the more playful things are, the better they learn and the harder they try.

This is especially true with challenging boys. As I have discussed previously, challenging boys struggle to keep their arousal in the Goldilocks Zone. They can easily get overloaded (the Overwhelmed Zone), but they also can struggle to keep themselves alert and focused (the Low-Engagement Zone). Making things fun helps keep challenging boys engaged and learning skills that they would otherwise have a difficult time focusing on.

Coaches have fun too. They can be playful and goofy. As coach Jay Martin says, "Let's have fun and get this done." He is saying, "Let *us* have fun," not "You have fun, and I'll stay over here and be serious."

7. Great coaches are prepared.

Great coaches, like firefighters, are not winging it; they have plans and they are prepared. They go into each practice knowing what drills the team will be doing and what objectives they will be trying to accomplish. Great coaches also have game plans. They know their team, study their opponents, and make plans that address strategy and tactics for the game.

It's important to be prepared as the parent of a challenging boy. Preparation is in small things like having emergency food with you and in bigger things like knowing your exit strategy if you are entering a challenging situation. It means also knowing what skills you are currently working on with your son and what your "game plan" is for teaching them.

Game plans are like incident plans in firefighting. They give you the biggest chance of success. They let you know what to focus on and what your job is. You won't get confused, and you are less likely to get overwhelmed and lose your cool.

EMOTION COACHING

John Gottman's approach to emotion coaching a child in distress (as described in his excellent book *Raising an Emotionally Intelligent Child*) has five steps. Step 1: Tune in to your child's feelings. If your child is having a tantrum, explosion, meltdown, or shutdown, try to identify the feelings that are behind the misbehavior. We must inhibit our impulse to focus first on dealing with behavior. Step 2: Recognize your child's emotional distress as an opportunity for deepening your connection. Our gut reaction is to see distress as something negative. Step 3: Listen to your child empathically and validate his feelings. Step 4: Help your child put his feelings into words (to make them "mentionable and manageable"). Finally, Step 5: Problem solve and, if necessary, set limits on your child's behavior. Often, we make the mistake of skipping the important emotional processing work of Steps 1–4 and go straight to Step 5 and try to find solutions or set limits. Gottman's research suggests that this method of emotion coaching helps children learn to self-regulate and to develop better skills for solving emotional and interpersonal problems.

Gottman's emotion coaching framework is very useful to have in mind during an emotionally challenging situation with a child. Like any other form of coaching, it requires trust and connection in the parent-child relationship; the more work we have done on our relationship, the more likely our son will accept our emotion coaching. When doing Gottman-style emotion coaching with challenging boys, I'd add Step 6: Have an emergency plan and be prepared to remove the trigger or exit the situation.

Gottman's emotion coaching is analogous to a coach calling time-out during a game. Coaches call time-out when players are starting to get tired, dysregulated, or momentum is going against the team. Coaches use time-outs to co-regulate players, make adjustments, and to get the team refocused on the game plan.

Coaches don't just coach during games. They coach skill development during practice. Today's coaches are also more focused than ever on the mental and emotional aspects of their sports. Likewise, emotion coaching extends well beyond the coaching that happens during a challenging moment.

The biggest emotional challenge facing athletes is the fear of failure: "What if I make a mistake?" "What if I'm not any good?" "What if I never improve, no matter how hard I train?" "What if I commit myself to my goal, and give it my all and I still don't make it?" It's not just about falling short of a goal, but a fear of disappointing others, and of feeling worthless.

The fear of failure causes all types of problems for the athlete. It can lead him to avoid challenges or quit his sport altogether. It causes stress and negative physiological arousal, which impairs focus and performance. It can cause frustration, anger, and a loss of confidence.

One of the most important things a coach can teach a player is how to handle setbacks, frustrations, and defeats. A player can take risks if he knows that he can bounce back from the disappointment he'll experience if he fails. Athletes improve faster when they take risks. We need to stretch to be able to grow.

Challenging boys face similar struggles with fear of failure. Often, they feel that they can't succeed at school, can't please their parents, and can't manage their emotions. It can lead them to not try.

Modern coaches train athletes in strategies that help them with the mental and emotional aspects of sport. These strategies are vital for a challenging boy to adopt. Yet these boys frequently resist learning the "mental game." The discussion of emotion coaching below is meant to serve as an aspirational goal to strive toward. It's important to keep this framework in mind while you focus on creating more opportunities for coaching by building your relationship with your son.

Process Focus

I played competitive tennis growing up. I struggled with an intense fear of failure and felt terrible pressure every time I stepped on the court for a match. When I lost, I felt like a loser. This is how challenging boys feel in many areas of their lives. You might be able to relate this feeling to some of your own experiences.

My college coach, Thomas Johnston, was the first person to help me with this painful situation by teaching me how to have a process focus. Rather than focusing on the outcome (whether I won or lost), he advised me to focus on what I could control: how hard I worked in practice, my effort during a match, and sticking to my game plan.

When athletes focus on the process, losing is much easier to accept. Winning *and* losing are both experienced by the athlete as part of the process of growth and improvement. Mistakes become easier to bounce back from; they can be learned from and then let go. This helps players to take risks because their evaluation of themselves is based on whether they gave their best effort. Winning still feels great, and losing still hurts, but winning and losing are no longer the basis of your value as a person.

Adopting a process focus reduced the pressure I felt in matches because I no longer defined myself by winning and losing. I finally enjoyed playing the game. To my surprise, once I stopped focusing on winning, I won more than I ever had before. The reason being, I wasn't tight and stressed out. I wasn't judging myself based on a standard that I didn't control. With that stress removed I was in the Goldilocks Zone and could perform at my best.

Challenging boys have an especially difficult time handling disappointment and failure. As we have discussed, they are temperamentally prone to experiencing intense negative emotions and these emotions fade slowly. Also, the tendency to feel like a problem child leads the boy to turn disappointment into "I am a disappointment," a setback into "I am a failure," and a struggle to learn something into "I am stupid." We need to help him define himself by things in his control: his effort, his improvement, and his willingness to take risks and try.

We need to help our sons develop a process focus. Focusing on what you can control helps you feel in control. It's hard for challenging boys to do this because they so often face poor outcomes. They frequently lag behind their peers in their social and academic development. They also have a difficult time maintaining consistent effort because of challenges keeping their arousal in the Goldilocks Zone. They are often too low and unable to pay attention, or too high and unable to think.

It's easy to slip into outcome-oriented thinking as a parent. It's hard not to compare our son to his peers and feel that he's falling short. This leads to a lot of judgment. We judge ourselves as parents. We judge our son. Even if we never say any of these things, he can feel it.

When we are emotion coaching a challenging boy we need to deliver consistent, brief, and positive process-focused messages: "Mistakes are wonderful opportunities to learn" (Jane Nelson), "Do your best and forget the rest" (Tony Horton), "Focus on that which you can improve, correct, or change. Ignore what you can't control" (John Wooden).

Self-Regulation

We can do a lot to help keep our sons regulated through using co-regulation strategies. The ultimate goal of these efforts is for him to internalize this ability and regulate himself. One of the ways we can help with that as emotion coaches is to teach him techniques that he can use to calm down when he's overwhelmed. This is extraordinarily difficult to get a boy's buy-in on. We can easily relate. When we're in fight-or-flight mode what we really *want* is help addressing the problem that is triggering us, even if what we really *need* is to calm down and think clearly.

Coaches teach athletes to do breathing exercises to help them manage the anxiety and stress of games. Slow, deep breathing activates the body's calming response, which brings heart rate and arousal down and helps athletes stay calm and perform under pressure.

It's very popular now to teach children this tool for self-regulation. However, I see parents make several mistakes in trying to coach challenging boys in the use of their breath to self-regulate. First, we don't explain the "why" of breathwork to our sons so that they get it. "When you feel frustrated, take deep breaths to calm down" is not an intuitive idea. When we're in fight-or-flight mode, we believe that there is a real threat. That's a bad time to calm down. It's difficult to grasp that most of the time the actual threat is our dysregulation, not a thing happening in the world.

Remember the difference between teaching and learning. We might explain it, but if he doesn't get it, there won't be buy-in, and we won't have met a necessary condition of coaching. He'll just experience being told to breathe as yet another attempt to invalidate his experience and control him.

As I said in chapter 6, we need to practice any self-regulation strategies we want to teach our son. If we don't practice breathwork ourselves, we won't know what it does firsthand and it will be much harder to explain to our son why he should do it. Also, it will help us to realize that it is a practice, it's not magic.

Let him know when you use breathwork and what it does for you. For example, you could tell him how it helps you relax when you are in the dentist chair, or how it helps you feel more confident at work before a big presentation, or how it helps you not say hurtful things when something upsetting happens at home. Ultimately you want him to see breathwork as something that would be useful to him in moments of stress.

Second, we frequently introduce breathwork in the heat of the moment when we're desperate to get him regulated. This is sure to fail. Deep breathing, and other self-regulation techniques, must be taught and practiced in calm moments. The more our sons practice their breathing technique, the more that it will be there for them when they need it.

Third, we don't fully appreciate how using our breath to calm down is a big executive functioning challenge. Remember, the easiest thing to do is react. It takes a significant amount of inhibitory control to stop our reaction when we're overwhelmed. Then we need working memory to be able to call to mind that we should breathe instead. Finally, we need cognitive flexibility to shift our attention and efforts from "fighting or fleeing" an external threat and instead focus on our breath.

If we manage to get buy-in, there are many calming techniques that a child can be taught. Merely having him learn to monitor and slow down his breathing lowers his heart rate and has a calming effect on his nervous system. Other approaches include teaching abdominal breathing where the child focuses on inhaling using his diaphragm rather than raising his shoulders. Square breathing is yet another technique. In square breathing, the child is taught to breathe in a "square" pattern: inhale for a count of 4, hold the breath in for a count of 4, exhale for a count of 4, hold the breath out for a count of 4, and then repeat the sequence.

For boys who have difficulty focusing on their breath, progressive muscle relaxation (PMR) is a self-regulatory technique that can be tried. PMR typically starts at the feet. The muscles of the feet are contracted for five to ten seconds and then released. After a relaxation period of ten to twenty seconds, the calf muscles are contracted for five to ten seconds then released followed by ten to twenty seconds of relaxation. The procedure "progresses" one muscle group at a time all the way up to the muscles of the face. There are many wonderful resources—books, websites, YouTube videos—that show you how to teach these self-regulatory techniques.

Self-Talk

As preschoolers we all start to talk to ourselves. We do it to practice our developing language skills, as part of play, and to express our imagination. We also use self-talk to help regulate our emotions and to bolster executive functioning. It's as if we're a separate person supporting and encouraging ourselves as we perform tasks: to plan, focus, stay motivated and problem solve. Initially we talk to ourselves out loud, but by the time we're seven or eight self-talk happens silently as inner speech.

In addition to positive self-talk—where we enhance our emotion regulation and executive functioning by encouraging, reminding, and guiding ourselves—there is negative self-talk. Aaron Beck, founder of Cognitive Therapy, noticed that we all have a continuous stream of negative, self-critical inner talk that goes on almost unnoticed in the back of our minds: "I can't do this," "I'm stupid," or "I can't do anything right." This negative self-talk erodes confidence, harms self-esteem, and lowers motivation.

Coaches teach athletes to use positive self-talk to improve their performance and to keep negative self-talk at bay. They teach athletes phrases to repeat to themselves. To calm down: "Take a deep breath." To stay motivated: "You've got this!" To stay focused: "Play your game." To bounce back from a mistake: "You're still in this."

Challenging boys struggle to use positive, reassuring, and encouraging self-talk. They get flooded with harsh self-criticism: "You're a loser." "Nobody likes you." "Your parents hate you." As emotion coaches, we need to teach our challenging sons to use positive self-talk by giving them mantras they can repeat when stressed or upset: "I am strong enough to face my fears." "Mistakes are just opportunities to learn and improve." "This is tough, but so am I." "It's OK to feel upset, it will pass." Like a coach, he can use these mantras to give himself a pep talk.

To introduce the idea of self-talk, we can ask our son to think of a "mean" (critical, impatient) teacher or coach who made him feel discouraged and bad about himself. We can then contrast this with a supportive, encouraging coach and ask him to think about how much more confident he felt, how much more enjoyment he experienced, and how much better he did with this type of coaching. We can then explain that we have both types of "coaches" inside of us: a mean one who tears us down and an encouraging one who builds us up. We help him see that the goal is to strengthen the encouraging coach within us and quiet the critical one.

Reframe

We all have "lenses" or "frames" that we look at the world through. These frames can distort our perceptions. We can have a mental filter where we pay more attention to negative things that happen than to positive ones or where we blow negative events out of proportion. This type of negative bias can make us anxious or depressed and can impair performance. Coaches help athletes *re*-frame a negative frame into a positive one. For example, a negative frame on losses and mistakes is: "I'm a loser." A positive reframe is: "I can learn and grow from winning *and* losing." Coaches can help players reframe pregame nerves. Negative frame: "I'm nervous. I'll choke." Positive frame: "These butterflies are energy that will help me try hard in the game."

Helping challenging boys learn to reframe things is a challenging, but important emotion coaching task. They tend to have a pessimistic, disempowering frame. They are negative about the self: "I'm defective." They are negative about the world: "Things are stacked against me." And they are negative about the future: "I'll always be a failure." They experience setbacks as confirmation of their pessimistic view. If, for example, a boy did poorly on a test, he thinks: "I'm stupid" (defective self); "My teacher doesn't like me" (unfair world); or "I'll never go to college" (future failure). They also discount positive events, explaining them away as the result of luck or some other temporary and uncontrollable factor.

Challenging boys resist reframing. They can experience reframing as we're not taking their feelings seriously, that we're lying to them, that we're offering them false hope, or we're just being nice. Reframing should only be done after you have validated the boy's perspective. It would come in at Step 5 in Gottman's emotion coaching.

Psychiatrist David Burns suggests the following strategy for reframing. It is more likely to be effective with a challenging boy because it respects his need for the reframe to be convincing. Step 1: Identify the feelings. When a boy is upset about a bad grade, a problem with a friend, an issue with a teacher, a poor performance in a video game, a bad grade, etcetera, help him identify what he's feeling. For example, if your son isn't understanding what's going on in math class he might feel inadequate, hopeless, and frustrated. If he can't tell you, go through the list of emotion words from chapter 3 together and have him pick which feelings he's having. Step 2: For each of the main feelings, help him identify the negative thoughts behind the feelings. Along with feeling inadequate he has the thought: "I am stupid." With hopeless he thinks: "I'll never have a good job." Initially, he probably won't be aware that he has any thoughts connected to his feelings. You might have to suggest possibilities. Step 3: Ask him how much he believes the thoughts. This is a very important step. Challenging boys engage in all-or-none thinking. The purpose of this step is to help him learn how to get out of black-or-white thinking and into the grays. When we ask him, "How much do you believe you are stupid? 90 percent, 80 percent, 50 percent?" he will usually realize that he doesn't 100 percent believe the negative thought. If he says "100 percent," then you can respond, "So there's no part of you that believes even a little bit that you are not stupid?" Step 4: Look for a more believable positive reframe. The more believable part is key. He won't accept the reframe if it isn't convincing. Often your son will have trouble coming up with a more believable positive thought. If that is the case, you can offer him what you believe is a truer reframe. "Here's what I believe is true: You're not stupid, but math is hard. Lots of people who find math difficult still get good jobs. Look at your Uncle Jeff. He was terrible at math and he's doing well." Step 5: Ask him how much he believes the positive reframe. Also ask him how much he now believes his initial negative thought. You know you are succeeding if, after going through the steps, he believes his negative thought less and the positive reframe more. Remember your son is the judge of what is most believable.

Do this exercise yourself to reframe your own negative thoughts. It will help you feel better, and it will help you generate examples to give your son of how reframing works for you. Look at David Burns's book, *When Panic Attacks*, for more detailed instructions on how to do this type of reframing.

When facing an anxiety-provoking challenge, challenging boys expect it will go badly. Another reframing tool is to help him get more specific about his fears. When we're anxious, our fears tend to be very vague. Psychologist Ellen Hendricksen suggests asking four questions to make fears more specific and more manageable: (1) What exactly are you afraid of? (2) How likely is it to happen? (3) How bad would it be? And (4) How would you cope? Asking these questions can reduce anxiety tremendously. In taking the boy through the questions, and eventually teaching him to ask them himself, he might find that the thing he fears is very unlikely, or wouldn't be so bad, or he could cope with it easily. This helps him to feel less anxious.

Practice and Visualization

Coaches and firefighters understand the importance of practice. To be able to perform a difficult skill, especially to perform it under pressure, requires that it be well learned and well practiced. Coaches set up drills in practice to simulate game situations. They often also add a competitive element to make it even more like a game. Similarly, firefighters use smoke generators and burn buildings to practice under conditions that simulate real fires. Practice is crucial for challenging boys. As discussed in chapter 8, practice is often an important part of jump-starting a rewards program.

Athletes also use visualization to prepare themselves for games. They visualize how they want to feel and how they want to perform. For situations where it's hard to practice, we can use visualization with our challenging sons. If our son gets overwhelmed during math class, we could help him visualize the situation. He could imagine not being able to understand a concept and starting to get upset. Then he could imagine employing his self-regulation skills. He could visualize himself remembering to breathe, saying his mantra ("you don't understand this now, but you will get it"), and reframing ("math is hard").

EXAMPLES OF COACHING INTERVENTIONS
Phone Use

Thirteen-year-old Daniel's parents are concerned about his phone use. He reaches for it the minute he gets up. He has it on in the bathroom when he's getting ready in the morning, he watches it while he eats breakfast, and it's on in the car on the way to school. After school he often lies in bed with his phone instead of getting started on homework.

Daniel and his parents fight frequently over his phone. His parents set a rule that his phone should be left in the hall when he goes to bed and no phones at the dinner table. Daniel refuses to comply. His mom tries motivating him by citing research that identifies mental health problems associated with this type of compulsive phone use. It has no effect. His parents consider shutting the phone off, and sometimes the conflicts escalate to the point where they are physically fighting with Daniel over the phone.

It's probably obvious from this description that this is not a situation where coaching will be effective. There is little cooperation between Daniel and his parents. They do not agree on what the problem is and therefore on what the goal is. In his parents' minds, Daniel's phone is the problem. In *his* mind it is the solution.

If the communication was better between them, Daniel might acknowledge that the problem is that he feels anxious and that his phone is the only reliable coping strategy that he currently has. Even if they could agree on what the problem is—that Daniel feels bad—his parents, quite logically, would think that the appropriate thing to do would be to teach him a new coping strategy while limiting his phone use. Daniel, on the other hand, has never found any of the strategies that his parents have tried to teach him helpful. Unfortunately, Daniel also feels significant mistrust toward his parents; it doesn't feel safe to work together with them. He experiences them as trying to control him and impose things on him. They say they want to help, but then do unhelpful things. They take his phone away, and he ends up feeling more alone and awful than ever.

A contrasting situation is Grant, also thirteen, who also spends a lot of time on his phone. He doesn't bring the phone to the dinner table, but he does turn to it first thing in the morning and spends a lot of time on it after school when he needs to be doing homework. Grant's phone frustrates his parents, and they can get reactive and try to control his use, leading to friction and fights (he is a challenging boy after all!). Grant's parents have worked hard to improve their communication and trust with him. They decide it's worth trying a coaching approach. Grant's dad asks Grant if he thinks his phone use is getting in the way of other things, like homework. Grant is reluctant to agree and insists that he can handle things if his parents would just leave him alone. Grant's dad says that he himself is on his phone too much checking work emails and scrolling Facebook. They don't yet agree on goals, so Grant's dad focuses on the coaching approach of *getting buy-in*. He proposes a plan. He and Grant's mother will not say anything about Grant's phone use for the following week. In exchange, he and Grant will both try to reduce their phone use during the week. At the end of the week, they will look at their screen time together. Grant agrees.

Grant's parents upheld their side of the plan and didn't nag, although it was very difficult because Grant was on his phone a lot. As a result, there was no fighting over the phone. Grant also did his part. He and his dad looked at their screen time at the end of the week. The dad's screen time was slightly reduced while Grant's almost doubled. Grant acknowledged that he had a lot of difficulty controlling his phone use without his parents' nagging and it was leading to him getting started on his homework late. They brainstormed some options. Grant and his dad agreed to set screen time limits on their phones (Tik Tok for Grant and Facebook for his dad) and give the other person the password.

As you can see in this example, the fights over phone use were able to be solved in a collaborative way. Grant's relationship with his parents was a key ingredient. They had trust and the ability to work together. His father's willingness to lead by example was also important.

Getting Ready for School

Fourteen-year-old Noah was having a hard time getting up for school in the morning. His mom, Amanda, would go into his room and raise the shades and nag him to get up. This would invariably lead to arguments. Noah and Amanda did have the same goal. They both wanted him to get to school on time. They disagreed, however, on how to achieve that goal. Amanda thought Noah needed help getting up. Noah wanted to get himself up. Amanda decided to take a coaching approach and *empower* Noah. She told Noah that she respected his desire to handle getting to the bus on time himself and she would let him figure it out. She said she was available to give him any help he needed but would wait to be asked. Noah thought this was a good plan.

The next morning, Noah didn't get up and missed the bus. It was very difficult for Amanda to stand by and watch this, but she didn't say anything. When Noah finally got up, he was upset and stressed out about being late for school. Amanda, who was working from home, offered him a ride. Some would argue that Amanda shouldn't have driven Noah to school, that he should feel the natural consequence of getting up late. Amanda thought that Noah was clearly trying, and he was upset enough at not getting up on time. She thought driving him in would reinforce the fact that they were working together.

On the drive to school, Noah talked about his ideas for how he would be sure to get up the next day: setting two alarms and placing his phone across the room so he'd have to get up out of bed to turn it off. Amanda said that those sounded like great ideas. She reminded Noah that she'd be going to the office the next day, so she wouldn't be able to drive him in if he was late. On the second day of Noah being in charge, he missed the bus again. He had to ride his bike and was late for school. That evening, Noah told Amanda that he realized that he did need her help getting up in the morning. She agreed to start helping him again. Because now it was done with his permission (an important part of coaching), it didn't lead to fights.

Emotion Coaching and Reframing during a Meltdown
Nine-year-old Mason had recently made a new friend, Eli. Mason came home from a playdate at Eli's and set to work trying to make something in the game platform, Scratch. It was for a project that he and Eli had started on the playdate. After a few minutes

Mason became very frustrated and started hyperventilating. His dad, Jonathan, came in to try to help. He had Mason breathe into a bag. Empathizing, he asked Mason if he was so upset because he couldn't figure out Scratch, or if he was worried that Eli would stop liking him and not want to be his friend anymore—the same way his former friend Nate had. Through his sobbing, Mason stuttered out, "Th-the sec-ond one."

Jonathan tried the coaching approach of *reframing*. He reminded Mason that the stories we tell ourselves determine how we feel. He said that Mason's story is that Nate rejected him, and it felt terrible. Mason agreed. Jonathan said that his memory of the situation was different. What he remembered was that Mason felt that Nate was mean and wasn't a good friend and that Mason decided to not be friends with him anymore. After that, Nate got mad and tried to make Mason feel bad. "In my story," Jonathan continued, "which in my view is the true story, you rejected Nate." Mason thought about it and decided his dad was right and it helped him calm down.

Exercise and Fun

Sometimes coaching interventions can be simple, but highly effective. Justin, dad of twelve-year-old challenging boy Alexander, was concerned about Alexander's lack of physical activity. After a number of failed attempts to encourage Alexander to exercise more, Justin's dad decided to try the coaching approach of motivation through *making things fun*. He bought two inexpensive step tracker watches and challenged Alexander to a competition to see who could do more steps in a week. At the end of the week, they'd go out to dinner and the winner would get to pick the restaurant. Justin also made a big chart and put it on the side of the fridge to track the progress of the competition. They had fun looking at the numbers on the chart and trash talking each other about their progress. For Alexander and Justin, the fun of this competition got them both moving more. It also had the added benefit of helping them connect in the shared activity of the competition and in going out to eat together.

Supporting Your Son in Pursuing His Goals

In parenting, it's so much more rewarding to coach your child to achieve his goals. Twelve-year-old Tyler loved video games. He told his dad, Brian, that he wanted to be a game designer for his favorite video game company when he grew up. Brian decided to do some research on what it took to become a video game designer. He found an online game design course for kids and suggested that he and Tyler take it together. They made a basic game, and Tyler was thrilled to play it with his friends.

With challenging boys sometimes these interests fade, but Tyler's desire to work for a video game company increased. Brian found more and more ways to support Tyler's goal. He found them other classes to take, branching out into coding languages like C++. For his thirteenth birthday, Brian booked a tour at the game company where Tyler wanted to work. He also got Tyler to look at job listings at the company with him. They saw that becoming a software engineer was the way to get the kind of job that Tyler wanted. They researched how to be a software engineer and saw that it required math and science skills. Brian and Tyler, for the first time, were able to work together on *Tyler's goal* of doing well in math, instead of Brian fighting with him to get his homework done.

COACHES AS ROLE MODELS

Coaches understand that their influence extends far beyond the skills that they teach. Players look to them as models for how to conduct themselves in practice, at games, and in life. Similarly, challenging boys learn much from modeling their parents.

As emotion coaches, it is particularly important to model healthy self-regulation strategies. By doing so, we not only improve our own lives, but we also become better equipped to teach these strategies effectively. We need to set an example of taking responsibility for one's own feelings and reactions. We need to practice using our breath to navigate through challenging episodes, monitor our self-talk, and develop positive mantras to help us stay positive, confident, and composed in challenging moments. Additionally, we need to develop our capacity to reframe our negative biases so that we don't overreact to, and overgeneralize from, disappointments and frustrations.

Finally, as role models, we need to take a process approach, not just with our sons, but also with ourselves. We need to stay focused on effort and improvement rather than blaming ourselves or feeling like failures because of our son's challenges. Our parenting mistakes should be viewed as opportunities to learn rather than reasons to beat ourselves up. We need to set an example of working hard, having fun, and accepting our successes and setbacks as part of the process of growth.

KEY IDEAS

- Our ultimate aim is for our challenging son to develop the skills and motivation necessary to take responsibility for his challenging nature and his life. To accomplish this, we must transition from being the chief who is in charge to being a coach who supports him in taking charge of his own life.

- For coaching to succeed, certain conditions need to be met: trust and connection in the parent-child relationship, a regulated parent and a regulated child, shared goals, and mutual openness to influence.

- A coaching mindset includes an emphasis on emotional connection as the foundation of growth, gentleness, getting buy-in, being a great listener, empowerment, making things fun, and being prepared.

- Emotion Coaching involves teaching the boy process focus, self-regulation strategies, positive self-talk, reframing, as well as teaching him to use practice and visualization.

- Being a good coach also means striving to be a good role model.

PARENTING JOURNAL EXERCISES

- Ask yourself: How does it feel for my son to be parented by me? How would I feel if someone interacted with me the way I treat him?

- Ask your son: "How am I doing as a parent? What is going well? What needs to change?" What can you learn from his answers?

- Reflect on your beliefs about discipline. How do these beliefs shape your interactions with your son? How do they interfere with taking a more collaborative approach with him?

- Where are you and your son regarding discipline tools? Does it feel like the only thing that gets his attention is punishment? Have you been able to create a successful reward program? Do you have experience taking a coaching approach to a problem?

- Are there any problems, like the ones in the examples above, where you might take a coaching approach? If there is, describe your coaching plan. If there isn't, which of the preconditions for coaching haven't you met: trust? shared goals? openness to influence?

- What aspect of emotional self-care is the most important for you to improve: having a process focus, breathwork, self-talk, or reframing?

- Write about a time when your son resisted your attempts to coach him. What might have been the underlying reasons for his resistance, and how can you address these in the future?

CHAPTER TEN

Bringing It All Together

Congratulations! I want to thank you and applaud you for taking your valuable time to read *Challenging Boys*. We've covered a lot of territory. At the end of chapter 6, I likened our journey to that of going through the fire academy. In the fire academy cadets learn how fires start and behave, the techniques of firefighting, and about fire prevention strategies. In the *Challenging Boys Academy*, you've learned where challenging behavior comes from, tactics for managing challenging episodes, and the tools and strategies for preventing challenging behavior in the future. You're now prepared for active duty.

I hope after reading this book that compassion for yourself has replaced criticism. No one knows better than you how hard it is being the parent of a challenging boy. Other people have no idea what you're up against—unless they have a challenging child themselves. It feels incredibly isolating. Not only does no one understand what you're going through, they judge you. Family, friends, and strangers believe that your son's challenges are your fault. You used to believe it was your fault too. You thought, "I must be doing something wrong because no one else's kid is acting like this." You felt like a complete failure as a parent. It is terrible to have to deal with all the intense feelings that challenging behavior evokes—frustration, rage, sadness, helplessness, hopelessness, despair—and believe that it is the result of your bad parenting. I hope that I've convinced you of the truth of

Dr. Greenspan's words: "You're not the cause, but you can be the solution."

You can stop blaming yourself for your son's problems with challenging behavior because it's not your fault. You can stop blaming your child's other parent. It's not their fault either. You can stop blaming your son also. He's not a bad kid. Your son doesn't want to defy you, disrespect you, fight with you, or challenge your authority. He wants to get along. He wants to succeed. He wants you to be happy with him. It's not *willfulness* that causes challenging behavior. It's a lack of *skillfulness*. He simply does not have the skills he needs to comply.

You've learned that his challenging behavior actually results from his being born with a challenging temperament that includes difficulties with negative emotion (the frequent and intense experience of anger, frustration, sadness, fear, and anxiety) and challenges with self-regulation (the ability to manage and control emotion, attention, impulses, and behavior). As he grows up, his challenging temperament is amplified by struggles with the core executive functioning skills of inhibitory control, working memory, and cognitive flexibility. These factors create conditions for your son where it's extremely difficult for him to follow rules and comply with requests that his peers can handle easily.

I hope this new understanding has helped you take his challenging behavior less personally. I hope also that it has helped you feel more empathy and compassion for your son. It's very difficult being a challenging boy. The adults in your life are frequently mad, upset, or disappointed in you. Other kids often don't want to play with you. It feels like you're constantly being told that there's something wrong with you and that you need to be different from how you are. It can feel like the whole world is against you. You don't feel like a child with a problem. You feel like you *are* the problem. You feel like a problem child.

One of the hardest parts of being the parent of a challenging boy is knowing that you are supposed to remain calm in challenging moments, but despite your best efforts you are frequently unable to do so. You get caught in a painful cycle of resolving to not lose your cool, trying hard to stay calm, often doing great for a while, but then finally losing it. This is followed by the experience of intense shame, guilt, and feeling like you are the worst parent in the world.

You now know why it's so incredibly difficult to stay calm during a challenging episode. First, challenging behavior is highly provocative. Frequently our sons challenge us personally: they blame us ("You're ruining my life!"), they reject us ("I wish you weren't my parent!"), they defy our authority ("I don't have to listen to you!"), they malign our character ("You're an idiot!"), and they attack our confidence ("No one could be a worse parent than you!"). They fight with us, or what can be even harder to deal with, they just refuse to do things. As if life as a parent wasn't hard enough! It's so upsetting, maddening, and disruptive.

It's also incredibly hard to stay calm during a challenging episode because we feel so much pressure. We feel under a microscope with all the judgment from others. They think they are parenting experts because they have typical children. Having typical kids makes you feel like a good parent because they'll do fine pretty much no matter what you do. You can even be a "my way or the highway" parent and things will probably work out. This is not true for challenging boys. Holding the line, setting hard limits, and never giving in will only lead to awful escalation.

Yet another reason it's difficult to stay calm during a challenging episode is that challenging behavior tends to polarize parents. Most couples begin parenthood with similar parenting values. One parent is typically somewhat more oriented toward empathizing with the child's experience but thinks that being firm is important also. The other parent is a little more focused on being firm, but also values understanding the child's experience. When challenging behavior enters the equation, parents tend to become more extreme in their positions. The empathic parent becomes increasingly identified with the child, while the firmer parent moves toward a more and more hardline stance. This creates tension in the home, which significantly stresses challenging boys, as they sense on some level that they are the cause of it. The tension also makes their parents less patient. As a result, this strained climate in the family increases the likelihood of a challenging episode, and once an episode has started, the conflict between the parents fuels an escalation. They get caught in pulling against each other believing that they must "protect" their child from the other parent's permissiveness or harshness. Add blended families into the mix and it gets even more complicated.

Finally, on a very deep level, we've learned that it's so incredibly difficult to remain calm during a challenging episode because of the powerful feelings that challenging behavior triggers in us. Of course there is the pain of our misplaced self-blame, but beyond that, challenging behavior sends us back in time emotionally and we reexperience the painful feelings from the traumas of our own childhoods. We *feel* the bad feelings, but we don't consciously remember the past events. This makes it feel vividly as if our intense reactions are about what is going on in the here and now of the challenging episode. We're triggered into fight-or-flight mode, which shuts down our thinking, and we overreact rather than being thoughtful and responsive.

Given all these strong feelings and pressures, no wonder you haven't been able to consistently keep your cool. Also, during challenging moments we've mostly been winging it. We don't receive any training on how to be a parent, especially not the parent of a challenging boy. We end up doing some combination of what our parents did, what our instincts tell us, what others tell us to do, and what we've read or heard. In *Challenging Boys,* we learned that the way to stay calm is to have a plan for challenging episodes. Plans help us be like firefighters. Firefighters remain calm and effective because they are not trying to make decisions during the stress of a fire scene. We need to have emergency plans worked out ahead of time so that in the heat of a challenging episode all we have to do is execute the plan.

In chapter 3, we started using our parenting journal to gather data about our son's challenging episodes so that we could start building our emergency plan. Our journal entries helped us discover where and when our son gets triggered, as well as how his challenging episodes typically play out. It also helped us learn about our own triggers and about what types of feelings and reactions from the past the challenging episodes evoke in us. I hope that you have been taking the time to work on the journal exercises. When we're caught up in a cycle of challenging behavior problems, it's very difficult to see what is happening objectively. Working in the journal helps us get some distance from the situation and see it more clearly. If you take the time to do the parenting journal exercises and have a written plan, you'll be amazed at the results.

Let's return to the Ross family, eight-year-old Josh and his parents, Chris and Andrea, from chapter 1. Andrea learned from her journal that one of Josh's main triggers is going to unstructured social situations: playdates, sports practices, birthday parties. He might say that he wants to do these things, but when the time comes, he can refuse to go. Andrea could also see in her journal entries that setting a firm limit almost always led to a huge escalation where Josh would get physically aggressive, run out of the house, or do some other very upsetting thing.

Andrea also learned from her journaling how she and Chris get triggered by Josh's challenging episodes. Chris wouldn't act like himself. His reaction to Josh's refusals would, at first, be way too intense. Andrea would feel in these moments that she needed to protect Josh from Chris's anger. However, her actions to get Chris to calm down only inflamed him more. Then he'd abruptly abandon her with a massively dysregulated Josh. She felt frightened and utterly alone in these moments.

Andrea's journaling helped her connect her intense feelings during challenging episodes to childhood experiences. At first, Chris's angry reaction evoked feelings of fear and anger related to her mom who would fly off the handle at the slightest provocation. In these moments Andrea would try to calm her mother down and protect her little sister. Chris's walking away from her and Josh would bring up how she felt as a kid when her father would travel for business and leave Andrea and her sister alone to handle their emotionally volatile mother. All these intense feelings were taking a toll on Chris and Andrea's relationship.

Before journaling, Andrea believed that her feelings during these challenging events were about what was happening with Chris and Josh today, but she now understood that she was triggered. She didn't know exactly what was going on with Chris, but the extreme nature of his reactions made it clear to her that Chris was triggered also. What was happening with Josh wasn't good, but being triggered into their childhood traumas made the situation much worse. Armed with this data, Andrea was able to approach Chris with what she'd learned, and they were able to make an emergency plan together.

Their plan looked like this. Step 1: If Josh refused to go to some scheduled event, they would first focus on his feelings. They'd empathize with and validate his anxiety about social situations. Step 2: If Josh seemed responsive and was starting to calm down, they would then try reminding him that he'll have fun and that his friends and teammates will miss him if he doesn't go. Step 3: If Steps 1 and 2 aren't gaining any traction, then they will stop encouraging Josh to go and see if that will help him calm down. Step 4: After fifteen minutes or so of giving him room to calm down, they will see if Josh is open to going late. If he isn't, then they'll give him fifteen more minutes. If after two of these attempts, he still isn't able to go, they will stop trying.

Steps 3 and 4 were extremely hard for Chris. He felt like it was giving in and letting the inmate run the prison. Andrea assured him that the emergency plan was a temporary measure to de-escalate things in their family. She proposed that she be the one to implement the plan when she is around (which she almost always was). All that Chris had to do was stay present and not interfere. The most important part of the plan is that they agreed that they would support each other emotionally. Chris and Andrea created a code word they could use during challenging episodes to remind each other to follow the plan and remain a team.

Andrea's journal entries were helpful in getting Chris to buy-in. He didn't want to set up their son to fail. He could see that trying to force Josh almost always led to an explosion. Andrea could show Chris how challenging episodes typically started, how they escalated, and how they ended with all three of them—Chris, Andrea, and Josh—all feeling bad about themselves and feeling bad about each other.

Their emergency plan didn't go perfectly at first. It was very hard for Chris to not insist that Josh go. Andrea and Chris were able to debrief after trying to implement the plan in a few challenging episodes. They decided it would work better if Chris disengaged right away and went to another room to calm down. Because his walking away was part of an agreed upon plan, it didn't feel like an abandonment to Andrea. It felt like they were on the same team. Tweaking their plan soon led to far fewer power struggles and it helped Andrea and Chris to feel better about themselves, each other, and Josh. It was a vast improvement.

Empowered with the success of their emergency plan, Chris and Andrea were able to plan together for a special circumstance that came up that had a very high risk of leading to a bad challenging episode. Chris's brother was finally getting married. Chris and Andrea knew that the ceremony and reception afterward would be potentially overwhelming situations for Josh. He might refuse to go, or demand to leave once there. He might cause a scene and shine a painful spotlight on Chris and Andrea's parenting in front of the judgmental eyes of Chris's parents and extended family. It was very stressful to think about and led to a lot of worry.

They decided on the following emergency plan for the wedding. You might remember from chapter 1 that Andrea and Chris were afraid to leave Josh with a sitter because of his challenging nature. In working the journal exercise about what one thing they could change that would make a big impact, Andrea thought about the problem of not being able to use a sitter. She got Chris to brainstorm with her. They eventually came up with the idea of placing an ad at a local college for a "big brother." From that ad, they hired Sean. He had been a high school athlete and was up for endless hours of soccer in the backyard or basketball in the driveway. There was no fear of Sean being physically overpowered by Josh, and it never happened anyway. Josh looked up to Sean and thought he was very cool. Also, all the exercise they did together helped keep Josh in the Goldilocks Zone.

Andrea and Chris got Chris's brother and fiancée's agreement to bring Sean to the wedding as a guest. Sean and Josh could stay as little or as long as Josh wanted. If Josh refused to go to the wedding, Sean and Josh would stay home. If Josh needed to leave the ceremony or reception, they felt confident that Sean could handle getting Josh home with minimal disruption. This allowed Chris and Andrea to actually look forward to the wedding rather than approach the day with dread.

Having an emergency plan isn't the end of the story. It's just the beginning. However, for most parents it's a huge relief. It takes a lot of pressure off to know that you don't need to take a hardline approach when your son is being challenging. You can finally relax as tension in the house decreases with the decrease in conflict. Most of all, it is a big boost of confidence to know exactly what to do when challenging behavior occurs. Everyone feels better and you're finally able to remain calm.

After creating an emergency plan, in chapter 4 you set out on the vital work of rebuilding your relationship with your son. Challenging behavior starts a negative spiral that leads to reactions in parents that worsen and escalate the situation. Eventually the parents and the boy feel alienated from each other and trust and connection in the parent-child relationship is eroded. You learned that your relationship repair work will become the foundation for your son's growth and change. It is what will enable you to finally move past the challenging behavior problems that have had such a negative impact on all of your lives.

In this book I told you about three "magic ratios" to keep in mind when it comes to rebuilding your relationship with your son. First is Jay Martin's 22:2. This ratio refers to the amount of time that needs to be devoted to building our relationship with our sons (22 hours) per every 2 hours that we spend working on teaching him new skills and helping him to change. Change and growth happen in the context of a strong relationship. This ratio helps us to remember to always prioritize relationship building work as we seek to help our son learn to master his challenging nature.

The second magic ratio is John Gottman's 5:1. Too often challenging behavior problems lead parent-child relationships to become overwhelmingly dominated by negativity. Gottman's ratio reminds us to think about engaging in five times as many positive interactions with our sons as negative ones. A positive tone leads to a strong parent-child relationship and forms the basis for the boy's development of confidence, healthy self-esteem, and resilience.

To achieve Gottman's magic ratio we learned to decrease negative interactions like criticizing our son's character ("you're lazy"), condescension ("you'll thank me later"), and defensiveness ("how dare you speak to me that way!"). We also learned ways to increase positive interactions. Being playful, paying careful attention, giving affection, and expressing appreciation are all great positive things to do daily. We learned that a particularly positive action is focusing on accepting our son as fully as we can. Acceptance is very healing and paradoxically clears the way for change. Understanding, accepting, and validating our son's feelings helps convey our acceptance of him.

Of course nobody is perfect. We're all going to slip and do hurtful things, or things that will otherwise set us back in our efforts to rebuild our relationship. When this occurs it's very positive to apologize and make amends. A thoughtful, heartfelt apology can sometimes leave our relationship even stronger than if we had never slipped up at all. Apologizing also models for our sons how to take responsibility for one's mistakes and do the work of repair.

The last "magic ratio" that we learned about is my 9:1 ratio of validation to influence. If we are going to be able to help our son overcome his problems with challenging behavior, we need him to be open to our influence. It is paradoxical that validating what our son thinks, feels, and believes is precisely the way to get him to change what he thinks, feels, and believes. Validation lowers resistance and leads to greater openness. We lay the groundwork for influence by helping our child feel understood, accepted, and *validated*. It takes effort and persistence. My 9:1 ratio reminds us that we need to do a lot of validating (validation that our son experiences as accurate and sincere) before we will have prepared the way for his openness to our influence.

Returning to Andrea and Chris, their emergency plan was a temporary measure. Chris couldn't have signed on to it if it were not. Andrea and Chris want Josh to be someone who can honor his commitments, do the things he enjoys, and not be overwhelmed and paralyzed by anxiety. They set to work to improve their relationship with Josh to create the foundation for change.

One area that Andrea and Chris particularly needed to focus on was acceptance. Josh's older sister, Mia, was easygoing, friendly, hardworking, and seemed to effortlessly succeed at everything she tried. She was an easy child who always made them feel good and look good as parents. They often felt guilty about how much of their time and attention was devoted to Josh. It felt to them like they were neglecting Mia. Andrea and Chris had to accept that Josh was going to need more from them than Mia and that life for Josh was simply going to be more challenging.

As Andrea and Chris worked on understanding and accepting Josh, they were able to appreciate how thoughtful and empathic he could be when he was in a good emotional space. As they let go of feeling pressured to get him to practice and games, when he did go, they were able to appreciate how physically gifted he is. In an effort to find an activity for him and Josh to do together, Chris stumbled across an article that said that fishing was a good activity for kids with challenging behavior. It turned out that Josh loved it. It became a regular activity. It also gave them additional ways to connect when they weren't fishing. They would search online together to find new fishing spots, look at equipment, and find places they were interested in traveling to for fishing trips. Things were really improving in their relationship.

In chapter 5, we learned important lessons about communication. We learned that there are two distinct goals in communication with our sons and that we should avoid mixing the two goals in a single conversation. One goal of communication is to get our son to talk to us and open up to us. We want to be closer to him and to build an increasingly more accurate understanding of how he thinks and feels. We learned that it's important to prioritize, above all else, making talking with us a positive experience. The second goal of communication is that we also want our son to listen to us. We can't teach if he won't listen. We learned some helpful guidelines to encourage him to listen: listen to be heard, begin with a gentle start-up, and keep our conversations brief (remember the rule that it's better to have twenty-five one-minute conversations than one twenty-five-minute conversation).

Chris discovered that fishing provided a great setting for talking with Josh. Chris could bring something up, they could talk for a minute and then let the silence fall again (a version of twenty-five one-minute conversations). Chris learned quite a bit from these talks. He learned that Josh felt that he and Andrea didn't understand him. It upset him that they got mad when he didn't get off his video games right away. They didn't understand that he needed to finish the game because there were other kids playing with him on a team. Weren't they the ones who said it's important to honor your obligation to your teammates? Josh also felt that Andrea and Chris didn't understand boys. In Josh's view, boys are hyperactive and they like video games. It seemed to him that his parents preferred girls because they are quieter and like to read, like Mia.

Josh eventually let Chris know that he felt very bad about himself. He felt they (Andrea, Chris, and Mia) were all so perfect and he ruined the family. Josh also knew that his high energy and impulsivity bothered people. It was part of what made him anxious in social situations; he didn't know who he was going to upset. Of course, it was painful for Chris to hear how much Josh was suffering, but it was hopeful too. Now they could start working on these problems instead of fighting.

In chapter 6, we learned that our son needs to be well regulated to be able to learn well. He needs to be in that sweet spot of arousal that is not too high and not too low, but just right: the Goldilocks Zone. We learned strategies for tuning in to ourselves so that we can be open to our son's emotions and arousal. We learned strategies for co-regulation through helping him manage his environment, his body, and his emotions. These strategies help our son get into the Goldilocks Zone so that he's ready to learn.

Beginning in chapter 7, we learned about the tools of discipline: punishments, rewards, and coaching—and when and how to use each. We learned about the pitfalls of punishments and the power of positive reinforcement—especially catching our sons being good. We also learned how to set up an effective rewards program for teaching new skills. Finally, we learned about the power of coaching. We learned that when the conditions are met (trust and connection, regulated parent and child, shared goals, and openness to influence), we can be on the same team with our son. Helping him to achieve his goals.

Armed with an emergency plan and with an improving relationship, things were much happier and more peaceful in the Ross household. Josh still had difficulties getting to playdates, practices, games, and birthday parties, but these situations didn't escalate anymore. Chris and Andrea felt much better about each other also and were taking advantage of the opportunity Sean provided to go on dates.

In the past, Chris and Andrea had primarily relied on punishments to deal with Josh's challenging behavior. They took away his Xbox, they lectured him on his responsibilities, they made him write apology letters, and even made him take a season off from soccer (remember from chapter 7, don't take away as punishments things that you want your son to be doing). This approach did not work, and things were frequently escalating to the point where they were yelling and threatening Josh with punishments. On one occasion things got so heated that Chris physically forced Josh into the car to take him to a game. Chris and Andrea hated losing their cool, but they believed that punishments were the only leverage they had. And they felt it would be irresponsible parenting to back down and not punish Josh for leaving his teammates in the lurch by not going to practice or games.

Persuaded by the benefits of the emergency plan and of his work to improve his relationship with Josh, Chris found it easier to shift his focus from punishments to rewards. He and Andrea made it a point to stop unintentionally reinforcing Josh's negative behavior with their angry attention and they began looking for opportunities to catch him being good. They also decided to create a rewards program. They focused the program first on helping Josh get to practice, which was the most frequent cause of his refusal. They created a program where Josh would get three points for going to practice on time, two points for going fifteen minutes late, and one point for going thirty minutes late. Andrea and Chris made a prize box of small items and the big prize at the end of the program was earning a special fishing trip with Chris. Almost immediately, the plan enabled Josh to get to practice more often, even if late—a dramatic improvement.

Another thing that Chris and Andrea decided was to seek help from a mental health professional. They could see now, after all the progress they'd made, that Josh really wanted to do well: for them to be pleased with him and to have friends. They could also see that Josh was really suffering from big negative feelings. They could use the help of an expert. After speaking with Josh's pediatrician, the psychologist at school, and friends, they came up with the names of a few potential therapists. After interviewing each to find out about their experience in working with families like theirs and kids like Josh, Chris and Andrea decided on a therapist who felt like a good fit.

With the power struggles over, gradually Josh could see that *he* wanted to be on the team. *He* loved soccer. *He* wanted to be a good teammate. And *he* wanted to be at practice. However, his anxiety paralyzed him and made it hard to go. He finally felt that it was *his* responsibility to get to practice, but he did need his parents' help. He was ready for coaching.

Wherever you started on this journey, the tools and concepts I have presented here will help you move your son along the path of greater cooperation, of improved ability to regulate himself, and of taking increased responsibility for his feelings and his life. My goal has been to help you feel confident and not confused as a parent, so that no matter what challenges your son presents, you will know how to make a plan for how to respond to them.

I've also wanted to present a philosophy of parenting that you can apply to any challenge with any child. The philosophy has three pillars. (1) As Ross Greene says, "Kids do well if they can." This actually applies to almost everyone: spouses, bosses, teachers, siblings, parents, and us. We all want to do well, but we don't always have the skills to do so. If your kid is being challenging, let's no longer view it as opposition. Instead, let's understand that he wants to do well, but that he is lacking some skill that we need to help him acquire. (2) Our relationship is the foundation for all change. If our child is having problems, we need to invest the majority of our efforts into cultivating trust, connection, and communication between us. (3) Our ultimate goal is to find ways to work together. Let's limit the use of punishments and use reward programs instead. Let's work on building our relationship and collaboration so that we are working together as a team. As trust, connection, understanding, and acceptance increase, we can gradually shift to focusing on coaching as our primary approach to discipline. If we hold in mind these three principles—understanding our child's challenges in a positive light, seeing our relationship as central to change, and working to make our relationship a collaboration in the service of bettering everyone's life—we'll be ready to confidently handle almost any situation.

I hope that you have already seen benefits from this program and that your home is happier and more connected than it has been in a long time. It's important to keep in mind that change isn't linear and that regressions are bound to happen. A few examples of the many situations that can lead to temporary setbacks are if your son gets sick, changes school, or goes through puberty. Every fall season, because they so desperately want to do well, challenging boys feel a swell of motivation to have a better year at school. "This year is going to be different," they pledge to themselves. They start off strong, but by October or November many of them find their motivation weakening and there is backsliding. If this happens, don't panic. It's natural. Growth is often a process of two steps forward, one step back. Get your journal out. Write about what is going on. Figure out the problem and make a plan for responding.

In the fire service, firefighters know that there's no such thing as a perfect fire call. At the scene, the focus is on the overall objective of the plan: "getting the wet stuff on the red stuff" to extinguish the fire. When battling the fire, you often don't see the holes in the planning or the mistakes you make in its execution. You learn about these things back at the station debrief, after all the equipment has been cleaned and put away and the hoses are packed carefully on the engines. At the debrief the call is reviewed, actions are analyzed, and lessons are learned. This becomes the basis for making modifications to firefighting planning, tactics, and future training. For our emergency plans for challenging episodes, debriefing questions include: Did the adults remain calm? Were buttons well managed? Could the episode have been prevented? Did parental actions lead to de-escalation? For the prevention plan: Is our relationship more trusting? Is communication better? Are skills improving? Do we see a trajectory of fewer episodes of challenging behavior? Do we see our son becoming increasingly better able to manage his emotions and triggers? Answers to these questions are used to revise the prevention plan. These new emergency and prevention plans, in turn, will be implemented, and then analyzed and modified at future debriefs.

While there are no "quick fixes," I am confident that if you apply the methods described in this book and stick with your plans, your son will increasingly learn the skills he needs to thrive. You'll also see your relationship transformed from conflict to connection, from opposition to teamwork, and to enjoying each other more and more. You will experience the immense satisfaction of helping your son grow from a challenging boy into a young man who can pursue worthy goals, foster relationships, take responsibility for managing his challenging nature, and face life's challenges with skill and resilience.

Additional Resources

Recommended Reading

Ross Greene, *The Explosive Child: A New Approach for Understanding and Parenting Easily Frustrated, Chronically Inflexible Children* (HarperCollins, 1998).
This is an essential read for any parent with a challenging child. It provides a comprehensive introduction to Greene's Collaborative Problem Solving (CPS) method, which helps children develop better frustration tolerance and flexibility.

Alan Kazdin, *The Kazdin Method for Parenting the Defiant Child* (Houghton Mifflin Harcourt, 2008).
The Kazdin Method is the ultimate resource for parents looking to use reward programs to address challenging behavior. It offers concrete steps and real-world examples to help parents successfully implement reward-based strategies.

John Gottman, *Raising an Emotionally Intelligent Child* (Simon & Schuster, 1998).
This book guides parents on how to tune in to their child's emotions. Gottman explains how to use emotion coaching to be responsive to a child's feelings while setting appropriate limits on misbehavior.

Adele Faber and Elaine Mazlish, *How to Talk So Kids Will Listen and Listen So Kids Will Talk* (Scribner, 1980).
This is a timeless guide for parents seeking to improve communication with their children.

Peg Dawson and Richard Guare, *Smart but Scattered: The Revolutionary "Executive Skills" Approach to Helping Kids Reach Their Potential* (Guilford Press, 2009).
Dawson and Guare offer a valuable resource for parents wanting to help their children with executive skills deficits. The book provides practical strategies to support kids in developing these critical skills.

David Burns, *When Panic Attacks: The New, Drug-Free Anxiety Therapy That Can Change Your Life* (Harmony, 2006).
Burns teaches parents how to identify and challenge their own negative self-talk and cognitive biases, promoting healthier thought patterns and better emotional regulation. By mastering these techniques themselves, parents can more effectively teach them to their children.

Peter Wright and Pamela Wright, *Wrightslaw: From Emotions to Advocacy—The Special Education Survival Guide* (3rd ed.) (Harbor House Law Press, Inc, 2023).
If your son's behavior is getting him into trouble at school or he is struggling academically, consider whether he needs an Individualized Education Program (IEP) at school. *Wrightslaw* offers a thorough introduction to the IEP process, the law behind it, what services your child might get from an IEP, and how to apply for one from his school.

GENERAL INFORMATION USEFUL TO PARENTS OF CHALLENGING BOYS
ADDitude Magazine (additudemag.com)
Understood (understood.org)
Challenging Boys (challengingboys.com)

RESOURCES RELATED TO EMOTION COACHING
Gottman Institute, Parenting (gottman.com/parenting/)

RESOURCES RELATED TO COLLABORATIVE PROBLEM-SOLVING

Lives in the Balance: CPS Materials (livesinthebalance.org/cps-materials-paperwork/)
CPS Connection (cpsconnection.com)
Think:Kids (thinkkids.org)

RESOURCES RELATED TO THE IEP PROCESS

Wrightslaw (wrightslaw.com)

RESOURCES FOR FINDING A THERAPIST IN YOUR AREA

Psychology Today Therapist Finder (psychologytoday.com/us/therapists)
American Psychological Association Locator (locator.apa.org)

BIBLIOGRAPHY

Aristotle. *Nicomachean Ethics*. Translated by W. D. Ross. Batoche Books, 1999. (Original work published 350 BCE.)

Barkley, Russell A. "Attention-Deficit/Hyperactivity Disorder, Self-Regulation, and Time: Toward a More Comprehensive Theory." *Journal of Developmental and Behavioral Pediatrics* 18, no. 4 (1997): 271–79.

———. *Taking Charge of ADHD: The Complete, Authoritative Guide for Parents*. Fourth edition. New York: The Guilford Press, 2020.

Beck, Aaron. *Cognitive Therapy and the Emotional Disorders*. New York: International Universities Press, 1976.

Blair, Clancy, and C. Cybele Raver. "School Readiness and Self-Regulation: A Developmental Psychobiological Approach." *Annual Review of Psychology* 66 (2015): 711–31.

Bracha, H. Stefan. "Freeze-Flight-Fight-Fright (and Faint): Adaptationist Perspectives on the Acute Stress Response Spectrum." *CNS Spectrums* 9 (2004): 679–85.

Burns, David. *When Panic Attacks: The New, Drug-Free Anxiety Therapy That Can Change Your Life*. New York: Harmony, 2006.

Cannon, Walter Bradford. *Bodily Changes in Pain, Hunger, Fear, and Rage*. New York: D. Appleton and Co., 1915.

Carrère, Sybil, and John M. Gottman. "Predicting Divorce among Newlyweds from the First Three Minutes of a Marital Conflict Discussion." *Family Process* 38, no. 3 (1999): 293–301.

Cohen, Lawrence J. *Playful Parenting*. New York: Ballantine Books, 2002.

Covey, Stephen R. *The 7 Habits of Highly Effective People: Powerful Lessons in Personal Change*. New York: Free Press, 1989.

Diamond, Adele. "Executive Functions." *Annual Review of Psychology* 64 (2013): 135–68.

Dreikurs, Rudolf. *Children: The Challenge*. New York: Dutton, 1964.

Espinosa, Gad. *How Your Child Can Become Unstoppable*. Espinosa Publishing, 2020. (Kindle edition, www.amazon.com/dp/B08XYZ1234).

Faber, Adele, and Elaine Mazlish. *How to Talk So Kids Will Listen and Listen So Kids Will Talk*. New York: Scribner, 1980.

———. *Siblings without Rivalry: How to Help Your Children Live Together So You Can Live Too*. New York: W.W. Norton & Company, 1998.

Felitti, Vincent J., et al. "Relationship of Childhood Abuse and Household Dysfunction to Many of the Leading Causes of Death in Adults: The Adverse

Childhood Experiences (ACE) Study." *American Journal of Preventive Medicine* 14, no. 4, May 1998, 245–58.

Garbarino, James. *Parents Under Siege: Why You Are the Solution, Not the Problem in Your Child's Life.* New York: Free Press, 2001. (YouTube Video: https://youtu.be /5ZP22SeGL-E?feature=shared)+.

Gershoff, Elizabeth T. "The Case against Spanking." *Monitor on Psychology* 43, no. 4 (April 2012). https://www.apa.org/monitor/2012/04/spanking.

———. *Report on Physical Punishment in the United States: What Research Tells Us about Its Effects on Children.* Columbus, OH: Center for Effective Discipline, 2008.

Ginott, Haim G. *Between Parent and Child.* New York: Macmillan, 1965.

Goldsmith, Wayne. "It's Time for Coaching Educators to Start Teaching Coaching and Stop Teaching Sport. In *Changing the Game Project* (podcast), 2017. https://changingthegameproject.com/podcast/50-time-coaching-educators-start -teaching-coaching-stop-teaching-sport-science-olympic-coaching-educator -wayne-goldsmith/.

Gottman, John M. *Raising an Emotionally Intelligent Child.* New York: Simon & Schuster, 1998.

———. *Why Marriages Succeed or Fail: And How You Can Make Yours Last.* New York: Simon & Schuster, 1994.

Gottman, John M., and Nan Silver. *10 Lessons to Transform Your Marriage.* New York: Harmony, 2006.

Gottman, John M., Lynn Fainsilber Katz, and Carole Hooven. *Meta-Emotion: How Families Communicate Emotionally.* New York: Routledge, 1997.

Greene, Ross W. *The Explosive Child: A New Approach for Understanding and Parenting Easily Frustrated, Chronically Inflexible Children.* New York: HarperCollins, 1998.

Greenspan, Stanley I., and Serena Wieder. *The Challenging Child: Understanding, Raising, and Enjoying the Five "Difficult" Types of Children.* Boston: Da Capo Press, 1996.

Hendricksen, Ellen. *How to Be Yourself: Quiet Your Inner Critic and Rise Above Social Anxiety.* New York: St. Martin's Press, 2018.

Horton, Tony. Quoted in *Beachbody. P90x*, 2005. https://www.90dayworkoutplan .com/about/what-is-p90x/.

Howard, Ron, dir. *Apollo 13.* DVD. Universal Pictures, 1998.

Jay, Meg. "Lessons from the Best Coach." *Soccer Journal*, 2016.

Karp, Harvey, producer. *The Happiest Toddler on the Block: How to Eliminate Tantrums and Raise a Patient, Respectful, and Cooperative One- to Four-Year-Old.* New York: Bantam, 2004.

Kazdin, Alan E. *The Kazdin Method for Parenting the Defiant Child.* New York: Houghton Mifflin Harcourt, 2008.

Kibler, Lindsay. "How Can Coaches Influence Players and Motivate Athletes." *University of Denver Sports Sense Blog*, 2020. https://www.du.edu/sport-sense/news /how-can-coaches-influence-players-and-motivate-athletes.

Murray, Desiree W., Katie Rosanbalm, Christina Christopoulos, and Amelia L. Meyer. "An Applied Contextual Model for Promoting Self-Regulation Enactment across Development: Implications for Prevention, Public Health, and

Future Research." *Clinical Child and Family Psychology Review* 21, no. 1 (2018): 19–42.

Nelson, Jane. *Positive Discipline: The Classic Guide to Helping Children Develop Self-Discipline, Responsibility, Cooperation, and Problem-Solving Skills*. New York: Ballantine Books, 2006.

Nixon, Charisse. "What Adolescents (or Teenagers) Need to Thrive." Video. YouTube, 2014. https://youtu.be/S05PBOIdSeE?feature=shared.

PBS LearningMedia. "What Is Mentionable Is Manageable: Mister Rogers." In *Meet the Helpers*." (https://ny.pbslearningmedia.org/resource/mentionable-manageable-mister-rogers-video/meet-the-helpers/?student=true&focus=true). Accessed 8 July 2024.

Pennebaker, James W., and Joshua M. Smyth. *Opening Up by Writing It Down: How Expressive Writing Improves Health and Eases Emotional Pain*. Third edition. New York: Guilford Press, 2016.

Pollack, William. *Real Boys: Rescuing Our Sons from the Myths of Boyhood*. New York: Owl Books, 1999.

Rohner, Ronald P. "Deep Structure of the Human Affectional System: Introduction to Interpersonal Acceptance-Rejection Theory." *Journal of Family Theory & Review* 9, no. 4 (2017): 426–40.

Rosanbalm, Katie D., and Desiree W. Murray. *Promoting Self-Regulation in Early Childhood: A Practice Brief*. OPRE Brief #2017-79, Office of Planning, Research, and Evaluation, Administration for Children and Families. Washington, DC: U.S. Department of Health and Human Services, 2017.

Rothbart, Mary K. *Becoming Who We Are: Temperament and Personality in Development*. New York: Guilford Press, 2011.

Thomas, Alexander, and Stella Chess. *Temperament and Development*. New York: Brunner/Mazel, 1977.

Wooden, John. Quoted in *The American Almanack*, 2019. https://theamericanalmanack.com/john-wooden/.

Wooden, John, and Steve Jamison. *Wooden: A Lifetime of Observations and Reflections On and Off the Court*. New York: McGraw-Hill, 1997.

Yerkes, Robert M., and John D. Dodson. "The Relationship of Strength of Stimulus to Rapidity of Habit Formation." *Journal of Comparative Neurology and Psychology* 18 (1908): 459–82.

Index

acceptance: basic need for, 70; challenge of accepting our son's feelings, 71–72, 78, 89, 103, 204; cornerstone of strong parent-child relationship, 70, 77, 83, 91, 99, 116, 126, 131, 203, 208; essential before problem-solving, 76; foundation for son accepting our guidance, 77, 170–71, 203, 208; foundation of good communication, 87, 90, 95–96, 99–100, 103, 105, 171; impact on self-esteem, 70, 72, 131; role in co-regulation, 122–23

Aiden (9 y/o), reward program for getting ready for school on time, 155–57, 159

anger: apologies, 80, 82; constructive vs. destructive expressions of, 64; emotional backdraft, 95; Gottman definition of, 74; meta-emotion and, 114–16, 128; Overwhelmed Zone, 109, 113; parental anger, xv, 2, 6, 8, 10, 23, 62–63, 78, 199; sign of parent being triggered, 16–19. *See also* punishment; temperament (negative emotion)

anxiety, xxi, 52–53, 63, 86, 93, 113, 118, 150, 168, 181, 185–86, 196, 200, 204, 207. *See also* temperament (negative emotion)

Apollo 13 (movie) 6–8, 61

apologies: four *R*s: Recognition, Responsibility, Remorse, Repair, 81–82, 143; importance of apologizing to your son, 80–83, 104, 203; making amends, 79, 80–83,

143, 203; teaching son to apologize, 143, 203, 206

Aristotle, xviii

attention deficit hyperactivity disorder (ADHD), xvii, xxi, 118

attention seeking behaviors, 36, 68, 69, 112, 135–36

autism spectrum disorder (ASD), xvii, xxi, 118

Bacon, Kevin, 6

Barkley, Russell, 33, 35

blame: directed at the challenging boy, 8–10, 22, 60, 136; interferes with problem solving, 6–12, 51, 61; parents being blamed, 4; parents blaming each other 8–9, 22, 61; parents blaming themselves, 4–5, 10, 12–13, 15, 22–23, 25, 52, 60, 192, 198; vs. taking responsibility, 11, 81

Bracha, Stefan, 2

bribes, 2–3, 11, 133, 162

bullying, 35, 88, 92, 115; of siblings, 16, 44, 73, 144; parents' experience with sibling bullying, 16, 47, 49, 51

Burns, David, 184–85

calm: challenges in staying calm, xiv, 2, 13, 15, 18, 197; strategies for staying calm, xvi, xxi, 22, 44, 54, 60, 95, 126, 198, 202

Cannon, Walter, 2

Carrère, Sybil, 172

Chess, Stella, 27–28

coaching, 165; coaching mindset 171–77, 192; emotion coaching 165, 177–86, 192; necessary conditions

About the Author

Dr. J. Timothy Davis is a clinical psychologist with thirty years of experience specializing in child, adolescent, couples, and family therapy. He has conducted research on male development at Harvard's renowned Study of Adult Development and served on the faculty of Harvard Medical School for twenty-five years. Dr. Davis's work emphasizes understanding the underlying causes of challenging behavior and equipping parents with proactive strategies to remain calm and connected while they teach their son the skills he needs to face life's challenges with resilience.